WATER MANAGEMENT AND AQUATIC ECOSYSTEM

ENV BOOKS SERIES

WATER MANAGEMENT AND AQUATIC ECOSYSTEM

Editors

Dr. Resham Bhalla
M.Sc. M.Phil. Ph.D., FASEA, FNESA, FFNSC
Associate Professor
LVH ASC College, Nasik
(Maharashtra)
(India)

&

Dr. Pawan Kumar 'Bharti'
Society for Environment, Health
Awareness of Nutrition & Toxicology (SEHAT)
B-225/5D, Top Floor, Subhash Gali, Road No. 7, Block B
Ashok Nagar, Shahdara
Delhi-110093
(India)

DPH

DISCOVERY PUBLISHING HOUSE PVT. LTD.
INDIA

Published by:
Namit Wasan

DISCOVERY PUBLISHING HOUSE PVT. LTD.
4383/4B, Ansari Road, Darya Ganj
New Delhi-110 002 (India)
Phone : +91-11-23279245; 23253475; 43596065
E-mail : discoverybooksindia@gmail.com
discoverypublishinghouse@gmail.com
namitwasan9@gmail.com
web : www.discoverypublishinggroup.com

***First Edition:* 2019**

ISBN: 978-93-86841-96-4

Water Management and Aquatic Ecosystem

Printed at:
Infinity Imaging Systems
Delhi

PREFACE

Water occurs as a liquid on the surface of Earth under normal conditions, which makes it invaluable for transportation, for recreation, and as a habitat for a myriad of plants and animals. The fact that water is readily changed to a vapour (gas) allows it to be transported through the atmosphere from the oceans to inland areas where it condenses and, as rain, nourishes plant and animal life.

Water is a valuable resource that is critical for the health, vitality and long-term sustainability of all natural ecosystems. For humans, water plays an essential role in food and energy production, transportation and recreation.

Worldwide, however, water resources are at a risk. Unsustainable population growth, land-use changes, pollution, and global climate change all threaten the distribution, quantity, and quality of the water on which all life depends.

Protecting and preserving our water resources requires that we take a "big picture" approach that addresses where water comes from, where it goes, how it travels, how it is used by living things, what's in it and how to remediate problems and develop policies to protect water.

The interdisciplinary study in Water Science & Policy educates people to address the complex challenges that we face today; to develop solutions that are socially acceptable, economically viable, and environmentally sustainable; and to be true stewards of our environment.

The present book updates the subject content of water quality, water management, water pollution assessment, aquatic biodiversity, aquatic ecosystem, aquatic scientific studies, flora and fauna of water bodies.

Thanks are due to publisher and contributors from various institutions and universities.

The book will be helpful for the researchers, academia working in the field of water quality, water management, water pollution assessment, aquatic biodiversity, aquatic ecosystem, aquatic scientific studies, flora and fauna of water bodies.

Editors
(envbooks@gmail.com)

CONTENTS

Water Management and Aquatic Ecosystem **Pages 1-6**
Edited by: Dr. Resham Bhalla & Dr. Pawan Kumar 'Bharti'
ISBN: 978-93-86841-96-4
Edition: 2019
Published by: Discovery Publishing House Pvt. Ltd., New Delhi (India)

1

Water

An Introduction

[1]Soubam P. Singh

Water, a substance composed of the chemical elements hydrogen and oxygen and existing in gaseous, liquid, and solid states. It is one of the most plentiful and essential of compounds. A tasteless and odourless liquid at room temperature, it has the important ability to dissolve many other substances. Indeed, the versatility of water as a solvent is essential to living organisms. Life is believed to have originated in the aqueous solutions of the world's oceans, and living organisms depend on aqueous solutions, such as blood and digestive juices, for biological processes. In small quantities water appears colourless, but water actually has an intrinsic blue colour caused by slight absorption of light at red wavelengths.

Although the molecules of water are simple in structure (H_2O), the physical and chemical properties of the compound are extraordinarily complicated and they are not typical of most substances found on Earth. For example, although the sight of ice cubes floating in a glass of ice water is commonplace, such behaviour is unusual for chemical entities. For almost every other compound, the solid state is denser than the liquid state; thus, the solid would sink to the bottom of the liquid. The fact that ice floats on water is exceedingly important in the natural world, because the ice that forms on ponds and lakes in cold areas of the world acts as an insulating barrier that protects the aquatic life below. If ice were denser than liquid water, ice forming on a pond would sink, thereby exposing more water to the cold temperature. Thus, the pond would eventually freeze throughout, killing all the life-forms present.

Water occurs as a liquid on the surface of Earth under normal conditions, which makes it invaluable for transportation, for recreation, and as a habitat for a myriad of plants and animals. The fact that water is readily changed to a vapour (gas) allows it to be transported through the atmosphere from the oceans to inland areas where it condenses and as rain, nourishes plant and animal life.

[1] Manager, Operation Centre at United Register System Certification Ltd, Noida, UP, India

Water is a valuable resource that is critical for the health, vitality, and long-term sustainability of all natural ecosystems. For humans, water plays an essential role in food and energy production, transportation, and recreation.

Worldwide, however, water resources are at a risk. Unsustainable population growth, land-use changes, pollution, and global climate change all threaten the distribution, quantity, and quality of the water on which all life depends.

Protecting and preserving our water resources requires that we take a "big picture" approach that addresses where water comes from, where it goes, how it travels, how it is used by living things, what's in it, and how to remediate problems and develop policies to protect water.

The interdisciplinary study in Water Science & Policy educates people to address the complex challenges that we face today; to develop solutions that are socially acceptable, economically viable, and environmentally sustainable; and to be true stewards of our environment.

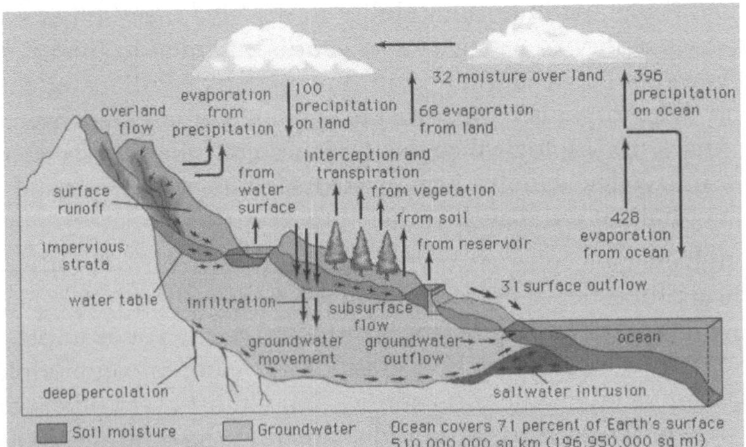

Fig. 1.1: Water cycle on Earth

The water on the surface of Earth is found mainly in its oceans (97.25%) and polar ice caps and glaciers (2.05%), with the balance in freshwater lakes, rivers and groundwater. As Earth's population grows and the demand for fresh water increases, water purification and recycling become increasingly important. Interestingly, the purity requirements of water for industrial use often exceed those for human consumption. For example, the water used in high-pressure boilers must be at least 99.999998 percent pure. Because seawater contains large quantities of dissolved salts, it must be desalinated for most uses, including human consumption.

Water is the transparent, tasteless, odorless and nearly colorless chemical substance that is the main constituent of Earth's streams, lakes, and oceans, and the fluids of most living organisms and that is vital for all known forms of life, even though it provides no calories or organic nutrients. Its chemical formula is H_2O, meaning that each of its molecules contains one oxygen and two hydrogen atoms connected by covalent bonds. Water is the name of the liquid state of H_2O at standard ambient temperature and pressure. It forms precipitation in the form of rain and aerosols in the form of fog. Clouds are formed from suspended droplets of water and ice, its solid state. When finely divided, crystalline ice may precipitate in the form of snow. The gaseous state of water is steam or water vapor. Water moves continually through the water cycle of evaporation, transpiration (evapo-transpiration), condensation, precipitation, and runoff, usually reaching the sea.

Water covers 71% of the Earth's surface, mostly in seas and oceans. Small portions of water occur as groundwater (1.7%), in the glaciers and the ice caps of Antarctica and Greenland (1.7%) and in the air as vapor, clouds (formed of ice and liquid water suspended in air) and precipitation (0.001%).

Water plays an important role in the world economy. Approximately 70% of the freshwater used by humans goes to agriculture. Fishing in salt and fresh water bodies is a major source of food for many parts of the world. Much of long-distance trade of commodities (such as oil and natural gas) and manufactured products is transported by boats through seas, rivers, lakes, and canals. Large quantities of water, ice, and steam are used for cooling and heating, in industry and homes. Water is an excellent solvent for a wide variety of chemical substances; as such it is widely used in industrial processes, and in cooking and washing. Water is also central to many sports and other forms of entertainment, such as swimming, pleasure boating, boat racing, surfing, sport fishing, and diving.

Water (H_2O) is a polar inorganic compound that is at room temperature a tasteless and odorless liquid, nearly colorless with a hint of blue. This simplest hydrogen chalcogenide is by far the most studied chemical compound and is described as the "universal solvent" for its ability to dissolve many substances. This allows it to be the "solvent of life". It is the only common substance to exist as a solid, liquid, and gas in normal terrestrial conditions.

Water Cycle

The water cycle (known scientifically as the hydrologic cycle) refers to the continuous exchange of water within the hydrosphere, between the atmosphere, soil water, surface water, groundwater and plants.

Water moves perpetually through each of these regions in the water cycle consisting of following transfer processes:

- Evaporation - from oceans and other water bodies into the air and transpiration from land plants and animals into air.

- Precipitation- from water vapor condensing from the air and falling to earth or ocean.
- Runoff- from the land usually reaching the sea.

Most water vapor over the oceans returns to the oceans, but winds carry water vapor over land at the same rate as runoff into the sea, about 47 Tt per year. Over land, evaporation and transpiration contribute another 72 Tt per year. Precipitation, at a rate of 119 Tt per year over land, has several forms: most commonly rain, snow, and hail, with some contribution from fog and dew. Dew is small drops of water that are condensed when a high density of water vapor meets a cool surface. Dew usually forms in the morning when the temperature is the lowest, just before sunrise and when the temperature of the earth's surface starts to increase. Condensed water in the air may also refract sunlight to produce rainbows.

Water runoff often collects over watersheds flowing into rivers. A mathematical model used to simulate river or stream flow and calculate water quality parameters is a hydrological transport model. Some water is diverted to irrigation for agriculture. Rivers and seas offer opportunity for travel and commerce. Through erosion, runoff shapes the environment creating river valleys and deltas which provide rich soil and level ground for the establishment of population centers. A flood occurs when an area of land, usually low-lying, is covered with water. It is when a river overflows its banks or flood comes from the sea. A drought is an extended period of months or years when a region notes a deficiency in its water supply. This occurs when a region receives consistently below average precipitation.

Effects on Life

Overview of photosynthesis and respiration. Water (at right), together with carbon dioxide (CO_2), form oxygen and organic compounds (at left), which can be respired to water and (CO_2).

From a biological standpoint, water has many distinct properties that are critical for the proliferation of life. It carries out this role by allowing organic compounds to react in ways that ultimately allow replication. All known forms of life depend on water. Water is vital both as a solvent in which many of the body's solutes dissolve and as an essential part of many metabolic processes within the body. Metabolism is the sum total of anabolism and catabolism. In anabolism, water is removed from molecules (through energy requiring enzymatic chemical reactions) in order to grow larger molecules (e.g. starches, triglycerides and proteins for storage of fuels and information). In catabolism, water is used to break bonds in order to generate smaller molecules (e.g. glucose, fatty acids and amino acids to be used for fuels for energy use or other purposes). Without water, these particular metabolic processes could not exist.

Water is fundamental to photosynthesis and respiration. Photosynthetic cells use the sun's energy to split off water's hydrogen from oxygen. Hydrogen is combined with CO_2 (absorbed from air or water) to form glucose and release oxygen. All living cells use such fuels and oxidize the hydrogen and carbon to capture the sun's energy and reform water and CO_2 in the process (cellular respiration).

Water is also central to acid-base neutrality and enzyme function. An acid, a hydrogen ion (H^+, that is, a proton) donor, can be neutralized by a base, a proton acceptor such as a hydroxide ion (OH^-) to form water. Water is considered to be neutral, with a pH (the negative log of the hydrogen ion concentration) of 7. Acids have pH values less than 7 while bases have values greater than 7.

Aquatic Life Forms

Earth surface waters are filled with life. The earliest life forms appeared in water; nearly all fish live exclusively in water, and there are many types of marine mammals, such as dolphins and whales. Some kinds of animals, such as amphibians, spend portions of their lives in water and portions on land. Plants such as kelp and algae grow in the water and are the basis for some underwater ecosystems. Plankton is generally the foundation of the ocean food chain.

Aquatic vertebrates must obtain oxygen to survive, and they do so in various ways. Fish have gills instead of lungs, although some species of fish, such as the lungfish, have both. Marine mammals, such as dolphins, whales, otters, and seals need to surface periodically to breathe air. Some amphibians are able to absorb oxygen through their skin. Invertebrates exhibit a wide range of modifications to survive in poorly oxygenated waters including breathing tubes (see insect and mollusc siphons) and gills (Carcinus). However, as invertebrate life evolved in an aquatic habitat most have little or no specialization for respiration in water.

Aquatic Ecosystem

An aquatic ecosystem is an ecosystem in a body of water. Communities of organisms that are dependent on each other and on their environment live in aquatic ecosystems. The two main types of aquatic ecosystems are marine ecosystems and freshwater ecosystems.

Aquatic ecosystems perform many important environmental functions. For example, they recycle nutrients, purify water, attenuate floods, recharge ground water and provide habitats for wildlife. Aquatic ecosystems are also used for human recreation, and are very important to the tourism industry, especially in coastal regions.

The health of an aquatic ecosystem is degraded when the ecosystem's ability to absorb a stress has been exceeded. A stress on an aquatic ecosystem can be a result of physical, chemical or biological alterations of the environment. Physical alterations include changes in water temperature, water flow and light availability. Chemical alterations include changes in the loading rates of biostimulatory nutrients, oxygen consuming materials, and toxins. Biological alterations include over-harvesting of commercial species and the introduction of exotic species. Human populations can impose excessive stresses on aquatic ecosystems. There are many examples of excessive stresses with negative consequences. Consider three. The environmental history of the Great Lakes of North America illustrates this problem, particularly how multiple stresses, such as water pollution, over-harvesting and invasive species can combine. The Norfolk Broadlands in England illustrate similar decline with pollution and invasive species. Lake Pontchartrain along the Gulf of Mexico illustrates the negative effects of different stresses including levee construction, logging of swamps, invasive species and salt water intrusion.

REFERENCES

http://www1.udel.edu/watersciencepolicy/

https://en.wikipedia.org/wiki/Water

https://www.britannica.com/science/water

https://en.wikipedia.org/wiki/Aquatic_ecosystem

Water Management and Aquatic Ecosystem **Pages 7-36**
Edited by: Dr. Resham Bhalla & Dr. Pawan Kumar 'Bharti'
ISBN: 978-93-86841-96-4
Edition: 2019
Published by: Discovery Publishing House Pvt. Ltd., New Delhi (India)

2

Water Management in Flower Crops

[1]A. Palanisamy, [2]A. Solaimalai, [3*]M. Jayakumar and [4]A. Rajkumar

Introduction

Water is an essential resource for all life on the planet. Of the water resources on Earth only three percent of it is fresh and two-thirds of the freshwater is locked up in ice caps and glaciers. Of the remaining one percent, a fifth is in remote, inaccessible areas and much seasonal rainfall in monsoonal deluges and floods cannot easily be used. At present only about 0.08 percent of all the world fresh water is exploited by mankind in ever increasing demand for sanitation, drinking, manufacturing, leisure and agriculture.

Water Management is important since it helps determine future irrigation expectations. Water management is the management of water resources under set policies and regulations. Water, once an abundant natural resource, is becoming a more valuable commodity due to droughts and overuse. Water resource management is the activity of planning, developing, distributing and managing the optimum use of water resources. Water resource management planning has regard to all the competing demands for water and seeks to allocate water on an equitable basis to satisfy all uses and demands.

Field water management practices are the most effective factors affecting crop yield particularly in irrigated agriculture in arid and semi-arid regions. Sandy soils are particularly critical for water management in irrigated agriculture because of their low water-holding capacity and low clay contents. The productivity of these soils is limited by high infiltration rate, high evaporation, low fertility level, low water-holding capacity and low organic matter content (Suganya and Sivasamy, 2006).

---

[1] Assistant Professor (Horticulture), Sethu Bhaskara Agricultural College & Research Foundation, Karaikudi (Tk), Sivagangai (Dt), Tamil Nadu – 630306, India.
[2] Associate Professor (Agronomy), Department of Fruit Crops, Horticultural College & Research Institute, TNAU, Periyakulam – 625 604, Tamil Nadu, India.
[3] Scientist, Regional Coffee Research Station, Thandigudi, Dindigul (Dt), Tamil Nadu, India.
[4] Assistant Professor (Horticulture), Krishna College of Agriculture & Technology, Sree Rangapuram, Usilampatti (TK), Madurai (Dt), Tamil Nadu, India.

At present and most probably also in the future, as a result of global warming, irrigated agriculture will take place under water scarcity. Hence, sustainable methods to increase crop water productivity are gaining importance in arid and semi-arid regions. In other words, irrigation management in arid and semi-arid regions will shift from emphasizing production per unit area towards maximizing the production per unit of water consumed (Fereres and Soriano, 2007).

The pressure for using water in agriculture sector is increasing to create ways to improve water-use efficiency and take a full advantage of available water. Therefore, the adoption of modern irrigation techniques is needed to increase water-use efficiency. High water application efficiencies are often possible with drip irrigation, since there is reduced surface evaporation, less surface runoff, as well as minimal deep percolation (Jiusheng *et al.* 2003).

On the contrary, eliminating unnecessary irrigation water could help in conserving irrigation water and preventing pollutants such as pesticides and fertilizers leaching to groundwater, provided that it can be done with low yield losses. The estimation of soil water content in the root zone is essential for a better irrigation management (Aydinsakir *et al.*, 2011).

The cut flower grew in the world presently begun in the beginning of the 20th century and it has become an important commercial activity in many developed and developing countries, especially after the end of World War II. The total production land for ornamental plants reached about 610.000 ha. It is known that there are more than 50 countries in the world performing cut flower growing. The most important producers of the European Union are Italy, the Netherland and Spain. The countries of European Union produce 47% of the total cut flower production of the world. (AIPH, 2007).

Plant growth and survival depend on availability of soil and water, as crop growth is associated with the losses of a huge quantity of water through transpiration by plants and evaporation from the soil surface. Irrigation is done to supplement the deficit in soil water content. While applying irrigation, the major aspects to be considered are related to the time, quantum and methods of irrigation. In most of the cases, the magnitude of yield and losses depends almost as much upon the timing of the deficit as on the total quantum of seasonal shortage of water. Thus proper scheduling of irrigation water is important to achieve maximum productivity. This involves the judicious use of soil, plant and climatological parameters.

Scheduling Irrigation

Scheduling irrigation is very critical for obtaining optimal crop yields. For optimum irrigation scheduling, sound knowledge of the soil water status, crop water requirements, crop water stress status and potential yield reduction under water-stressed conditions is prerequisite to maximize profits and optimize the use of water and energy.

Irrigation scheduling is conventionally based on "soil water balance calculations," where the soil moisture status is estimated by water balance approach, in which the change in soil moisture storage over a period of time is given by the difference between the inputs (irrigation + precipitation) and the losses (runoff + drainage + ET). Irrigation scheduling involves the timing of irrigation and the amount of water applied. There are different methods of irrigation scheduling *viz.,* critical crop growth stage approach, soil moisture depletion approach (whether in terms of soil water content or soil water potential), atmospheric evaporativity approach, IW at different cumulative pan evaporation (CPE) approach, etc. can be adopted for optimizing the timing of irrigation. There are different methods of irrigation scheduling *viz.,* critical crop growth stage approach, soil moisture depletion approach, and irrigation based on atmospheric evaporativity etc. which may be adopted for optimizing the timing of irrigation. Irrigation scheduling technique based on atmospheric evaporativity has been used extensively for several crops.

Drip Irrigation in Greenhouse Cultivation

The plant is required to take up very large amounts of water and nutrients, with a relatively small root system, and manufacture photosynthates for a large amount of flower per unit area with a foliar system relatively small in relation to required production.

Watering System

Micro irrigation system is the best for watering plants in a greenhouse. Micro sprinklers or drip irrigation equipments can be used. Basically the watering system should ensure that water does not fall on the leaves or flowers as it leads to disease and scorching problems. In micro sprinkler system, water under high pressure is forced through nozzles arranged on a supporting stand at about 1 feet height. This facilitates watering at the base level of the plants.

Equipments Required for Drip Irrigation System Include

(*i*) A pump unit to generate 2.8 kg/cm^2 pressure

(*ii*) Water filtration system – sand/silica/screen filters

(*iii*) PVC tubing with dripper or emitters

Drippers of Different Types are Available

(*i*) Labyrinth drippers

(*ii*) Turbo drippers

(*iii*) Pressure compensating drippers – contain silicon membrane which assures uniform flow rate for years (*iv*) Button drippers- easy and simple to clean. These are good for pots, orchards and are available with ide outlet/top outlet or micro tube out let

(*v*) Pot drippers – cones with long tube

Water Output in Drippers

(*a*) 16 mm dripper at 2.8 kg/cm^2 pressure gives 2.65 litres/hour (LPH).

(*b*) 15 mm dripper at 1 kg/cm^2 pressure gives 1 to 4 litres per hour

Filters: Depending upon the type of water, different kinds of filters can be used.

Gravel filter: Used for filtration of water obtained for open canals and reservoirs that are contaminated by organic impurities, algae etc. The filtering is done by beds of basalt or quartz.

Hydrocyclone: Used to filter well or river water that carries sand particles.

Disc filters: Used to remove fine particles suspended in water

Screen filters: Stainless steel screen of 120 mesh (0.13 mm) size. This is used for second stage filtration of irrigation water (http://agritech.tnau.ac.in/horticulture/horti_Greenhouse%20cultivation.html#drip).

Water Productivity

Water productivity (WP) which refers to the yield of produce obtained per unit of water (kg m^{-3}) reported by Kijine *et al.* (2002).In the absence of new irrigation projects, bringing more area under irrigation would mostly rely on the efficient use of water. In this context, micro irrigation could play a key role in higher productivity and increased water use efficiency (WUE) besides fulfilling sustainability mandates with economy in use and higher crop productivity.

Adoption of micro irrigation helps in raising the irrigated area, crop productivity and WUE (Sivanappan, 1985).

Patil *et al.* (2008) stated that scheduling of drip irrigation in hybrid cotton at 50 per cent potential evapotranspiration throughout the crop growth period will save 50 per cent irrigation water and enhances WUE (53.2 g ha^{-1} cm^{-1}) and cotton productivity without affecting the quality on a medium black soil. Patil *et al.* (2008) pointed out that under water scarcity area or low rainfall years drip irrigation is better than alternate furrow irrigation for obtaining higher water use efficiency.

Nutrient Dynamics under drip Fertigation

Under drip irrigation, the highest reduction in soil NO_3-N was observed in 30 to 60 cm depth (18 mg kg^{-1}), while the highest reduction in soil K was observed in 0 to 30 cm depth (7.42 mg kg^{-1}) and the soil pH was not affected by drip irrigation.

The increase in NH_4-N concentration immediately in the vicinity of the emitter is a consequence of the hydrolysis of urea (Haynes, 1990).

Drip Irrigation and Rooting Pattern

The rate of applying water in drip irrigation is an important factor which governs moisture distribution in soil profile. A high rate may cause deep percolation loss whereas, a very low rate may contribute to evaporation losses. Irrigation frequency and rate of water application in trickle system not only decide the size of the wetted soil surface, but also determine the geometry of the wetted zone. Moisture distribution profile of trickle irrigated summer squash for the daily irrigated treatment showed that downward water movement is restricted to the surface of 60 cm while lateral movement occurs no further than 60 cm from the emitter (Earl and Jury, 1977).

Sivanappan *et al.* (1987) studied the water movement pattern for a discharge rate of 8 lph and observed it upto 30 and 40 cm distances in horizontal and vertical direction, respectively. The moisture content after 48 hours at the surface (below the emitter) decreased from 37.8 to 27.8 per cent for discharge rate of 4 lph. The moisture content after 48 hrs at 30 cm depth below the dripper was found to be stabilized at 23.9 per cent in 0-30 cm depth and at 40 cm distance away from the dripper was 21.8 to 22.7 for discharge rate of 4 lph. Goel *et al.* (1993) reported that the moisture content on weight basis showed that in beginning, the water at higher application rate saturated the soil near the dripper and infiltration was slower whereas, the water penetrated deeper with lower application rate because of availability of more time for infiltration.

Visalakshi *et al.* (2007) reported that the pattern of wetting of soil surface was circular and that of soil profile was elliptical under a single emitter. Under twin emitters the nature of wetting at the soil surface tends to become elliptical whereas, the moisture front advance in the profile changed from a three dimensional to almost two dimentional, after the moisture front of the two emitters touched each other and the pattern of soil moisture distribution under drip was bulb shaped. Suganya *et al.* (2007) stated that soil moisture content was higher near the dripper (0-30 cm) and it decreased with the increase in lateral distance from the emitter. Similarly, it was higher in the surface layer (0-15 cm) and followed a decreasing trend with the depth. This uniform soil water content represented soil water near the field capacity indicating optimum soil water availability conditions for the crop. It implies that the drip system could maintain an ideal moisture regime for optimum crop growth condition and thus ensures water saving or increasing the water use efficiency.

In drip irrigation with the increase in water application, the moisture content of soil increased horizontally and vertically, respectively. Horizontal spread of moisture content at 4 lit hr-1 discharge rate of drip irrigation for 1 hr and 2 hrs was 0.3 m and 0.6 m, respectively on the soil surface. The depth attained by the outermost moisture profile in shallow soil was lower as compared to deep and medium types of soil for 1 hr and 2 hrs operation. The moisture content was in the range of 71 to 100 per cent of field capacity under drip irrigation (Arulkar *et al.*, 2008).

In general, root development under drip irrigation is constrained to the soil volume wetted by the emitters, near the soil surface with root length density decreasing with depth (Stevens and Douglas, 1994; Michelakis *et al.*, 1993). Roots are more concentrated near the water source for daily irrigated plots with 75 per cent of roots occurring within 50 cm of the emitter. In contrast, roots are more evenly distributed laterally in weekly irrigated plots with 63 per cent occurring within 50 cm of the emitter.

Regarding the root length, in the daily irrigated plots roots are highly concentrated in the surface layers, with 64 per cent occurring in the upper 45 cm and the density markedly decreasing below 75 cm. In comparison, roots are more evenly distributed in weekly irrigated plots, with 43 per cent occurring in the surface 45 cm and significant root penetration to below 120 cm (Earl and Jury, 1977).

Rooting patterns have traditionally been analyzed by means of root weight density or root length density (RLD). The distribution of RLD is an important indicator of potential water uptake (Sharp and Davis, 1985). However, studies have shown that actual water uptake patterns (root activity or effectiveness) reflect a complex interplay between RLD and other soil factors such as water, nutrient and aeration status of the root zone.

A good understanding of crop root distributions and water uptake patterns has become increasingly important as we seek to develop modern and environmentally-friendly practices involving high frequency irrigation and fertigation (Clothier and Green, 1994). Vanangamudi *et al.* (1990) reported that, the root length of chilli was higher when irrigation was scheduled at 83 mm CPE as compared to irrigation at 63 and 53 mm CPE, respectively.

Rose

Water requirement of roses depends upon the soil type and seasons. Therefore, irrigation be adjusted in such a way that soil will remain moist but not wet. Irrigation is done once in 2 days until plants establish and once a week thereafter. Avoid salt water for irrigation purpose. Drought stress leads to defoliation and sunburns of canes, and may contribute to spider mite problems. However, over watering or poorly drained soils may lead to root disease and nutritional deficiencies. Frequency and duration of irrigation will depend on weather conditions and soil texture. Roses do best when 50% of available water is depleted between irrigations. Checking after irrigation to determine soil moisture status and rate of depletion is helpful in scheduling irrigation. Daily irrigation should not be necessary. Water may be supplied via overhead sprays, flood irrigation, or drip tubing. Irrigation with over-the-top delivery should take place in the morning so foliage dries during the day. Mulches help to decrease water loss from the soil through evaporation and may enhance growth of the root system.

A better understanding of the effects of irrigation frequency on flower production and quality of rose plants can help to propose optimal irrigation scheduling. Irrigation scheduling was based on crop transpiration, and irrigation was performed whenever accumulative solar radiation outside the greenhouse reached 1600 kJ m^{-2} [high irrigation frequency (HIF)] and 3200 kJ m^{-2} (low irrigation frequency). The amount of water applied was 0·2 and 0·4 mm for high and low irrigation frequencies, respectively. The results showed that irrigation frequency influenced cut flower fresh and dry weight, since the total fresh and dry weight of cut flower shoots measured at the end of the experimental period was about 33% higher in the HIF treatment. As far as the number of shoots harvested is concerned, the results showed that the higher the irrigation frequency, the higher the production, as the total number of cut flowers measured at the end of the experimental period was 20·7 and 16·2 per cent greenhouse $m^{''2}$ for high and low irrigation frequencies, respectively, namely about 28% higher in the HIF. Furthermore, the results showed that the length of rose flowering shoots was not affected by the irrigation frequency. In conclusion, it seems that the higher irrigation frequency improved the biomass production but did not affect the quality of harvested flowers. (Katsoulas, 2006)

Optimal irrigation scheduling of greenhouse soilless crops is very important since it influences the rhizosphere environment, media water potential, and salt accumulation, which in turn affects plant growth and photosynthesis, and consequently crop production and quality (Raviv and Blom, 2001). Irrigation control involves the determination of both timing and quantity of water application. The most common and simple method used until now for scheduling irrigation consists in estimating the crop transpiration by means of the radiation-based method (Stanhill and Scholte, 1974).

A solar integrator gives a starting signal to a water supply system after a previously set level of radiation is reached. An irrigation system controlled by a solar radiation method can appropriately supply nutrient solution to plants without unnecessary water and nutrient emissions (Rohand Lee, 1996). However, this method implies the knowledge of a 'crop coefficient', which varies in the function of the crop phenological stage. The fact that roses, unlike most other crops, are being constantly harvested and thereby exhibiting large fluctuation of the transpiring area must be taken into consideration when attempting to formulate any model for scheduling irrigation. Optimal irrigation scheduling is very important to save water, while efficient use of water by irrigation is becoming increasingly important. Accurate supply of water and nutrients will result in better water use efficiency, avoid stress situations and control production (Raviv and Blom, 2001).

Caballero *et al.* (1996) reported that when stress occurs during leaf growth in the marketable stem, although it does not affect the stems quality, it causes a yield delay of 10–15 days. It has also been reported (Chimonidou-Pavlidou, 1996, 1999) that drought stress was very damaging to rose plants development, affecting the quantity (up to 70% reduction in production) and quality (reduction of stem length and fresh weight) of the flowering shoots produced. On the other hand, excessive water in the substrate can also be injurious to roses by reducing substrate aeration and causing abnormal development of plants. One other important parameter in a hydroponic system that affects crop growth and development is the electrical conductivity (EC) of the nutrient solution. The EC of the nutrient solution in the root environment must vary between a low value, which implies the availability of nutrients in the solution, and a high value, which must be determined from the ability of the plants to grow in a high EC root environment.

Frequency of irrigation depends on stage of growth, soil texture,climate etc. In lighter soils more frequent irrigation is needed than in heavy soils. After manuring each time watering is necessary. Generally plants are not watered before and after pruning. Thereafter watering once in 10 days is recommended. Irrigation is done once in 2 days until plants establish and once a week thereafter. Avoid salt water for irrigation purpose. Irrigate once in 7 - 10 days depending on field conditions. Adopt drip irrigation to get good quality flowers apart from saving water. Twice a week during October to March, Thrice a week during April to June. No irrigation is required during the rainy season. Irrigations should not result in water logging.

The increasing irrigation water amounts significantly increased the flower yield in rose. Considering yield and water use efficiency, it was concluded that the most efficient irrigation scheduling was $k_{cp:}$ 0.40 (Ucar, 2016).

Nagaraju *et al.* (2003) observed that the plant supplied with drip irrigation (2 L & 4 L/plant/day) performed well with respect to plant spread (EW and NS direction), flower characteristics of rose cv. Landora as compared to those provided with flood irrigation. However, there was no significant variation between fresh weight of rose flowers from plant receiving 4 L and 2 L water through drip irrigation. Koriesh (1989) established that sub surface (4 l/plant) or drip irrigated rose plants produced more flowers as compared to that of surface irrigation.

Chimonidou (1998) studied rose cultivation in pots and observed that the stem length was significantly lower when irrigation intervals were 6 days during summer. He also noted that stem and bud length and bud diameter decreased when water stress occurred in the beginning of sprouting. Folegatti *et al.* (2001) observed that there is a linear tendency of increasing length and diameter of stems buds with increasing irrigation water depth and maximum values was obtained from T125 (Irrigation water depth corresponding to a fraction of reduced pan evaporation equal up to 125%) in rose.

Nagaraju *et al.* (2003) reported that the 4 L drip irrigation treatment significantly increased the stem length, neck and bud diameter and percentage quality flower production as compared to those of flood irrigation in rose cv. Landora. In rose cv. Gladiator, maximum flower yield (7.23 lakh/ha) was obtained from 0.8 PEF irrigation treatment through drip and fertigation with 100 % of recommended dose of NPK (90-30-30 g NPK/plant) and black plastic mulch, which was 47% higher than control (Anon., 2008b). Patil *et al.* (2008) revealed that drip irrigation (0.8 PEF) produced comparatively higher number of flowers and stalk length of rose than surface irrigation. Weight of flowers was recorded higher in 0.8 PEF irrigation regimes.

Through drip irrigation, prevent water expense efficiency increased as compared to control was 199 mm/ha, 104 mm/ha and 64 mm/ha in I1 (0.4 PEF), I2 (0.6 PEF) and I3 (0.6 PEF), respectively in rose (Anon, 2008). Borrelli (1981) revealed that in rose, flower number and stem length increased with increase in irrigation and nitrogen but beneficial effects were much greater when irrigation and N supplies were both combined together. The presence of NH_4 - nitrogen in the nutrient solution increased the flower yield and dry matter production and the cumulative flower yields were highest with 1 : 4 ($NH_4 : NO_3$) ratio (Feigin *et al.*, 1986).

Chrysanthemum

Water management is important aspect. Need adequate water during active vegetative growth when new leaves are being formed. After flower bud formation no leaves are formed and less water is required. Drip irrigation with 8-9 litres of water/m^2/day. Many soilless systems have been studied for growing cut chrysanthemums. However, the production of chrysanthemum in soilless culture still has some problems to be resolved. Irrigation frequencies of 6 (400 mL) and 8 (533 mL) times/day can improve plant growth and flowering characteristics such as plant dry weight and number of flowers of chrysanthemum plants grown under restricted root conditions. This may be attributable to a higher availability of nitrogen and phosphorus. For cultivation efficiency, an irrigation frequency of 6times/ day can be suggested for growing chrysanthemums under restricted root volume. (Taweesak *et al.*, 2014)

As in all plants, irrigation is an essential practice for chrysanthemum growing, but its adequate handling has been neglected by growers, resulting in growing loss and consequent productivity and quality decreases in the final product (Farias *et al.*, 2009).In order to irrigate more extensive areas with the available water resources, such factors as soil, plant, and water resource must be taken into consideration. In addition, the values of plant water consumption under either sufficient or deficient water conditions should be known throughout the growing season of plants and water-yield relationships should be formed accordingly. These data can be obtained by making a large number of investigations for each plant (Doorenbos and Kassam, 1979).

The large amount of irrigation water applied increased the plant water consumption, and its effect was reflected positively on the quality parameters; hence, a longer stem and a higher stem weight were obtained from the treatments with a larger amount of water application and high plant water consumption accordingly (Turan *et al.*, 2015).The vital role of water presents a great barrier preventing the cultivation of such commercially and ornamentally important plant under arid zones conditions. For chrysanthemum, reduction of irrigation from sufficient to deficient decreased its growth by 25% (Schuch, 1998).

Irrigation of two week intervals can improve plant survival, vegetative growth and flowering characteristics such as stem length, number of leaves and number of flowers in chrysanthemum plants grown in pots under restricted root volume. For cultivation efficiency, an irrigation frequency of one time a week with fertilizer application of 3.0 g l as foliar spray can be 1 suggested for vegetative growth of chrysanthemums under restricted root volume. However, flowering would be stimulated at two week irrigation intervals and fertilization with 15.0 g l in irrigation water (Hassanein, 2015). Schuch *et al.* (1998) observed that plant height and leaf area were maximum with high irrigation i.e. average of 300 ml per pot in chrysanthemum.

Irrigation Water and Evapotranspiration

Turan *et al.*, 2015 reported that,the evapotranspiration varied at different irrigation intervals even if the same amount of irrigation water was applied. Since the soil surfaces of the treatments with short irrigation intervals were 421 continuously wet, the values of plant water consumption measured in these treatments were higher. The deep percolation values ranged from 27.72 to 18.90 mm according to the experimental treatments. Since the irrigation water amount applied at the beginning of the experiment was higher than the values of plant water consumption, the majority of deep percolation (18.90 mm) had taken place before making a transition to scheduled irrigation. After making a transition to scheduled irrigation, no deep percolation occurred in treatments T3: kcp 3 = 0.60 and T4: kcp 4 = 0.30 (Figure 2.1).

Harbaugh *et al.* (1989) studied irrigation and fertilization management of cut chrysanthemums and observed that plant height, whole plant fresh weight and weight of marketable stems were similar regardless of irrigation (overhead vs trickle irrigation) (soluble or controlled release fertilizers) in the cv. Monatce yellow Iceberg.

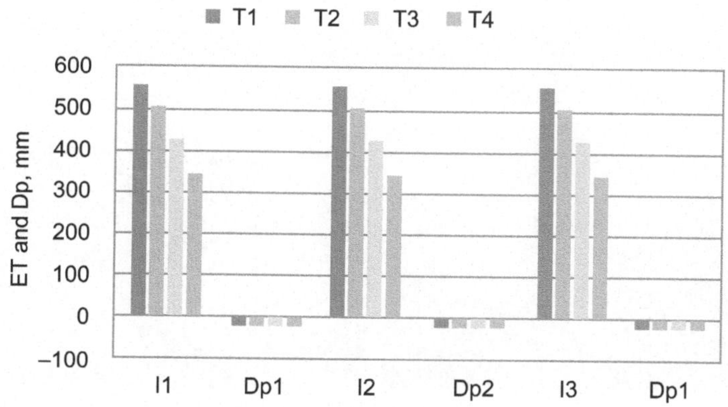

Fig. 2.1. Evapotranspiration and deep percolation values according to the experimental treatments (T1, T2, T3 and T4: The level of irrigation water amount; I1, I2 and I3: Irrigation interval; Dp1, Dp2 and Dp3: Deep percolation; ET: Evapotranspiration)

Anthurium

Anthurium require generous watering; Microclimate in green house, season, size of plant, plant stage, type of container, compost are factors that decide frequency of irrigation. More watering is needed in spring and summer, when plants are in flowering. Surface of soil is allowed to dry between successive watering.

Anthuriums can be given water either from above or below the plant. The top layer of the substrate may become very dry when plants receive water solely from below the pot (by using drip tubes or dripping spikes) during longer cultivation periods. Moreover the plants will assume a somewhat dull appearance due to the drier top layer and dust on the foliage. These problems can be avoided by watering the plants at intervals of 4-6 weeks, with water supplied either by sprinkler lines or spray booms.

When cultivating in beds a sprinkler system can be perfectly used for distributing the water.

However, for cultivation in pots it is better to use dripper spikes. The water must be free of chemical and visible contamination. Elements like sodium and chlorine must stay under 3 mmol/litre and also the bicarbonate cannot be too high. In the absence of supplies of good-quality water it will be necessary to make use of reverse-osmosis water.

The quantity of water required by the plants depends on the climate, the substrate, and the age of the crop. The capacity of the irrigation system should equal approximately 3 to 5 litres per m^2 per day. This amount should be dosed in three to five hours. For the irrigation system it is important that the drain water can easily be removed. The excess water should be removed to avoid the substrate getting too wet (Anthura and Bleiswijk, 2007).

Cultivation bed with 360° sprinklers (substrate is lava stones)

High greenhouse with 2 sprinkler lines, 180°sprinklers (substrate is oasis).

There are four methods of irrigation followed in green house anthurium cultivation. One is the ebb-and-flow system. When using this system, the pot must have an edge at the bottom to ensure good drainage of the pot. The absorbing capacity of the media is also important; pay attention to drying media at the top of the pot. A second method is an irrigation mat. The bottom of the pot should have two holes that are directly in contact with the mat. The absorbing capacity of the potting compost is important. The third method involves a PVC pipe with sprinklers. Wash off the fertilizers with clean water 30 seconds after every irrigation. This kind of overhead watering is used mostly with small pot sizes and young plants. The final method is drip irrigation. This system is especially effective with larger pot sizes due to longer growing time. The advantage is that the plants stay clean and use less water. With every drip, 50 ml per dripper is recommended. With pot sizes of 10 inches, two drippers per pot are advisable(Leeden, 2001).

Once the planting is finished watering may be carried out for 2 – 3 weeks without any fertilizer application. The growing media should be sufficiently wet all the time after 15 days of planting fertilizers may be added to the water. Normally two irrigations are ideal. The first in the morning and 2nd by afternoon. During very hot weather the 3rd watering may be added. (CCARI,2013- http://www.ccari.res.in/dss/Anthurium.html).

Mist or overhead sprinkler to provide water and to improve relative humidity. Anthuriums needs daily watering when rains are scarce. Hence a perennial water system has to be available as a prerequisite to establishing a farm. Water supplied to plants should be of good quality. (http://agritech.tnau.ac.in/horticulture/horti_flower%20 crops_anthurium.html)

Carnation

Over watering and poor drainage causes root death and stunted growth. Water logging would cause deprival of oxygen to plants. The growing medium should be evenly moist. Irrigation is provided with drip system once in 2-3 days according to soil moisture to maintain water holding capacity at 60% to 65%. The optimum water requirement of the crop is drip system with drippers at 30 cm spacing (5-6 l/m^2/day).(http://agritech.tnau.ac.in/horticulture/horti_flower%20crops_carnation.html)

Jasper (1966) reported that the maximum yield and the best quality could be obtained when the soil water tension is kept at -0.04 bars. Hanan (1969) pointed out that, when the solar radiation is about 600 cal m^{-2}, water use of carnation grown in greenhouse covered with glass is 12.28 mm whereas it is 8.19 mm for carnation grown in greenhouse covered with plastic. Khristov and Parlov (1977) reported that the carnation should be irrigated when 40% of the available soil moisture is depleted. Taylor *et al.* (2008) reported that the maximum flower yield and the best quality were obtained when the soil moisture tension was kept at – 45 kPa.

Water usage is a vital issue for all agricultural crops as well as for ornamental crops. To obtain high quality flowers, it is essential to supply water when it is required. A problem which is common with cut flower growers are determining when to irrigate and the amount of water to apply. Irrigation water amount and irrigation frequency are significantly important in order to obtain higher yield of carnation grown in unheated plastic greenhouses under the Mediterranean climatic conditions. Irrigation intervals and different pan coefficients applied had significant effects on all the characteristics of yield and flower quality of D. caryophyllus L. cv. Judith except for flower stem diameter. The highest yield and quality characteristics were obtained from cumulative CAP evaporation reached 10 mm and CAP coefficient of 1.20. It is concluded that flower stem length, flower stem diameter, flower diameter, stem weight, vase life, and yield were increased depending on higher irrigation intervals and pan coefficients compared to lower ones. It is concluded that low frequency irrigation water regimes may improve water use efficiency by reducing water consumption, not only low regimes but also high irrigation water regimes reduced plant size and decreased its ornamental quality. (Aydinsakir *et al.*, 2011).

An ideal soil for carnation growth is loamy sand or sandy loam soils well drained to a depth of 0.75 to 1.0 m and slightly alkaline. Agricultural use of water is an important issue for cut flower growers. Water use in greenhouse cut flower production is frequently at excessive levels. To obtain better flower yield and flower quality, irrigation under arid climates and greenhouses conditions is essential. The amount of irrigation water and frequency in carnation depends on soil texture, photoperiod, relative humidity, temperature, air convection, growing period and variety. As a general rule, it is required that the soil cultivated with carnation should be always moist. When the soil moisture level drops below the wilting point, the flowering and flower quality are affected negatively. One of the consequences of exposing plant to deficit irrigation regimes in terms of plant growth is the production of smaller leaves and shorter internodes sections and reductions in flower number, size and quality (Cameron *et al.*, 1999; Sanchez-Blanco *et al.*, 2004).

The soil for growing carnation needs to be kept near field capacity. Rooted cuttings need watering immediately after planting. Drip irrigation or Sprinkler system is effective and economical than soil surface irrigation. During first 3 weeks after planting you will need overhead sprinklers to prevent young plants from drying out. It is possible to gradually shift to drip irrigation (3 tubes per bed). Irrigation may be provided with drip system once in 2-3 days according to soil moisture to maintain water holding capacity at 60-65%. The optimum water requirement of the crop is 4-5 litres /m^2/day (http://agroan.com/carnation-cultivation/#_Toc459571969).

Rooted cuttings should be watered immediately after planting. Spraying of water through misting has to be done for at least two weeks. After 3 weeks of planting, drip irrigation has to be adopted. Drip irrigation system is being followed in carnation cultivation. Laterals are laid out every alternate row and emitters are spaced at 30 cm intervals. The amount of water to be given per irrigation depends upon factors like air temperature, light intensity, humidity, soil type and soil temperature. Fully grown carnation plants require 4-5 lit of water/m^2 /day. It is advisable to check the irrigation water quality in terms of EC and pH. Stagnation of water should be avoided to minimize the incidence of diseases. (Jawaharlal *et al.*, 2010).

Aydinsakir *et al.* (2011) observed that WUE values decreased when the amount of water use increased. In carination the highest WUE was obtained from I1PC1 (10mm pan evaporation and 0.60 Epan coefficient) treatment as 0.51 and 0.30 number m^{-2} mm^{-1} in the first and second year of the experiment, respectively.

Aydinsakir *et al.* (2011) observed that flower stem length was maximum with I1Pc1 treatment (10 mm pan evaporation and 0.60 pan coefficient) in carnation, whereas flower stem diameter and flower diameter were obtained maximum with I1Pc3 treatment (10 mm pan evaporation and 1.20 mm pan coefficient). The longest vase life (23.3 days) was obtained in I2Pc3 treatment (20 mm pan evaporation and 1.20 mm pan coefficient) in carnation. Flowers grown under the low frequency irrigation treatment (I1Pc1) had a significantly shorter vase life as compared to other treatments.

Kazaz *et al.* (2010) reported that both irrigation interval and crop pan coefficients significantly affected total yield of carnation flowers and noted that the highest total number of flowers was obtained from I1kcp-4 treatments (One day interval and 1.0 crop pan coefficients) followed by I1kcp-5 treatment. Kazaz *et al.* (2010) noted longest stem length (71.04 cm) from Kcp-5 (1.25 CPC) while shortest from Kcp-1 (0.25 CPC) in terms of irrigation intervals, the longest stems were obtained from I1 (One day interval of irrigation) in carnation.

Irrigation Water and Water Use in Carnations

Aydinsakir *et al.*, 2011 reported that,the irrigation water (I) in Table 2.1 includes also the amount of 100 mm water applied equally in all the treatments for rooting. In the first year, the amount of water applied to Pc1, Pc2, Pc3 and Pc4 treatments were 319.8, 429.7, 539.5 and 649.4 mm, respectively. In the second year, the amount of water applied to Pc1, Pc2, Pc3 and Pc4 treatments were 600.1, 850.2, 1100.2 and 1350.3 mm, respectively.

Deep percolation from the root zone was also one of the important components in soil water balance. The difference of drainage amount between treatments depended on the amount of total irrigation. As the amount of water applied in each treatments increased, depending on CAP coefficients, deep percolations increased also.

On the other hand, when the irrigation intervals increased, a decrease in deep percolation was observed because of the increased deficiency in soil water storage as a result of transpiration by carnation plants and evaporation over soil surface. I_1Pc_4 (I1: 10 mm pan evaporation and Pc4 = 1.50 Epan) irrigation application had the largest deep percolation amount and treatment I2Pc1 (I2: 20 mm pan evaporation and Pc1 = 0.60 Epan) had the least amount of deep percolation (Table 2.1).

Table 2.1. The Components of Water Balance and WUE in Carnations

Year	Treatment	Yield number (m^{-2})	I (mm)	Dp (mm)	DSW (mm)	WU (mm)	WUE number (m^{-2} mm^{-1})
2006	I1Pc1	147.5	319.8	51.4	21.8	290.2	0.51
	I1Pc2	160.0	429.7	72.9	19.9	376.9	0.42
	I1Pc3	167.5	539.5	97.1	18.8	461.2	0.36
	I1Pc4	162.5	649.4	110.3	13.2	552.3	0.29
	I2Pc1	140.0	319.8	19.1	23.5	324.2	0.43
	I2Pc2	150.0	429.7	21.5	24.8	433.0	0.35
	I2Pc3	157.5	539.5	29.7	19.0	528.8	0.30
	I2Pc4	147.5	649.4	38.9	14.4	624.9	0.24

2007	I1Pc1	150.0	600.1	122.2	23.2	501.1	0.30
	I1Pc2	162.5	850.2	157.1	9.2	702.3	0.23
	I1Pc3	170.0	1100.2	199.0	4.2	905.4	0.19
	I1Pc4	165.0	1350.3	229.6	3.0	1123.7	0.15
	I2Pc1	140.0	600.1	36.0	13.7	577.8	0.24
	I2Pc2	155.0	850.2	49.6	9.8	810.4	0.19
	I2Pc3	157.5	1100.2	60.9	5.8	1045.1	0.15
	I2Pc4	150.0	1350.3	99.8	3.9	1254.4	0.12

Seasonal water use (WU) varied from 290.2 to 624.9 mm in the first year and 501.1 to 1254.4 mm in the second year of the experiment. As seen in Table 2.1, water use increased with increasing pan coefficient in each irrigation intervals. For a given pan coefficient, although the same irrigation water was applied, as irrigation interval increased, water use also increased as a result of decreasing deep percolation and increasing amount of water taken from the soil water storage (Table 2.1).

WUE values decreased when the amount of water use increased (Table 2.1). The highest WUE was obtained from I1Pc1 treatment as 0.51 and 0.30 number m-2 mm-1 in the first and second year of the experiment, respectively. Halepyati *et al.* (1995) also obtained similar WUE values for *Polianthes tuberose* crop. The authors reported the highest value of WUE in the treatment, where applied irrigation water was 40% of pan evaporation while the highest flower yield was obtained from treatment where irrigation water was 120% of pan evaporation. Similar to their results, in both years of this study, the highest flower yield was obtained from the treatment where pan coefficient was 120% while the highest WUE value was obtained from the treatment, where pan coefficient was 60.

China Aster

Maintain an even moisture content in the container; excessive drying will cause leaf browning and drop. Overhead watering or drip irrigation is adequate. Irrigate once in 7 - 10 days depending upon the weather conditions. China aster [Callistephuschinensis (L.) Ness.] a member of the family Asteraceae, is one of the important commercial flower crops of our country. Among annual flower crops, it ranks next to chrysanthemum and marigold. In India China aster occupied approximately more than 5000 ha grown in few states like Maharastra, Karnataka, Tamil Nadu, West Bengal and Andhra Pradesh (Chowdhuri *et al.*, 2016). Application of 8 litre of irrigation water and 100 per cent water soluble fertilizers per square metre was found beneficial compared to control in china aster cv. Kamini and cv. Violet Cushion (Vijaya Kumar *et al.*, 2011).

Gerbera

Drip irrigation is done once in 2 – 3 days @ 3.75 litre/drip/plant for 15 – 20 minutes. Average water requirement is about 500 – 700 ml/day/plant. Gerberas should receive a thorough watering and then be allowed to dry somewhat. This limits growth of the flower stem and discourages soilborne diseases. Gerberas should never be allowed to wilt, however. Plants allowed drying out too much and too frequently having short flower stems that may be hidden in the foliage. It is also a good practice to water early in the day so the foliage is completely dry before evening. (http://agritech.tnau.ac.in/horticulture/horti_flower%20crops_gerbera.html).

Higher yields can be obtained through drip irrigation. Lay plastic pipe (laterals) between two rows. Install drips at distance of 2 - 5 feet with capacity to discharge 4 ltr. of water per hour. Drip and micro sprinklers desirable. pH of the water 6.5 to 7.0. EC 0,5 to 1 mS/cm. One drip/plant. Water requirement –700 ml to 1 lit/day/plant. Micro-sprinklers-early stage-encourage uniform and good root development-practised upto first flowering. Resort to drip. Foggers for humidity maintenance. Morning irrigation is best. Soil should be wet uniformly. Excess water and RH led to deformed flowers. 500-700 ml of water/day/plant to be given through drip. In drip system- place drippers of 2 l /hr capacity at 5-10 cm away from plant Irrigate 4-10 times a day.

Gerbera's require 80 – 90% humidity immediately after planting. This is possible by irrigation with overhead irrigation system or spraying the same until a month or so. This helps in uniform root development. Thereafter gradually change the drip irrigation. Generally 1 drip per plant is required. If hard watering is adopted then a jerry can may be used. The quantity of water required for a plant varies from season to season. Watering should be completed before 12 noon. The relative humidity of the air should not exceed 90 – 92% as it cause deformity of flowers. Soil may always be moist and never soggy or dry (CCARI).

Junges (1964) observed that the difference in number of flowers in gerbera due to seasonal differences in light intensity could partly be reduced by irrigation and stem length increased with the water supply at flower initiation. Patil *et al.,* (2008) noted maximum stalk length, stalk thickness and number of flowers/plant in gerbera with the application of irrigation at 0.4 PEF and it was also statistically at par with 0.6 PEF of irrigation level. Water requirement of gerbera under polyhouse condition was found to be 1184, 888 and 592 mm under 0.40 PEF, 0.60 PEF and 0.80 PEF irrigation levels, respectively. They are noted that WUE of gerbera was found maximum in 0.40 PEF i.e. 0.35 flowers/m^2-mm or 3520 flowers/m^2-mm. The WUE decreased considerably with increase in the levels of drip irrigation (Anon, 2007).

Gladiolus

Gladiolus plants re-quire plenty of water during the entire growth period. The most critical period a water requirement, however, starts with the formation of third leaf and ends when the seventh leaf appears. Watering should be done early in the morning. The crop should not be allow to suffer from moisture stress especially when the spikes are emerging wherever the facility is available the field is the 7-10 days. Irrigation should be withheld at least 4-6 weeks before lifting of corms. Lack of soil moisture during spike differentiation and emergence often leads to blindness. Mulching materials like polythene sheet, dry grass, saw dust etc., may be used to preserve soil moisture.

Gladiolus is a water loving plant and needs sufficient moisture in the soil till the harvesting of spikes. Flower bud initiation and spike elongation are the most critical stages in gladiolus. Moisture stress during these stages results in a considerable damage to growth and yield. Water requirement and frequency of irrigation depend on the soil type, weather conditions and stage of the crop. Lateritic soils need more number of irrigations compared to sandy loam soils. Irrigation is not required in rainy season unless there is a dry spell. In lateritic soils, irrigation should be given once in a week during winter and twice in a week during summer whereas in sandy loam soils once in a week during summer and once in a week or 10 days during winter. Normally, irrigation can be cut down after the harvest of spikes and withheld completely once leaves start yellowing. If the soil is hard, a light irrigation may be given to facilitate the lifting of corms from the soil. Irrigate the crop once in 10 days when it is grown under partial shade of coconut gardens during summer season. It can tolerate high summer temperature and comes up well if sufficient moisture is maintained in the soil during the crop period. So, the success of the crop in summer is mainly dependant on the irrigation (CCARI).

Flower bud initiation and spike elongation are the most critical stages in gladiolus. Gadiolus is a water loving plant and needs sufficient moisture in the soil till the harvesting of spikes. Normally, irrigation can be cut down after the harvest of spikes and withheld completely once leaves start yellowing (FRS, 2017).

Howell (1972) suggested that 50 mm of weekly water application in well-drained soil would maintain a strong development of gladiolus. Maggio *et al.* (1993) concluded that flower weight and length were the highest when 1500 m^3/ha water was applied, but 700 m^3/ha water application were enough to reach standard yield of gladiolus. Bastug *et al.* (2006) reported that the highest flowering per cent in I3 treatment i.e. 1.0 Epan (86.2%) followed by I2 i.e. 0.75 Epan (75.2%) and I3 i.e. 0.50 Epan (58.1%) in gladiolus. The total water use of I1, I2 and I3 irrigation treatments during the entire growing period were found to be 203.6, 246.8 and 289.6 mm, respectively. Begum *et al.* (2007) reported the highest spike yield of gladiolus with three irrigation applied at sprouting, 4 leaves and spike initiation stage, while the lowest spike yield of gladiolus was obtained from control treatment.

Begum *et al.* (2007) noted that the total water expense (TWE) by gladiolus varied with the variation of irrigation water applied to the soil. The highest TWE bearing was found in I4 (irrigation at plant emergence, 4 leaves, spike initiation and flower initiation) and the lowest in I0 (no irrigation). El Gamassy *et al.* (1977) observed that the yield and quality of flowers were best when the plants were watered at an interval of 12 or 17 days and a minimum soil moisture content of 58% field capacity for successful gladiolus cultivation in sandy clay soil. Alvino *et al.* (1998) found that the water use efficiency of CO_2 enriched plots was higher than that of the control plots. They also observed that irrigation was based on pan evaporation and the crop co-efficient were changed depending on the growth period in gladiolus.

Heliconia

Heliconia love water. They should be watered as often as possible, at least once in the morning and once in the evening. The soil should never be allowed to dry out completely. Rotting of established plants as a result of over-watering is unlikely as long as the soil is free-draining. In fact, some species of *Heliconia*can even be adapted to grow completely in water, such as *Heliconiastandleyi* and *Heliconiadensiflora* 'Fireflash'. However, the watering of newly-planted rhizomes is a completely different matter, as they are prone to fungal attacks in excessively water-retentive soil.

Jasmine

Irrigation is most important for jasmines. Constant and adequate water supply (irrigating twice a week) in light soils during peak flowering season (March –October) is essential for high yield of flowers. After flowering is over, the water supply can be cut off. Constant and adequate water supply during peak flowering season is essential for high yield of flowers. After flowering is over, the water supply can be cut off. During summer, irrigate twice a week (CCARI). Irrigate the plants once in a week depending on soil and climatic conditions. Irrigation is essential during summer months. Irrigate the crop at the time of applying fertilizers. Frequent irrigation is essential during flowering stage. Irrigate the crops once in 4 days during summer months and earth up the plants. (UAS, Bangalore).

Thamburaj *et al.* (1984) reported that the *Jasminum grandiflorum* plants were irrigated when available soil moisture (ASM) reached to 60, 40 and 20% of field capacity with control plants being irrigated weekly. Irrigation at 60% ASM increased flower yield by 20.33% over control. Whereas, irrigation at 20% ASM decreased the flower yield by 9.02%. Drip irrigation with 10 litres of water per day (LPD) and 75 percent of recommended dose of fertilizers (RDF) with black polyethylene mulch recorded highest values for growth and flower quality parameters in jasmine (Vijayselvaraj, 2007).

Marigold

At all stages of vegetative growth (55-60 days) and during flower production sufficient amount of moisture in soil is essential. Moisture stress at any stage affects normal growth and flowering. In lighter soils more frequent irrigations are required than in heavy soils. In sandy loam soil, weekly irrigation is necessary between September and March while during summer months between April to June irrigation at 4-5 days intervals is required.

It is a herbaceous plant and makes required growth rapidly in earlier stages. It takes 50-68 days to complete vegetative stage and enter to reproductive stage. At this stage terminal flowers bud appears which breaks the apical dominance and side branches starts growing. At all stages filling flower production sufficient amount of soil moisture is essential moisture stress affects growing weakly irrigation is necessary in sandy loam soil and during summer month frequent irrigation us given at an intent of 4-5 days. Irrigation is done once in a week or as and when necessary. Water stagnation should be avoided. (http://agritech.tnau.ac.in/horticulture/horti_flower%20crops_marigold.html)

Razvi and Omer (1994) obtained the highest plant growth parameters in *Tagetespatula* with 0.5 litre of water per pot applied at 10 days interval. Ram *et al.* (1999) studied the effect of irrigation regimes on growth and herb production of *Tagetesminuta*during winter season at foothills of UP. Plant height and number of primary branches per plant were highest when crop was irrigated at 0.4 IW: CPE and highest herb yield was obtained at 0.2 IW: CPE. Halepyati *et al.* (2001) reported that higher growth in terms of plant height, leaf production and dry matter production of marigold was obtained with irrigation scheduled at 100% Epan. However, the lowest values were recorded with irrigation scheduled at 40% Epan.

Halepyati *et al.* (2002) observed that tuberose was tallest in plant height (26.8 and 40.5 cm), number of leaves (17.5 and 23.2) and leaf area (1001 and 1217.3 cm2/plant) in 1992 and 1993, respectively, when the crop was irrigated at 100% Epan during the entire crop growth. Halepyati *et al.* (2001) obtained maximum flower yield (7240.8 kg/ha) in marigold when irrigated at replenishing 120% Epan. Irrigation at 0.5 IW : CPE ratio also resulted in the highest herbage and oil yield in *Tagetesminuta*. Halepyati *et al.* (2001) revealed that the highest flower yield (7240.2 kg/ha) was obtained when irrigation scheduled at 120% Epan. It may be due to differences in number of flowers per plant and diameter of flowers.

The flowering characters like flower diameter, number of flowers per plant, weight of ten flowers and flower yield were found better when marigold plants irrigated at 1.2 IW / CPE ratio (Chawla *et al.*, 2008). Chawla *et al.*,(2008) revealed that maximum proline and total sugar from fresh leaves at 90 DAT were recorded with irrigation at 0.6 IW/CPE ratio, which were lower with irrigation at 1.2 IW/CPE ratio in marigold. Ram *et al.* (1999) observed at 1.2 IW: CPE ratio, 338.5 mm CUW and the WUE value was 0.31 kg oil ha-1 mm-1 in marigold.

Chawla *et al.*, (2008) observed that consumptive use of water increased significantly with increase in levels of irrigation regimes up to 1.2 IW/CPE ratio, whereas water use efficiency decreased up to irrigation at 1.2 IW/CPE ratio in marigold. Halepyati *el al.* (2001) noted average highest water use efficiency (15.59 kg ha-1/mm-1) in marigold with irrigation replenishment of 40 % Epan. Chawla *et al.*,(2008) reported that plant height, plant spread and number of branches per plant were higher with irrigation scheduled at 1.2 IW/CPE ratio. It may be due to fact that adequate soil moisture provided resulted in greater development of green tissue areas contributing to higher photosynthesis and assimilation in marigold.

Sunflower

Vivek and Chakor (1992) recorded maximum plant height (106.66 cm and 116.50 cm) leaf area index (4.70 and 4,18) and functional leaves at flowering (23.16 and 24.39) in sunflower in rainfed condition in 1988 and 1989, respectively, with the application of irrigation at 0.9 IW: CPE ratio. Sharma (1994) reported maximum plant height (176.2 cm), number of leaves per plant (27.3) and stem diameter (1.79 cm) in sunflower (*Helianthus annus*) cv "EC 68415" with the application of 3 irrigations (1st at pre sowing + 2nd at 3-4 leaves +3rd at flowering stage).

Vivek and Chakor (1992) reported the highest seed yield of 18.16 and 18.39 q/ha in 1988 and 1989, respectively at 0.9 IW: CPE ratio which was significantly higher than other irrigation levels i.e. 0.3 and 0.6 IW: CPE ratio in sunflower. Sharma (1994) reported maximum head diameter (17.8 cm) and seed yield (15.83 q/ha) in sunflower cv. "EC 68415" with the application of 3 irrigations (1st at pre-sowing + 2nd at 3-4 leaves + 3rd at flowering stage). Singh *et al.* (1997b) recorded highest disc diameter (17.0 cm), weight of 1000-seeds (41.3g) and seed yield (1.72 t/ha) in sunflower with the application of 4 irrigation (25 DAS + flower bud initiation + complete flowering + seed setting).

The low productivity of sunflower in India in general, is due to its cultivation in unfavorable environmental conditions such rain feed condition in marginal and sub marginal lands with poor nutrient supply, improper irrigation scheduling and inadequate plant protection measures. Water being a natural resource input and now a scare and costly input in the production of agricultural crops, has direct influence on the availability of nutrients from the soil. Judicious irrigation management is crucial in sunflower production.

In post–rainy /simmer season sunflower responds better to man agreement factors, especially irrigation. More than 62 per cent increase in seed yield has been observed due to irrigation compared to rainfed condition (Sunilkumar *et al.*, 1992).

Turan *et al.*, 2015 revealed that, higher head diameter (14.34), number of seeds per head (662) and seed weight per head (25.61 g) (Table 2.2) were recorded in 0.8 IW/CPE ratio over rest of irrigation schedules (0.4, 0.6 IW/CPE ratio and critical stages). Increase in these yield components is mainly attributed to better performance of plants with respect to growth parameters like plant height, number of leaves, leaf area index and total dry matter production. This is mainly due to optimum moisture available in the root zone which favoured plant growth throughout growing period reflecting better growth attributes.

Table 2.2 : Yield Parameters of Sunflower at Harvest as Influenced by Irrigation Schedules and Mulcheses

Irrigation schedules (I)	Head diameter (cm)				Number of seeds per head				Seed weight per head (g)			
	Mulches (M)											
	M1	M2	M3	Mean	M1	M2	M3	Mean	M1	M2	M3	Mean
I1	12.39	13.18	13.74	13.10	576.6	560.0	589.0	573.8	18.67	20.93	22.45	20.68
I2	13.68	14.10	14.17	13.99	567.6	586.6	613.3	589.2	21.76	22.64	24.39	22.93
I3	14.26	14.24	14.52	14.34	597.0	675.0	715.0	662.3	24.16	26.24	26.44	25.61
I4	12.04	12.91	13.55	12.83	519.3	555.3	608.3	562.6	18.74	20.27	21.65	20.22
Mean	13.09	13.61	13.99		565.1	590.5	634.4		20.83	22.50	23.73	
For comparison	S.E.±		C.D. (P = 0.05)		S.E.±		C.D. (P = 0.05)		S.E.±		C.D. (P = 0.05)	
Irrigation schedules (I)	0.18		0.64		10.4		36.0		0.40		1.40	
Mulches (M)	0.14	0.44	13.7	41.3	0.33	0.99						
I x M	0.30	NS	24.8	NS	0.67	NS						

Note : I1 : 0.4 IW / CPE
I2 : 0.6 IW / CPE
I3 : 0.8 IW / CPE
I4 : Critical stages

M1 : No mulch NS-Non significant
M2 : Mulch with maize straw
M3 :Mulch with polythene

Mishra *et al.* (2012) revealed significantly higher seed yield, stalk yield and harvest index of sunflower under 0.9 IW/CPE irrigation schedule based on critical stage than other treatment. However, significantly lower values were recorded under irrigation schedule of 0.7 IW/CPE. The consumptive use of water and water use efficiency increased with increase in irrigation level. Maximum water use efficiency of 4.79 kg/ha/mm was recorded under irrigation at 25 DAS + flower bud initiation + complete flowering + seed setting in sunflower (Singh *et al.* 1997b).

Orchid

Mist irrigation or fogging or micro sprinkler is ideal. Water should have natural pH and free from dissolved salts. As orchid is grown on very porous substrate, it is important to supply the water to the crown portion by using sprinkler. The water must be free from any harmful chemicals or contamination. The quantity of water required by the plants depends on climate, substrate and the age of crop. The irrigation system must be capable of supplying between 5 to 12 liters of water per meter per hour. It is very important to ensure that plants are provided with appropriate drainage (CCARI).

Tuberose

In India it has gained considerable importance and is being commercially grown in West Bengal, Tamil Nadu, Maharashtra, Karnataka and hilly areas. It is grown for long stem cut flowers, flowers, beds, borders and pot plant. It is also grown for perfumery as its flowers contain about 0.1 per cent oil.

It is very essential to irrigate before planting to provide optimum moisture for sprouting and further irrigation should be avoided until the bulbs are sprouted. During summer, irrigation should be given at weekly interval or even earlier in case soil dries out and during winter at 10 days interval. (http://eagri.org/eagri50/HORT281/pdf/lec41.pdf).

Soil should have 60-90 per cent moisture and no watering is required until bulbs sprout. Depending upon weather 8-12 irrigations of 2.5-5 cm depth are required. Stage immediately after sprouting and 4-6 leaf stage are very sensitive to water deficit. Irrigation once a week is ideal. Mulching reduce the water requirement up to some extent. However, irrigation should be avoided at maturity stage of bulbs.(http://www.hillagric.ac.in/edu/coa/vegetables/lectures/VSF_231_Flori/VSF_231_Flori_Lect_17_Tuberose.pdf).

Soil moisture is an important factor affecting the growth, flowering and bulb yield of tuberose. Field should be irrigated after planting the bulbs and further irrigation should be avoided until the sprouting of bulbs. The crop should be irrigated at weekly interval in the absence of rainfall. However, irrigation should be avoided at the maturity stage of bulbs during December-January.

Scheduled based on prevailing temperature nature of crop, soil, humidity etc. Over irrigation is harmful as it leads to rotting of flower irrigation once in a week – summer once in 15 days – winter immediately after planting, until the bulb germinate the field is not irrigated. Irrigation is an important factor affecting growth and flowering in tuberose. It is very essential to irrigate before planting to provide optimum moisture for sprouting and further irrigation should be avoided until the bulbs are sprouted. During summer irrigation should be given at weekly intervals or even earlier in case soil dries out and during winter at 10 days interval.

Halepyati *et al.* (1995) reported that spike length, rachis length and number of flowers/spike linearly increased with increasing the irrigation frequency and highest values of spike length, rachis length and number of flowers/spike were noted with 1.2 IW/CPE ration in tuberose. Tuberose production i.e. number of spikes, weight of flower, length of spike and vase life were found to be higher in drip irrigation at 0.8 PEF as compared to control (Patil *et al.*, 2008).

The application of irrigation based on IW/CPE ratio revealed that plant height of tuberose consistently increased with the increasing moisture regimes. However, the highest plant height of 54.97 was obtained with the irrigation at 1.0IW/CPE ratio, which was superior to other irrigation treatments. Maximum flower per spike (31.80) was observed at 1.0 IW/CPE ratio and the minimum number of flower/ spike (31.40) was recorded by irrigation schedule of 0.8 IW/ CPE ratios. The varietals effects in promoting the number of flower per spike, irrespective of irrigation levels, were significantly influenced. The maximum spike per plot was recorded at 1.0 IW/CPE which gave about 33.15 number of spike per plot, which was superior to 0.8 IW/CPE (32.25) and 0.4 IW/CPE (30.57) (Khanam *et al.*, 2017).

Table 2.3: Effects of Irrigation Levels on Diameter of Spike and Flower Per Spike of Three Varieties of Tuberose

Treatment	Diameter of spike (cm)				Flower/spike			
	Variety			Mean	Variety			Mean
	V1	V2	V3		V1	V2	V3	
I1	3.1	3.3	3.4	3.27	30.8	31.5	32.5	31.6
I2	3.2	3.4	3.4	3.33	30.3	31.4	32.6	31.39
I3	3.1	3.3	3.5	3.35	29.6	31.6	34.3	31.84
Mean	3.15	3.36	3.41	—	30.22	31.5	33.12	—
SEm (±)	I	V	I x V		I	V	I x V	
	0.05	0.05	0.08		0.38	0.38	0.66	
CD (5%)	NS	0.14	NS		NS	1.14	NS	

Note: I1 = Irrigation at 0.4 IW/CPE, I2 = Irrigation at 0.8% IW/CPE, I3 = Irrigation at 1.0 IW/CPE and V1 = Variety Prajwal, V2 = Variety Calcutta single, V3 = Variety Calcutta double

Khanam *et al.*, 2017 reported that, for computing the net profit and benefit cost ratio, the prevailing cost of cultivation and the gross return from the flower crop as per market value was taken into consideration. The result showed that the higher net reruns was recorded at higher moisture regime (IW/CPE at 1.0) followed by intermediate moisture regime (IW/CPE at 0.8) and lower moisture regime (IW/CPE at 0.4). However, the benefit-cost ratio was just opposite to net return values. This indicated that the economic yield of tuberose was not high enough in response to the higher irrigation regimes, thereby giving lesser gross return as well as the net return values as compared to the lower moisture regime.

However, the benefit-cost ratio was just opposite to net return values. This indicated that the economic yield of tuberose under higher moisture level was not high enough/or optimal in response to the higher irrigation regimes, thereby giving lesser gross return as well as the net return values as compared to the lower moisture regime.

Table 2.4: Economics of Tuberose Cultivation under Different Moisture Regimes

Particulars	Irrigation levels		
	0.4 IW/CPE	0.8 IW/CPE	1.0 IW/CPE
Cost of Cultivation (Rs/ha)	125000	135000	140000
Yield (Spike/ha)	254750	268750	276250
Selling price (Rs./ spike)	0.75	0.75	0.75
Gross return (Rs./ha)	191062	201562	207187
Net return (Rs/ha)	66062	66562	67187
Benefit : cost ratio	0.53 : 1	0.49 : 1	0.48 : 1

Halepyati *et al.* (2002) observed that irrigation at 100% Epan during entire of tuberose produced maximum spike length (85.3 and 88.1 cm), rachis length (21.7 and 22.9 cm), number of florets per spike (37.6 and 40.6) and flower yield (78.49 and 84.59 q/ha) in 1992 and 1993. Halepyati *et al.* (2002) also noted that the WUE was highest with irrigation given to replenishment of 50 % Epan during vegetative as well as reproductive period in tuberose. Halepyati *et al.* (1995) also obtained similar WUE values for *Polianthestuberosa.*

Conclusion

In Indian context, water is a factor of prime importance in agriculture industry. Water resources are continuously been overburdened with excessive drafts and water sources are shrinking at faster rate. Groundwater levels are dropping at the rates faster than ever. If the current trend continues perennial streams will be converted to intermittent and intermittent streams will be nonexistent. Under this type of scenario judicious use of water is with due attention to key issues of water conservation and increasing water productivity is imperative. Area under horticultural plantations is increasing at exponential rate. The unproductive uplands and low productive midlands and lowlands are brought under fruit based horticultural plantations. For example farmers in the eastern plateau region are changing their rice based mono cropping system to more remunerative horticultural plantations. Four technologies that are best suited for the optimal use of water in this region are described in following sections. These technologies are water harvesting and utilization for horticultural development, Doba technique of water harvesting, Drum Kit drip irrigation system and sub surface drip in vegetables water harvesting and utilization for Horticultural development Eastern Plateau and hill zone (Zone-III) is characterized by semi humid climatic conditions; it has high average annual rainfall of about 1350 mm. Distribution of rainfall is not uniform throughout the year. It is concentrated in only four monsoon months and rest part of the year remains almost without rain. Topography is undulating which does not allow stagnation of water, and the precious water flows out of the area. To irrigate the upland horticulture one has to pump the water from lowlands which requires an extra cost on the irrigation. Retaining the water in upland area itself can overcome this fact. Moreover the highly permeable nature of soils gives rise to high seepage. The only way to ensure the availability of water during non-monsoon months is water harvesting and it is imperative to build a water harvesting structure in the midlands and uplands. In uplands and midlands, unless some water harvesting structure is built up it is not possible to retain the water for future use.

Irrigation is in short supply in most locations and therefore demands a careful and economic use. Economy of water helps to bring more areas under protective irrigation and leads to a greater crop production in areas of limited water supply. On areas where water is scarce, farmers are not able to apply normal irrigation to crops and are forced to skip some irrigation. It is therefore necessary to decide a priority of stages of crops when irrigations are to be applied and the stages when one or more irrigations can be skipped. The critical stages of water need of crops receive the foremost attention. It is necessary to simultaneously consider and weigh the relative importance of the various stages for irrigation and the availability of water. A preferential status of crop stages according to their relative importance to yield should be considered for irrigation in areas of water scarcity.

REFERENCES

AIPH. 2007. International Statistics Flowers and Plants. Volume 55, Ed. by Florian Heinrichs, Institutfür Gartenbauökonomie der Leibniz Universitat Hannover, ISBN 90.74486-16-3. Belgium.

Alvino, A., Andrina, R., Cerio, L., Mori., Sorrentino, G. 1998. Physiological Response of Gladiolus to Carbonated Water Application Under Two Water regimes. *Adv. Hort. Sci.* 12:145-152.

Anonymous. 2007. Effect of Drip Irrigation with Fertigation Levels on Growth and Flowering in Chrysanthemum var. 'Red Lady'. *Annual Report, PFDC, Jorhat,* pp. 13-14.

Anonymous. 2008a. Performance Evaluation of Tuberose Under Drip Irrigation System. *AGRESCO Report of GAUS.* pp. 63-68.

Anonymous. 2008b. Irrigation, Fertigation and Mulching Studies in Rose var. Gladiator. *AGRESCO Report of GAUS,* pp. 18-42.

Anthura and Bleiswijk B.V. 2007. Anthurium Cut Flower Cultivation Guidelines. Anthuriumweg 12, 2665 KV, The Netherlands.

Arulkar, K. P., S. C. Sarode and R. C. Bhuyar. 2008. Wetting Pattern and Salt Distribution Indrip and Micro Sprinkler Irrigation. Agric. Sci. Digest., 28(2):124-126.

Aydinsakir, K., I. H.Tuzel and D. Buyuktas. 2011. The Effects of Different Irrigation Levels on Flowering and Flower Quality of Carnation *(Dianthus caryophllus L.)* Irrigated by Drip Irrigation. African Journal of Biotechnology, 10(66).14826-14835.

Bastug, R., Karaguel, O., Aydinsakir, K. and Buyuktas, D. 2006. The Effects of Drip Irrigation on Flowering and Flower Quality of Glasshouse Gladiolus plant. *Agril. Water Management,* 81: 132-144.

Begum, R. A., Rahman, M. N., Mondol, A. T. M. A. I., Rahman, M. J. and Khan, F. N. 2007. Effect of Different Moisture Regimes on the Growth and Quality of gladiolus.*Int. J. Sustain. Crop Prod.* **2**(5): 43-45.

Borrelli, A. 1981. The Influence of the Water Regime and Nitrogen Feretilising on the Production of Roses under glass. Rivistadellaortoflorofrutticoltura Italiana, 65(2):109-117.

Caballero, M., Mansito P, Zieslin N, Rodrigo J, Melia J, Renz O. 1996. Water Use and Crop Productivity of Roses Growing on Volcanic lapilli (picon) in Canary Islands. Acta Horticulturae, 424, 41–44

Cameron RWF, Harrison-Murray RS, Scott MA. 1999. The Use of Controlled Water Stress to Manipulate Growth of Container-grown Rhododendron cv. Hoppy. J. Hort. Sci. Biotechnol. 74: 161-169.

Chawla, S. L.,Mohd, S and Mahawer, L. N. 2008. Role of Irrigation Frequencies on Growth, Yield and Flower Quality and Water Use Pattern of African marigold (*Tageteserecta*). *The Hort. J.* 21(2): 77-80.

Chimonidou, P. D. 1998. Yield and Quality of Rose 'Madelon' as Affected by Four Irrigation and Three Shading Regimes. *Acta Hort.,* 458: 95-102.

Chimonidou-Pavlidou D. 1996. Effect of Water Stress at Different Stages of Rose Development. Acta Horticulturae, 424, 45–51.

Chimonidou-Pavlidou D. 1999. Irrigation and Sensitive Stages of Rose Development. Acta Horticulturae, 481, 393–401.

Chowdhuri, T.K, Rout, B, Sadhukhan R. and Mondal, T. 2016. International Journal of Pharmaceutical Science Invention. Volume 5 Issue 8, pp. 15-18.

Clothier, B. E. and S. R. Green. 1994. Rootzone Processes and the Efficient use of Irrigation Water. Agric. Water Management, 25: 1-12.

Doorenbos J., Kassam A.H. 1979. Yield Response to Water. Food and Agriculture Organization, Irrigation and Drainage Paper No. 33, 193. Rome.

Earl, K. D. and W. A. Jury. 1977. Water Movement in Bare and Cropped Soil Underisolated Trickle Emitters: II. Analysis of Cropped Soil Experiments. Soil Sci. Soc. Am. J., 41:856-861.

EI-Gamassy, A. J., EI-Barkousky, M and Hashem, M., 1977. Tech. Bull. *Gubba Botanic Garden,* pp. 18-19.

Farias M.F., De Saad J.C.C, Denise M.C.. 2009. Effect of Soil-water Tension on Cut Chrysanthemum Floral Quality And Longevity. Applied Research & Agrotechnology 2(1): 141-145.

Feigin, A., C. Ginsburg and S. Gilead and A. Ackerman. 1986. Effect of NH_4/NO_3 Ratio in Nutrient Solution on Growth and Yield of Greenhouse Roses. Acta Hort., 189: 127-135.

Fereres E, Soriano MA. 2007. Deficit Irrigation for Reducing Agricultural Water Use. J. Exp. Bot. 58: 147-159.

Folegatti, M. V., Casarini, E. and Blanco, F. F. 2001. Greenhouse Irrigation Water Depths in Relation to Rose Stem and Bud Qualities. *Scientia Agricola,* 58(3): 465-468.

FRS. 2017. Package of Practices of Flower Crops. Floricultural Research Station, Sri Konda Laxman Telanagna State Horticultural University, Rajendranagar, Hyderabad-30.

Goel, A. K., R. K. Gupta and R. Kumar. 1993. Effect of Drip Discharge Rate on Moisture Distribution Pattern. J. Water Management, 1(1): 50-51.

Halepyati, A. S., Sujata, K. and Prabhakar, M. 2001.Effect of Irrigation and Nitrogen Levels on Growth, Yield and Water Use of marigold.*J. Orna. Hort.,* New Series, 4: 30-32.

Halepyati, A. S., Sujatha, K. and Prabhakar, M. 1995.Effect of Irrigation Regimes and Nitrogen on dry Matter Accumulation and Floral Characters of Tuberose during Winter. *Indian J. Hort.* 52(1): 74-76.

Halepyati, A.S., Sujatha, K. and Prabhakar, M. 2002.Growth, Yield and Water Use of Summer Tuberose as Influenced by Irrigation Regime and Plant Densities. *J. Orna. Hort., New Series,* **5**: 47-50.

Hanan JJ. 1969. Effect of Watering Frequency and Inert Medium on Carnations. Colorado Flower Growers Assoc. Bull. 234: 1-3.

Harbaugh, B. K., C. D. Stanley, J.F. Price and J.B. Jones. 1989. Irrigation and Fertilization Management of Cut Chrysanthemums. Hort. Sci., 24(1):150.

Hassanein, A. M. A. 2015. Effects of Irrigation and Method of Fertilization on Growth and Flowering Responses of Potted Chrysanthemum. Journal of Horticultural Science & Ornamental Plants 7 (3): 80-86.

Haynes, R. J. 1990. Movement and Transformation of Fertigated Nitrogen Below Trickle Emitters and their Effects on pH in the Wetted Soil Volume. Fertilizer Res., 23:105-112.

Howell, E. A. 1972. Growing Season Care. In: the World of the Gladiolus Unknown: Book, N, Amer. Gladiolus coun. Edgewood Press, Edgewood, MD, pp. 52-53.

Jasper FDR.1966. Effect of Watering Treatment or Growth of Carnations. Colorado Flower Growers Assoc. Bull. 194: 1-3.

Jawaharlal, M., M.Ganga, K.Padmadevi, V.Jegadeeswari and S.Karthikeyan. 2010. Technical Guide on Carnation Cultivation. Department of Floriculture, TNAU, Coimbatore, p 27.

Jiusheng, L., Jianjun, Z. and Ren, L. 2003. Water and Nitrogen Distribution as Affected by Fertigation of Ammonium Nitrate from a Point Source. Irrigation Science, 22, 19-30. http://dx.doi.org/10.1007/ s00271-003-0064-8.

Junges, W. (1964).*Arch Gartenb.,*12: 469-482.

Katsoulas, N., C. Kittas, G. Dimokas, C. Lykas. 2006. Effect of Irrigation Frequency on Rose Flower Production and Quality, Elsevier, 93(2): 237-244.

Kazaz, S., Yusuf, U. M., Askin, A., Aydinsakir, K., Senyigit, U and Kadayifci, A. 2010. Effects of Different Irrigation Regimes on Yield and Quality Parameters of carnation. *Scientific Research and Essays,* Vol. **5**(19): 2921-2930.

Khanam, R., D.Kundu, U. Thingujam and S.K. Patra. 2017. Effect of Different Irrigation Level on Growth, Yield and Water Use Efficiency of Tuberose in Lower Gangetic Plain of West Bengal. *Int.J.Curr.Microbiol. App. Sci., 6*(8): 1944-1952.

Khristov K, Pavlov P. 1977. Greenhouse Carnation Growth in Relation to Soil Moisture and Chlorcholine Chloride Treatment. Priroda-Bulgaria. 26(5): 88-89.

Kijine, J. W., T. P. Tuong, J. Bennett, B. Bouman and T. Osweis, 2002. Ensuring Food Security via Improvement in Crop Water Productivity. Challenge Programme on Water and Food Background Paper 1.

Koriesh, E. M. 1989. Effect of Some Irrigation Systems on Growth, Flowering and Some Mineral Contents in Rose Plants Grown in Sandy soil. *Assint Journal of Agricultural Science*, 20(1): 75-90.

Leeden,M. V. D. 2001. Crop Cultivation- Culture Tips for Anthurium. Anthura B.V. U.S.(https://gpnmag.com/article/culture-tips-anthurium/)

Maggio, A., Andria, R. and Morelli, G. 1993. Irrigation of Gladioli in Hilly area. *Colture-Protette*, 22: 63-69.

Michelakis, N., E. Vougioucalou and G. Clapaki. 1993. Water Use, Wetted Soil Volume, Root Distribution and Yield of Avocado Under Drip Irrigation. Agric. Water Management, 24: 119-131.

Mishra, S., Kumar, S., Tuteja, S. S. and Bhoi, S. 2012. Effect of Various Irrigation Scheduling, Source and Levels of Nutrients on Productivity Potential and Economics of Winter Hybrid Sunflower (*Helianthus annus*L.) at Vertisols of Chhattisgadh Plain. *Res. J. Agric. Sci.*, **3**(1): 222-224.

Nagaraju, C. G., Reddy, T. V. and Madaiah, D. 2003. Effect of Plant Density, Irrigation and Oil Cakes on Growth, Production and Quality of Field Grown Rose Cultivar Landora. *J. Orna. Hort.*, **6**(3): 172-179.

Patil, R. G., Patel, R. M. and Solia, B. M. 2008. Water Management in Flower Crops. In: Proc. of *National Symposium on Recent Advances in Floriculture*, pp. 21-27.

Patil, V. C, H. L. Halemani, S. S. Hallikeri, R. A. Nandagavi, T. T. Bandiwadder andC. M. Kalibavi. 2008. Comparitive Performance of Cotton Hybrids and Variety under Drip Irrigation. J. Indian Soc. Cotton Improvement, pp. 79- 84.

Ram, P., Kumar, B., Singh, A., Yaseen, M and Kothari, S. K. 1999. Response of Marigold *(Tagetesminuta)* to Irrigation and Nitrogen Fertilization under Himalayan Foot Hills of Tarai Region of Uttar Pradesh. *J. Medicinal and Aromatic Plant Sci.*, 21: 361-366.

Raviv M; Blom J. 2001. The Effect of Water Availability and Quality on Photosynthesis and Productivity of Soilless-grown Cut Roses. Scientia Horticulturae, 88(4): 257–276.

Razvi, A. M. and Omer, E. A. 1994. Effect of Water Regime on the Growth, Flower Yield and Volatile Oil Content of Marigold (*Tagetespatula*) *Egyptian J. Hort.*, 21: 195-202.

Roh M Y; Lee Y B. 1996. Control of Amount and Frequency of Irrigation According to Integrated Solar Radiation in Cucumber Substrate Culture. Acta Horticulturae, 440, 332–337.

Sanchez-Blanco MJ, Ferrandez T, Navarro A, Banon S, Alarcon JJ. 2004. Effect of Irrigation and Air Humidity Preconditioning on Water Relations, Growth and Survival of Rosmarinus Officinalis Plants During and After Transplanting. J. Plant Physiol. 161: 1133-1142.

Schuch, U.K. 1998. Cultivar, Fertilizer and Irrigation Affect Vegetative Growth and Susceptibility of Chrysanthemum to Western Flower Thrips. J. Amer. Soc. Hort. Sci., 123(4): 727-733.

Schuch, V. K., Redak, R. A. and Bethke, J. A. 1998. Cultivars, Fertilizers and Irrigation Effect on Vegetative Growth and Susceptibility of Chrysanthemum to Western Flower thrips. *J. American Soc. Hort. Sci.*, 123(4): 727-733.

Sharma, R. S. 1994. Influence of Irrigation Schedule and Fertility Levels on Yield of Sunflower *(Helianthus annus* L.). *Indian J. Agron.*, 39: 496-497.

Sharp, R. E. and W. J. Davis. 1985. Root Growth and Water Uptake by Maize Plants in Drying Soil. J. Exp. Bot., 36: 1441–1456.

Singh, V., Yadav, B. S. and Bhunia, S. R. 1997b. Effect of Planting Date and Irrigation Management on Growth and Yield of Spring Sunflower *(Helianthus annuus).Indian J. Agril. Sci.*, 67: 48-50.

Sivanappan, R. K. 1985. In Drip Irrigation in Action, Vol II, ASAE, Michigam, Pp: 736-740.

Sivanappan, R. K., O. Padmakumari and V. Kumar. 1987. Drip irrigation. Keerthi Publishing House, Coimbatore, India, p. 75-80.

Stanhill G; Scholte A J. 1974. Solar Radiation and Water Loss from Glasshouse Roses. Journal of American Society of Horticultural Science, 99, 107–110.

Stevens, R. M. and T. Douglas, 1994. Distribution of Grapevine Roots and salt Under Drip and Full-ground Cover Microjet Irrigation Systems. Irrig. Sci., 15: 147-152.

Suganya, S. and Sivasamy, R. 2006. Moisture Retention and Cation Exchange Capacity of Sandy Soil as Influenced by Soil Additives. Journal of Applied Sciences Researches, 2, 949-951.

Suganya, S., A. Anitha and K. Appavu. 2007. Moisture and Nutrient Distribution System under Drip Fertigation Systems. In: Third International Ground Water Conference on "Water, Environment and Agriculture - Present Problems and Future Challenges". February 7-10. 2007.

Sunil Kumar, Dixit, R.S. and Tripathi, H.P. 1992. Effect of Moisture Regimes and Nitrogen Levels on Growth and Yield of Sunflower (Helianthus annuus L). Narendra Deva J. Agric. Res., 7: 192-194.

Taweesak,V., T. L. Abdullah, S. A.Hassan, N. H. Kamarulzaman and W. A.W. Yusoff. 2014. Growth and Flowering Responses of Cut Chrysanthemum Grown under Restricted Root Volume to Irrigation Frequency. The Scientific World Journal, Volume 2014, Article ID 254867, 6 pages.

Taylor RD, Hill J, Grout WW. 2008. Does Irrigation Regime Affect the Post Harvest Quality and Vase Life of Cut Flower Carnations (Cv. Santorini). ActaHortic. 792: 663-668.

Thamburaj, S., Sambandamurthi, S., Chezhiyan, N., Abdul Khader, J.B.M. and Ponnuswami, V. 1984.Studies on Water Requirements of *Jasminumgrandtflorum* L. *South Indian Hort.,* 32:363-364.

Turan, A., Y. Ucarand S. Kazaz. 2015. Effects of Different Irrigation Treatments on Quality Parameters of Cut Chrysanthemum. Research gate. Horticulture. Vol. LIX. 2286-1580.

Ucar,F., S. Kazaz, F. Eraslan, H. Baydar. 2016. Effects of Different Irrigation Water and Nitrogen Levels on the Water Use, Rose Flower Yield and Oil Yield of Rosa *damascene.* Sciencedirect.182, 94-102.

Vanangamudi, K., K. S. Suramanian and M. Bhaskaran. 1990. Influence of Irrigation and Nitrogen on the Yield and Quality of Chilli Fruit and Seed. Seed Res., 18(2):114-116.

Vijaya Kumar, N. S., G. Gopinath and R. Krishna Manohar. 2011. Quality, Yield and Economics of China Aster var. Kamini and var. Violet Cushion as Influenced by Drip Irrigation and Fertigation. Mysore J. Agric. Sci., 45(1): 182-185.

Vijayselvaraj (2007). Standardization of Irrigation and Fertigation Techniques in Jasmine (*Jasminum grandiflorum*) var Co. 2. Ph.D (Hort.) Thesis, Horticultural College & Research Institut, Tamil Nadu Agricultural University, Coimbatore.

Visalakshi, K. P., R. Mathew, P. Suseela and T. K. Bridgit. 2007. Soil Moisture Distribution Pattern Under Surface and Subsurface Drip Irrigation. In: Proc. of Third International Ground Water Conference on "Water, Environment and Agriculture - Present problems and future challenges". 2007. February. pp. 7-10.

Vivek and Chakor, I. S. 1992. Effect of Nitrogen and Irrigation on Growth and Yield of Sunflower *(Helianthus annuus)* under Mid-hill Conditions of Himachal Pradesh. *Indian J. Agron.,*37: 500-502.

Water Management and Aquatic Ecosystem
Edited by: Dr. Resham Bhalla & Dr. Pawan Kumar 'Bharti'
ISBN: 978-93-86841-96-4
Edition: 2019
Published by: Discovery Publishing House Pvt. Ltd., New Delhi (India)

Pages 37-43

3 Water Management in Textile Processing Industry

[1]Ashok K. Rathoure

Summary

With the increasingly important requirement for textile manufacturers to reduce pollution in textile production, the use of enzymes in the chemical processing of fibres and textiles is rapidly gaining wider recognition because of their non-toxic and eco-friendly characteristics. They can be safely used in a wide selection of textile processes such as de-sizing, scouring, bleaching, dyeing and finishing, where the alternatives are very harsh chemicals whose disposal into the environment causes many problems. The textile industry plays an important role in the economy of the country like India and it accounts for around one third of total export. Out of various activities in textile industry, chemical processing contributes about 70% of pollution. It is well known that cotton mills consume large volume of water for various processes such as sizing, de-sizing, scouring, bleaching, mercerization, dyeing, printing, finishing and ultimately washing. Due to the nature of various chemical processing of textiles, large volumes of waste water with numerous pollutants are discharged. Since these streams of water affect the aquatic eco-system in number of ways such as depleting the dissolved oxygen content or settlement of suspended substances in anaerobic condition, a special attention needs to be paid.

Introduction

Water management is the activity of planning, developing, distributing and managing the optimum use of water resources. Textile industry is an intensive water use sector. Consequently, enormous quantities of wastewater are generated from different manufacturing processes. It is a fragmented and heterogeneous sector, with a demand mainly driven by three main end-uses: clothing, home furnishing and industrial use.

[1] Eco Chem Sales & Services; Ecosystem Resource Management Pvt. Ltd. Surat, Gujarat, India

Manufacturing Process for Dying and Printing of Gray Cloth

In a common textile processing industry, following steps are carried out for dyeing and printing of gray cloths.

(*i*) *Gray Cloth:* Gray cloth is distributed individually for measurement of length and width in the gray cloth department.

(*ii*) *Jet Dyeing Machine:* In this section, the gray cloth is washed at temperature 130°C and pressure 2.5 kg / cm^2. In the jet dyeing machine, cloth is washed. There are four types of washing.

- Normal
- Soap washing
- Scouring
- Weight reduction

(*iii*) *Dyeing:* Dyeing is carried out with disperse dyes at temperature 130°C for 25 - 35 minutes. Application of dispersing agents, dyes and Auxiliaries is done here. Acidification follows the dyeing to remove excess unfixed colour. Application of whitening agent (White - R) is done in jet dyeing to impart white colour on the cloth.

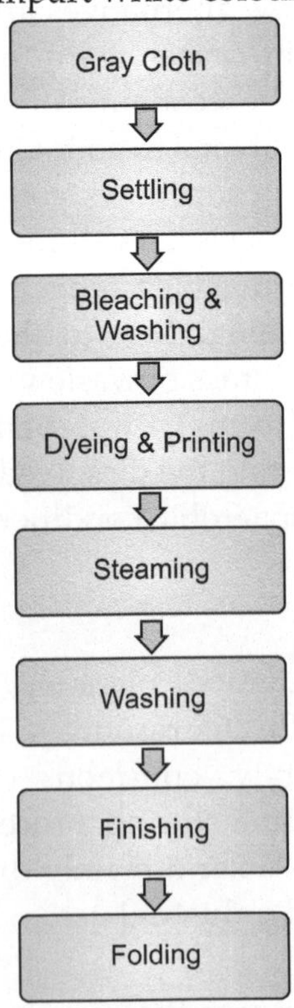

Fig. 3.1: Flow Diagram for Dying and Printing of Gray Cloth

(*iv*) *Thermosetting*: Dyed fabric coming from jet dyeing machine is taken to stanter machine where thermosetting is done at 180 °C - 190 °C for 30 - 40 seconds, which provides dimensional stability to the cloth.

(*v*) *Folding*: In this department the length is measured and designed as per the customer choice.

(*vi*) *Finishing*: It includes addition of finishing agents like softeners, elastomers, fillers, etc. to cloth coming from washing section, which is done as per the customer requirements.

(*vii*) *Zero-Zero:* Finally, the fabric is taken to zero - zero machines where smooth finishing is done. Water is continuously added into steam-heated blanket.

(*viii*) *Folding*: At last the fabric goes to the folding machine for measuring and sorting then the fabric is ready for dispatch.

Need of Conservation

The water supply is finite in the textile industry, which means that we do not have an endless supply. We only have the water that we have now. Water conservation programme can cut water consumption by up to 30% or more, and the cost savings can pay for the required materials in a very short time as well as it saves thousands of rupees per year.

Water Conservation Measures Lead To

- Reduction in processing cost.
- Reduction in waste water treatment cost.
- Reduction in thermal energy consumption.
- Reduction in electrical energy consumption.
- Reduction in pollutants loads an effluent volume.

Re-use of Waste Water

Water re-use measures reduce hydraulic loadings to treatment systems by using the same water in more than one process. Re-use of certain process water elsewhere in mill operations and reuse of uncontaminated cooling water in operations requiring hot water result in significant wastewater discharge reductions. Examples of process water reuse include:

- Re-use of cooling water.
- Cooling water in Jet dyeing machine can recycle totally.
- Concentration of effluent from jet dyeing machine and drum washer is on a lower side (dilution is higher side). This water can be recycled in printing machineries, blanket washing etc.
- RO rejected water; treated water of ETP, washing/dhulai water can be recycled in printing machineries and screen washing.

- Water from the Kundis (last nos.) can be recycled again for dhulai purpose.
- Instead of one large kundi, increase nos. of small kundis for dhulai purpose.
- Instead of Charkhi, use Pressure Rode.
- In processes like scouring, bleaching, dyeing and washing, where water is most utilized. These all the system should convert into PLC system. So that water consumption can be controlled efficiently. Due to this PLC system, industry can save water as well as color and chemical consumption also.
- Re-using wash water/Counter Current washing.

The counter-current washing method is relatively straightforward and inexpensive method and can be used for continuous as well as batch process for both water and energy savings. With this method the least contaminated water from the final wash is reused for the next-to-last wash and so on until the water reaches the first wash stage, where it is finally discharged. It is widely adopted in new textile mills and also easy to implement in existing mills.

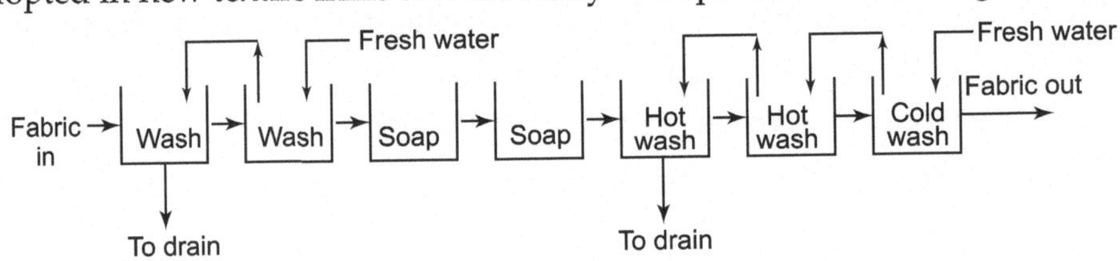

Fig. 3.2: Recommended Counter Current Flow of washing on a Soaper Range

Water Management

Due to adopting this water management system, industries can minimize their fresh water consumption on daily basis.

Table 3.1: Water Management in Different Sections

S.No.	Utilization	Machineries	Function
1.	Steam	Jet Dyeing machine	Scouring and Dyeing
2.	Steam	Drum Washers	
3.	Steam	Jigger Machine	
4.	Steam	Loops Steamer	Proper Colour Fixation
5.	Steam	Soaper	Reduce excess colour (washing/dhulai)
6.	Steam	Colour/Kitchen	for thickening of gum
7.	Steam	Zero-Zero	For anti-crease/ironing

8.	Condensate Recovery	Boiler	It raises the temperature of Boiler feed water from 30 °C to 85 °C, so it saves fresh water consumption.
9.	Water	Drum Level Indicator	Reduce fresh water consumption
10.	Water	Setting PLC System	Reduce fresh water consumption
11.	Batch Cycle/ Process Cycle	Process unit	Reduce fresh water consumption
12.	Water	Jet level Indicator	Reduce fresh water consumption
13.	RO-rejected water	RO System	Utilize for washing purpose and reduce fresh water consumption

Water Requirement for Production

Water required for the dyeing and printing of textiles in a typical textile industry is 0.010 to 0.0181 m^3/meter depending upon the material and process adopted for the dyeing and printing of textiles, whereas actually (technically) the water required is 0.009 to 0.0134 m^3/meter depending upon their manufacturing process, dye used and material to be processed. Variation in the actual and technical data is due to spillage of water from valves and taps, evaporation losses etc.

Fig. 3.3. Washing/Dhulai

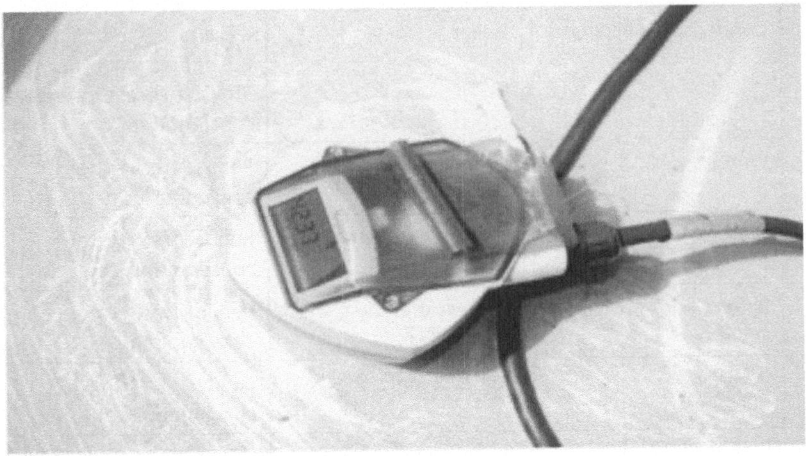

Fig. 3.4. Flow Meter

Fig. 3.5. ETP System

Water Conservation Methods

Water consumption in a textile factory can be reduced by implementing various changes ranging from simple procedures such as fixing leaks, optimizing water use, reducing the number of process steps etc. Some suggestions are outlined.

- Repair Leaks, Faulty Valves, etc.
- Turn off Running Taps and Hoses.
- Turn off Water when Machines are not running.
- Reduce the Number of Process Steps.
- Optimize Process Water Use.
- Recycle Cooling Water.
- Re-use Process Water.
- Using Water Efficient Processes and Equipment.
- Reusing Water from Auxiliary Processes.

Conclusion

Water management in the textile industries can save millions of money used for waste water treatment and final disposal of waste water as well as in sludge disposal. Process modification would reduce water consumption in the washers and ultimately reduce capital cost of plant. Also re-use of water from various industrial process and water conservation techniques can reduce fresh water consumption and alternately reduce capital cost of industry.

REFERENCES

Arslan I., Balcioglu, I.A. and Tuhkanen, T., (1999). *Environ. Technol.*, 20:921-931.

Asokan R. and Shavakumar, N., (2002). Effluent Treatment in Textile Wet Processing, Industrial Training Programme, Process Control in Textile Wet Processing, Bannari Amman Institute of Technology, 77-84.

Buckley C.A. (1992). Wat. Sci. Technol., 25:203-209.

Jurgens, Julian F., Reid, David J., Guthrie, John D. (1948). Textile Research Journal, 42-44.

Mali P.L., Mahajan, M.M., Patil, D.P. and Kulkarni, M.V., (2000).*J. Sci. Res.*, 59:221-224.

Mckay G, (1979). American Dyestuff Reporter, 68:29-34.

Namboodri C.G., Sperkins W. and Walsh W.K. (1994). American Dyestuff Reporter, 4:17-27.

Owen, G.R., (1978). Journal of Society of Dyers and Colourists, 94:243-251.

Sivaramakrishnan, C.N., (2004). Colourage, LI, No.9, 27-32.

Tanaka, K., Padermpole, K. and Hisanaga, T., (2000).Wat. Res., 34, 327-333.

Tang W.Z. and An., H., 1995, Chemosphere, 31, 4157-4170.

Vlyssides A.G. and Israilides, C.J., (1998). J. Environ. Sci. Health, A33 (5), 847-863.

Weeter O.W. and Hodgson, A.G., (1977). Dye Waste Water Treatment, 32nd Industrial Waste Conference, Lafayette, IN. Proceedings, 1-9.

Wu JN., Eiteman MA & Law S.E. (1998). Evaluation of Membrane Filtration and Ozonation Process for Treatment of Reactive Dye Wastewater. *Journal of Environmental Engineering-*ASCE, 124(3):272-277.

Yamuna R.T. (1995). Ph.D Thesis, Bharathiar University, Coimbatore.

Water Management and Aquatic Ecosystem **Pages 44-67**
Edited by: Dr. Resham Bhalla & Dr. Pawan Kumar 'Bharti'
ISBN: 978-93-86841-96-4
Edition: 2019
Published by: Discovery Publishing House Pvt. Ltd., New Delhi (India)

4

Agroforestry for Watershed Management

[1]Alok Kumar Patra

ABSTRACT

Watershed management is the process of creating and implementing plans, programmes and projects to sustain and enhance watershed functions that affect the plant, animal and human communities within a watershed boundary. It implies the judicious use of all the resources i.e. land, water, vegetation in an area to prevent soil erosion, improve water availability and increase food, fodder, fuel and timber on sustained basis. Adoption of agroforestry practices with the available technologies fulfils all the objectives of the watershed management. This helps in conservation of soil and water from land surface and will always add to the productivity of resource poor small and marginal farmers. An agroforestry system can provide ecological resilience and contribute to the maintenance of beneficial ecological functions. Maintaining a protective forest in the form of an agroforestry system as an integral part of the landscape provides a healthy watershed for reliable water supply, protection from soil erosion and a more secured supply of forest products for cash and home consumption. Watershed management through agroforestry practices offer a number of benefits to the marginal and small farmers living in a watershed area.

This chapter discusses the contribution of agroforestry systems towards improvement of soil water regime in watershed areas. An attempt has also been made to enumerate the various biological measures like alley cropping, boundary planting, homegardens, agri-horti-silvi-cultural, silvi-pastoral and horti-pastoral systems etc. for watershed management.

Introduction

The natural resources like soil, water and vegetation are nature's gift to the mankind and our survival depends upon their maintenance and proper management. However, overuse of these natural resources has resulted in

[1] Professor (Agronomy), All India Coordinated Research Project on Integrated Farming Systems, Orissa University of Agriculture and Technology, Bhubaneswar 751003, Odisha, India

depletion of groundwater, loss of forests and wild habitats, reduced capacity of ground to absorb water, thus causing water logging and increased salinity. The availability of resources for future generation depends on their sustainable management. In the last fifty years sustainability of natural resources had been threatened due to misuse and mismanagement of natural resources for human greed. Soil degradation and deforestation are the two major threats to the mankind. Thus, the proper maintenance and management of the natural resources are required for sustainable development of any country.

Soil degradation refers to decline in the productive capacity of land due to decline in soil quality caused by human activities. It is a global problem. Worldwide around 1.96 billion ha are affected by human induced soil degradation, mainly caused by water and wind erosion (1094 and 548 million ha, respectively). Chemical degradation accounted for 240 million ha, mainly nutrient decline (136 million ha) and salinization (77 million ha), physical degradation occurred on 83 million ha, mainly as a result of compaction, sealing and crusting.

It is also a very serious problem in India, which shares only 2.45% of the world's land resource and supports more than 17.5% of the world's human population and 16% of livestock population. Estimates of soil degradation are varied depending upon the criteria used. About 57% (187.8 m ha) of the total geographical area (329 m ha) is suffering from various forms of degradation like water erosion (79% of 187.8 m ha), wind erosion, chemical and physical degradation. Out of 400 m ha-m precipitation in the country, utilizable water is only about 112.3 m ha-m comprising 69.0 m ha-m surface water and 43.3 m ha-m ground water. About 115 m ha-m is lost as runoff resulting in drought in the catchments and floods in downstream. Over 5.3 billion tons of top-soil alone is lost annually which results in loss of around 8 million tons of plant nutrient and 3 million tons of food grains due to runoff processes.

The processes leading to soil degradation are generally triggered by excessive pressure on land to meet the competing demands of growing population for food, fodder, fibre and fuel. Therefore, the direct causes for soil degradation are unsustainable land use and inappropriate land management. The most common direct causes include:

- Deforestation of fragile lands
- Over cutting and grazing of vegetation
- Extension of cultivation on to lands of low capability/potential
- Improper crop rotations
- Unbalanced fertilizer use
- Non-adoption of soil conservation practices
- Inadequacies in planning and management of irrigation resources
- Overdraft of groundwater in excess of capacity to recharge

Deforestation refers to the transfer of forest land to non-forest uses and includes all land where the forest cover has been stripped off and the land converted to such uses as permanent cultivation, shifting cultivation, human settlements, mining, reservoirs etc. Deforestation continues to threaten and erode the area under forest cover in several countries of the world. Forests provide critical ecosystem services to the agricultural sector, including pollination and watershed protection, and support to fisheries. Millions of poor people and small-scale enterprises depend on forests for food, fibre, fodder and other materials, but are finding this increasingly hard as the natural forests shrink.

The forest coverage in India has shrunk from 33% in 1947 to 22.6% at present. As per the recommended norm of the National Forest Policy 1988, about 33% of the geographical area should be under the forest cover, which comes to about 110 million ha compared to 68.83 million ha presently under the forest cover in India. India has established an organization called the National Afforestation and Eco-development Board in 1992 to take up afforestation programmes and bring back the productivity from the degraded forestlands.

Watershed Concept

A watershed is a geohydrological unit or all the land and water area bounded by a divide which contributes runoff to a common point. In other words, a watershed is an area of land that drains into a common water body, such as a river or lake. Watershed is considered to be synonymous with 'catchment basin' and 'drainage basin'. A watershed is an ecosystem with complex interacting natural components. In watershed approach, development is not only confined to agricultural lands but also covers the area, starting from the highest point of the land to the outlet of the natural stream.

Watershed is a terrestrial ecosystem consisting of interacting biotic and abiotic components such as land, water, plants, animals and minerals. It is not simply the hydrological unit but also social, political and ecological entity which plays crucial role in determining food, social and economic security in terms of life-supporting services to rural people. It is a major site for residential, commercial, industrial, agricultural, educational, experimental, environmental, and forest land uses which are often conflicting and competing with each other for the limited watershed land resource (Tideman, 2007). The classification of watershed according the size of the area is given in Table 4.1.

Table 4.1: Classification of Watershed According to Size of the Area

Hydrologic unit	Size (in ha)
Region	> 300 lakh
Basin	30-300 lakh
Catchment	10-30 lakh

Sub-catchment	2- 10 lakh
Watershed	50000-200000
Sub-watershed	10000-50000
Mili-watershed	1000- 10000
Micro-watershed	100-1000
Mini watershed	1-100

Source: http://agropedia.iitk.ac.in/content/watershed-management-dryland

Watershed Management

Watershed management becomes increasingly important as a way to improve livelihood of people while conserving and regenerating their natural resources. Watershed management is the process of creating and implementing plans, programmes and projects to sustain and enhance watershed functions that affect the plant, animal and human communities within a watershed boundary. It implies, the judicious use of all the resources i.e. land, water, vegetation in an area to prevent soil erosion, improve water availability and increase food, fodder, fuel and timber on sustained basis.

The process of creating and implementing plans, programs, and projects to sustain and enhance watershed functions that affect the plant, animal, and human communities within a watershed boundary. It involves management of land, water, energy and greenery integrating all the relevant approaches appropriate to socioeconomic background for a pragmatic development of a watershed. It also involves the greening of watershed through proper management of land water and energy resource. The main components of watershed management are resource conservation, crop production and alternate land-use systems (Tideman, 2007).

Principles of Watershed Management

The main principles of watershed management based on resource conservation, resource generation and resource utilization are:

1. Utilizing the land based on its capability
2. Protecting fertile top soil
3. Minimizing silting up of tanks, reservoirs and lower fertile lands
4. Protecting vegetative cover throughout the year
5. In situ conservation of rain water
6. Safe diversion of gullies and construction of check dams for increasing ground water recharge
7. Increasing cropping intensity through inter and sequence cropping
8. Alternate land use systems for efficient use of marginal lands

9. Water harvesting for supplemental irrigation
10. Maximizing farm income through agricultural related activities such as dairy, poultry, sheep, and goat forming
11. Improving infrastructural facilities for storage, transport and agricultural marketing
12. Improving socio - economic status of farmers

Objectives of Watershed Management

The concept of National Watershed Development Project in Rainfed Areas (NWDPRA) is scientific utilization of natural and human resources to sustain production system which can meet the socio-economic need of the people and to maintain health, vigour and purity of production environment. The broad objectives of the NWDPRA are:

1. Recognition of watersheds as a unit for development and efficient use of land according their capabilities for production.
2. Conservation, development and sustainable management of natural resources including their use.
3. Restoration of ecological balance in the degraded and fragile rainfed ecosystems by greening these areas through appropriate mix of trees, shrubs and grasses.
4. Flood control through small multipurpose reservoirs and other water storage structures at the head water of streams and in problem areas.
5. Adequate water supply for domestic, agricultural and industrial needs.
6. Efficient use of natural resources for improving agriculture and allied occupation so as to improve socio-economic conditions of the local residents.
7. Enhancement of agricultural productivity and production in a sustainable manner.
8. Reduction in regional disparity between irrigated and rainfed areas.
9. Creation of sustained employment opportunities for the rural community including the landless
10. Abatement of soil and water pollution.
11. Expansion of recreation facilities such as picnic and camping sites.

Agroforestry Concept

The general concept of agroforestry is to integrate trees and agriculture so as to create a more diversified landscape, while providing the producers with new environmental and economic benefits. In other words, agroforestry is a method of farming that allows trees and shrubs to grow along with crops and/ or livestock, therefore that combining the best attributes of agriculture and forestry in the same production system (Bene, 1977).

A strictly scientific definition of agroforestry should stress two characteristics common to all forms of agroforestry and separate them from the other forms of land use.

1. The deliberate growing of woody perennials on the same unit of land along with agricultural crops and/or animals, either in some form of spatial mixture and in some temporal sequence.
2. There must be a significant interaction (positive and/or negative) between the woody and non- woody components of the system, either ecological and/or economical.

Several definitions of agroforestry have been suggested since its conceptualization as a land use approach in 1977 but, in short, agroforestry is generally perceived as the deliberate cultivation of several productive components, of which at least one is a woody perennial, on the same piece of land, combined either spatially or sequentially. The definition proposed in the early 1980s by International Council for Research in Agroforestry (ICRAF) gained wider acceptance. This definition which was used from the early 1980s to the mid-nineties is as follows:

Agroforestry is a collective name for land-use systems and technologies where woody perennials (trees, shrubs, palms, bamboos, etc.) are deliberately used on the same land-management units as agricultural crops and/or animals, in some form of spatial arrangement or temporal sequence. In agroforestry systems there are both ecological and economical interactions between the different components.

ICRAF in 1996 redefined agroforestry as a dynamic, ecologically based natural resource management system that, through the integration of trees on farms and in the agricultural landscape, diversifies and sustains production for increased social, economic and environmental benefits for land-users at all levels. Thus, in agroforestry systems there are both ecological and economical interactions between the different components (Lundgren and Raintree, 1982).

This definition implies that:

- Agroforestry normally involves two or more species of plants (or plants and animals), at least one of which is a woody perennial;
- An agroforestry system always has two or more outputs;
- The cycle of an agroforestry system is always more than one year; and
- Even the simplest agroforestry system is more complex, ecologically (structurally and functionally) and economically, than a mono-cropping system.

Additionally, there are three attributes which, theoretically, all agroforestry systems possess (Nair, 2008).

1. Productivity: Agroforestry systems aim to maintain or increase production of preferred commodities as well as productivity of the land.
2. Sustainability: Agroforestry can achieve and indefinitely maintain conservation and fertility goals by conserving the production potential of the resource base, mainly through the beneficial effects of woody perennials on soils.
3. Adoptability: Improved or new agroforestry technologies that are introduced into new areas should fit the social as well as environmental characteristics of the land use system for which it is designed and also confirm to local farming system.

Benefits of Agroforestry

Agroforestry systems play a great role in conservation of natural resources, especially soil. Adoption of agroforestry practices were always adds to the productivity of resource poor small and marginal farmers. Agroforestry has both productive and service functions. Among the productive functions, food, fuel wood, timber and fodder are the most important besides gums, resins, medicines, fibres and a host of other economic base and greater food security. The service functions include shade, reduction in wind speed, control of erosion and maintenance and improvement of soil fertility. Agroforestry systems increase nutrients inputs through nitrogen fixing trees and nutrient uptake from deep soil horizons. They reduce nutrient leaching losses through tree root and micorrhizal systems. Agroforestry systems recycle nutrients through decomposition of litter, pruning and root residues. Agroforestry is a medium and a combination of agricultural and forestry technologies to create integrated, diverse and productive land use systems (Garrity and Agus, 2000). While agroforests are typically less diverse than native forest, they do contain a significant number of plant and animal species. This diversity can, in time, provide ecological resilience and contribute to the maintenance of beneficial ecological functions. Benefits from agroforestry can be grouped under three broad categories; **environmental,** economic or social benefits.

Environmental Benefits

1. Reduction of pressure on natural forests.
2. More efficient recycling of nutrients by deep rooted trees on the site.
3. Better protection of ecological systems.
4. Reduction of surface run-off, nutrient leaching and soil erosion through impeding effect of tree roots and stems on these processes.
5. Improvement of microclimate, such as lowering of soil surface temperature and reduction of evaporation of soil moisture through a combination of mulching and shading.

6. Increment in soil nutrients through addition and decomposition of litter fall.
7. Improvement of soil structure through the constant addition of organic matter from decomposed litter.

Economic Benefits

1. Increment in an outputs of food, fuel wood, fodder, fertilizer and timber.
2. Reduction in incidence of total crop failure, which is common to single cropping or monoculture systems.
3. Increase in levels of farm income due to improved and sustained productivity.

Social Benefits

1. *Improvement in rural living standards from sustained employ-ment and higher income.*
2. Improvement in nutrition and health due to increased quality and diversity of food outputs.
3. Stabilization and improvement of communities through elimination of the need to shift sites of farm activities.

Objectives of Agroforestry in Watershed Areas

The primary objective of agroforestry systems in watershed areas is to maximise biomass production per unit area per unit time. The other major objectives of agroforestry systems in watershed areas include:

1. Conservation: Enormous loss of valuable, fertile topsoil is taking place with sediment and water. It has been estimated that on an average soil is displaced at the rate of about 16 t/ha/ year and washed in to the reservoir, which is much higher than the permissible limit. Some of the barren portion and wasteland of the watershed can be provided with a cover through agroforestry interventions in the watershed management programme.
2. Soil improvement: In addition to conservation of production based agroforestry practices enrich soil by nitrogen fixation and addition of organic matter. Thus it helps in meeting nutrient requirements of plants growing in association with trees and at the same time, the soil structure and infiltration rates are also improved.
3. Moderation of microclimate: The micro-climate in the neighbourhood of trees is moderated by adopting agroforestry systems and the field crops growing in association with trees get the benefit in various ways. Its pronounced effect is observed in semi-arid and arid regions.

4. Agro-based cottage industries: An agroforestry system in watershed management helps in promotion of agro-based cottage industries, such as paper pulp, herbal drugs, fibre, poultry, piggery, dairy, bee-keeping, sericulture cultivation etc. This will provide gainful employment and raise the standard of living of small and marginal farmers.

Traditional agroforestry systems in the mountains are very close to natural ecosystems as they provide ecosystem services similar to the forests such as the biodiversity, provision of food and fibre, water resources and its purification, climate regulation and carbon sequestration, nutrient cycling, primary production, production of oxygen, and soil formation, and recreation and the cultural services for the well-being of the people and society (Sharma *et al.*, 2007).

Agroforestry - A Sustainable Management Option for Watershed Management

Adoption of agroforestry practices with the available technologies will fulfil all the objectives of the watershed management. This will help in conservation of soil and water from land surface and will always add to the productivity of resource poor small and marginal farmers. Though the agroforests are typically less diverse than native forest the significant number of plant and animal species in an agroforestry system can provide ecological resilience and contribute to the maintenance of beneficial ecological functions. Forest watershed functions include maintenance of high quality water, regulation of water quantity and maintaining water-sediment balance in watersheds. These functions depend on the amount and type of forest and the various land use practices followed. Watershed functions are based on the three aspects of forests that together dominate the impact on the flow and quality of water.

1. **Vegetation:** Trees and understorey crops in an agroforestry system hardly allow any bare land. Trees are better at maintaining transpiration rates throughout the year than most other plants, and their annual water consumption often exceeds that of other vegetation. Tree canopies intercept more rainfall than other vegetation and this is returned to the atmosphere by direct evaporation.
2. **Soil conditions:** Forest soils have a high surface infiltration rate and substantial macroporosity (due to soil biological activity and tree root turnover) facilitate deep infiltration, and also sub-surface lateral flow of water.
3. **Landscape:** A landscape with a rough, uneven surface, including depressions and swamps, provide temporary water storage and sediment filter functions and very few pathways for rapid surface runoff.

Maintaining a protective forest in the form of an agroforestry system as an integral part of the landscape provides a healthy watershed for reliable water supply, protection from soil erosion and a more secured supply of forest products for cash and home consumption. Watershed management through agroforestry practices offer a number of benefits to the marginal and small farmers living in a watershed area.

1. More income if the agroforestry is commercially successful.
2. Annual crops around tree crops protect the soil from erosion and help maintaining soil fertility.
3. Diversity of agroforestry provides both cash crops and food for home consumption.
4. Less mechanization and a greater role for draft animals and their manure reduces the need for chemical fertilizer.
5. Less chemical fertilizers and pesticides reduce input costs.
6. The diversity of agroforestry is more resilient to weather and market fluctuations.

Trees Improve Soils in Watershed Areas

The approach of use of newly developed high yielding crop varieties, improved agronomic management practices, use of chemical fertilizers, efficient water management and timely plant protection measures has been successful in achieving large increases in crop productivity in recent years. On the other hand, continuous application of fertilizers at higher rates leads to environmental problems. Yield responses to fertilizers have declined because of soil physical degradation and micronutrient deficiencies. A new set of approaches has been recommended by Young (1988, 1997) to overcome these soil related constraints and to maintain or enhance the productivity level of soil.

- To find ways for sustainable use of marginal lands
- To reclaim and restore degraded lands
- To improve germplasm to produce plant varieties suitably adapted to soil constraints
- To maintain soil organic matter and biological activity, with benefits both for soil physical conditions and balanced nutrient supplies
- To improve nutrient cycling and nutrient use efficiency in agroecosystems
- To use fertilizers and other external inputs at moderate levels, seeking strategic use to overcome deficiencies that cannot otherwise be remedied
- To improve water use efficiency

Agroforestry can contribute to all these aspects and has a major role to play in some of them. The capacity of trees to grow under difficult climatic and soil conditions coupled with their ability for soil conservation and enhanced nutrient cycling gives agroforestry systems a potential in the marginal, semiarid and sloping soils. Tree litter and prunings can substantially help to maintain soil organic matter and improve soil physical properties resulting in a continuous supply of nutrients.

Agroforestry systems have the potential to make use of marginal and degraded lands through the soil improving effects of trees. Trees have a different impact on soil properties than annual crops, because of their longer residence time, larger biomass accumulation and more extensive root systems. 'Trees improve soils' – this hypothesis is substantiated by the following facts (Young, 2005).

1. The soil under natural forest is fertile. It is well structured, has a good water holding capacity and has a store of nutrients bound up in the organic matter. From time immemorial, farmers have known that they will get a good crop by planting in forest clearings.
2. In natural forests, nutrients are efficiently cycled with very small inputs and outputs from the system. A forest ecosystem is a relatively closed system in terms of nutrient transfer, storage and cycling in contrast to agricultural systems.
3. Reclamation of degraded land through afforestation or a similar type of tree-based land- use system is found to be best to restore soil fertility in many areas.
4. The practice of shifting cultivation demonstrated the power of trees to restore fertility lost during cropping.
5. The conversion of natural forest ecosystems to arable farming systems leads to a decline in soil fertility and a degradation of other soil properties unless appropriate corrective measures are taken.

Nitrogen fixation and a high biomass production are the two most desirable characteristics of a tree. However, many properties are specific to particular objectives of systems in which the trees are used. The properties which are likely to make a tree suitable for soil fertility maintenance or improvement are:

- A high rate of production of leafy biomass
- A high rate of nitrogen fixation
- The existence of deep roots and a dense network of fine roots with a capacity for abundant mycorrhizal association
- A high and balanced nutrient content in the foliage; litter with high nitrogen, low lignin and polyphenols
- An appreciable nutrient content in the root system
- Rapid litter decay, where nutrient release is desired, and a moderate rate of litter decay, where maintenance of a soil cover is required
- Absence of toxic substances in the litter or root residues
- A capacity to grow on poor soils for reclamation

- Absence of severe competitive effects with crops, particularly for water
- Low invasiveness
- Productive and service functions other than soil improvement

Contribution of Trees Towards Improvement of Soil Water Regime in Watershed Areas

Trees contribute a lot towards maintenance and improvement of soil fertility. Since tree is the primary component in an agroforestry system it maintains or improves soil fertility through the following processes.

(*a*) Processes, which increase additions to the soil

- Maintenance of soil organic matter, through carbon fixation in photosynthesis and its transfer via decay of litter and roots
- Nitrogen fixation, by many leguminous and some non-leguminous trees
- Nutrient uptake: the taking up by tree roots of nutrients released by rock weathering
- Atmospheric inputs: the provision by trees of favourable conditions for inputs by rain and dust, including transmission by through fall and stream flow
- Increased water infiltration, through better soil physical properties and effects of roots
- Water retrieval: taking up of water from depth by tree root systems

(*b*) Processes, which reduce losses from the soil

- Protection from erosion and losses of organic matter and nutrients
- Reduction in the rate of organic matter decomposition, by shading and mulching
- Reduction of water loss from evapotranspiration, by shade and litter
- Increased water storage capacity, through better soil physical conditions

(*c*) Processes, which affect soil physical conditions

- Maintenance of soil properties through organic matter and effects of roots
- Penetration of compact or indurated layers by roots
- Modification of extremes of soil temperature, by shade and litter

(*d*) Processes, which affect soil chemical conditions

- Reduction of acidity, or rate of acidification, through bases in litter
- Reduction of salinity and sodicity, by trees in association with other management measures
- Reduction of soil toxicities caused by pollution

(*e*) Soil biological processes and effects

- Production of leaf litter of high quality, containing a balanced nutrient supply, and its transfer to the soil by litter decomposition
- Improvement in nitrogen mineralization through the effects of shade
- Increased availability of phosphorus through mycorrhizal associations
- Increased nodulation on roots of nitrogen-fixing trees in close proximity to roots of non-nitrogen-fixing plants, with possible direct transfer of nutrients between root systems

However, the greatest advantage of trees is in controlling soil erosion by checking the rate of soil runoff. The reduction in runoff is to a small degree, caused by canopy interception and direct transpiration but the greater part of it results from higher infiltration capacity under trees. It helps in improving recharge of ground water, besides perennial flow of stream and better moisture availability through micro-climatic interventions.

Biological Measures for Watershed Management

Choice of suitable cropping system and appropriate agronomic management practices like selection of suitable crops and varieties, sowing time, seed rate, planting techniques, use of fertilizers etc. are the major biological considerations to tackle the problems of watershed areas. The following agroforestry practices can be adopted in watershed areas and the objectives of both watersheds and agroforestry can be achieved.

Alley Cropping

Alley cropping or hedgerow intercropping is a management-intensive agroforestry practice in which perennial, preferably leguminous trees or shrubs are grown simultaneously with an arable crop. The trees, managed as hedgerows, are grown in wide rows and the crop is planted in the interspace or 'alley' between the tree rows. The trees are pruned regularly during the cropping phase and allowed to grow freely to shade the inter-rows when there are no crops. Alley cropping retains the basic restorative attributes of the bush fallow through nutrient recycling, fertility regeneration and weeds suppression and combines these with arable cropping so that all processes occur concurrently on the same land, allowing the farmer to crop the land for an extended period.

Benefits from Alley Cropping

1. An important benefit of alley cropping is the addition of large amounts of organic materials from the prunings as mulch or green manure which can have favourable effects on soil physical and chemical properties, on microbiological activity and hence on soil productivity. This ultimately improves crop performance in alleys (Mohapatra and Patra, 2011).

2. There is a reduction in the use of chemical fertilizers which decreases environmental pollution and maintains soil health.
3. There is an overall improvement in the physical nature of the soil environment. The addition of mulch lowers soil temperatures, reduces evaporation, and improves soil fauna activity and soil structure resulting in better infiltration, reduced runoff and improved water use efficiency.
4. The tree rows on sloping land, act as a physical barrier to soil and water movement, resulting in significant reductions in erosion losses. The presence of prunings applied as mulch in the alleys also controls soil erosion.
5. Alley cropping provides additional products such as forage, firewood or stakes when a multipurpose tree is used as the hedgerow.
6. During the fallow period shading of the interspaces reduces weed growth, while in the cropping phase, the mulch inhibits germination and establishment of weeds.

Management of Alley Cropping Systems

Biologically, the effectiveness of alley cropping systems depends to some extent on the soil type and agroecological zone in which the system is used but it is also very dependent on management strategies adopted. Factors such as choice of tree species, orientation, layout and manipulation of the hedgerows and crop husbandry practices are all important in determining the outcome of the alley cropping system. Trees are planted as hedgerows in farm fields to maximize the positive and minimize the negative effects of trees on crops. Trees compete with agricultural crops for nutrients, soil moisture and solar energy. However, right kind of tree species planted at right spacing, with proper management practices can reduce competition and actually produce a net increase in yields per unit area (Patra, 2013).

The position and spacing of hedgerow and crop plants in an alley cropping system depend on plant species, climate, slope, soil condition and the space required for the movement of people and tillage equipments. Ideally, hedgerows should be positioned in an east-west direction so that plants on both sides receive full sunlight. The spacing adopted is usually 2 m to 8 m between rows and 25 cm to 2 m between the trees within rows. The closer spacing is generally used in humid areas and the wider spacing in semi-humid and semi-arid regions. On sloping land, hedgerows are densely planted along the contours to form a barrier against soil erosion. Grass strips planted alongside hedgerows will create a more effective barrier. If the desirable east-west orientation of hedgerows is not maintained on the slopes then regular pruning of tree branches is required to prevent excessive shading to the agricultural crops in alleys.

The choice of tree species for alley cropping is extremely important and to a large extent determines the success or failure of the system. The following attributes are to be considered when selecting a tree species for an ideal alley cropping.

- a rapid growth rate,
- ability to withstand frequent cutting,
- good coppicing ability (regrowth after cutting),
- ease of establishment from seeds or cuttings,
- nitrogen fixing capacity,
- deep-rooted with a different root distribution to the crop,
- multiple uses such as forage and firewood,
- ability to withstand environmental stresses such as drought, waterlogging, and extremes of pH,
- high leaf to stem ratio,
- small leaves or leaflets,
- dry season leaf retention
- freedom from pests and diseases

The suitable species for hedgerow planting are *Cassia siamea, Leucaena leucocephala, Glyricidia sepium, Calliandra calothyrsus, Sesbania sesban, Acacia mangium, Gmelina arborea, Albizia* spp., *Cajanus* spp., *Chamaecytisus* spp., *Desmodium* spp., *Erythrina* spp., *Flemingia* spp., *Inga* spp. and *Tephrosia* spp.

Agroforestry for Fuelwood Production

In this system, various multipurpose fuel wood species are interplanted in or around agricultural lands. The primary productive role of this system is to produce firewood. Tree species commonly used as fuel wood are *Acacia nilotica, Acacia* auriculiformis, *Acacia mangium, Gmelina arborea, Dalbergia sissoo, Albizia lebbeck, Casuarina equisetifolia, Prosopis juliflora, Cassia siamea, Eucalyptus tereticornis*, etc.

Multipurpose Trees and Shrubs on Field Bunds

In this system, trees are scattered haphazardly or according to some systematic patterns on bunds, terraces or plot/field boundaries, crop lands, pastures and rangelands. Multipurpose trees like *Acacia nilotica, Acacia albida, Casuarina equisetifolia, Azadirachta indica, Acacia senegal, Cocos nucifera, Leucaena leucocephala* and *Acacia mangium* are planted on field bunds and boundaries (Patra, *et. al.*, 2011).

Benefits

1. Farmers consider such trees not to be competitive against food crops.

2. Trees provide shade for livestock during intense heat of the long dry season.
3. The trees diversify farmers' products and increase crop production and the duration of cropping season without fertilizer use.
4. The system reduces soil erosion due to high wind velocity or rain water runoff.
5. Sale of non-timber products, such as charcoal, firewood, tree borne oil and fruits significantly increases income.

Boundary Planting

This is a simple but effective practice particularly for small farmers. It consists of planting trees all along the boundaries between the fields and farm or along the margins of roads and canals. It is also called four-sided forestry with object of gaining production from trees, whilst having no adverse effect on adjacent crops and possibly a beneficial effect through fertilization by nitrogen fixing tree species or their leaf litter, protection from wind or aiding soil conservation i.e. watershed protection. Tree species like *Acacia mangium, Acacia auriculformis, Acacia nilotica, Sesbania grandiflora, Azadirachta indica, Albizia lebbeck* etc. are most suitable for field bund or boundary plantation. Farmer's choice, land suitability, marketability of the produce etc are to be considered while selecting the tree and crop species for plantation.

Intercropping with Multipurpose Trees

In order to overcome the limitation of land and to attain self sufficiency, the farmers can resort to intercropping for increasing the efficiency of land use, both under limited soil moisture as well as under adequacy of resources. Inclusion of annual pulse crop in inter-row spaces of widely spaced multipurpose trees offers additional productive benefits as well as protective benefits.

Shelterbelts

A shelterbelt is a wide strip of vegetation consisting of several rows of trees that slows wind speeds, thereby reducing wind erosion, evaporation and damage farmlands by the wind. It is sometimes referred to as windbreak, although the latter often implies a single strip of trees and other vegetation. A shelterbelt presents a mechanical barrier to the impact of the wind, and separates two zones; the windward and the leeward zones. The windward zone refers to the side from which the wind blows, while the leeward zone relates to the side where the wind passes.

The main characteristics of shelterbelts are:

1. Shelterbelts have a typical triangular shape by raising tall trees in the centre.

2. A certain degree of penetration by wind is planned as by raising a solid wall of trees, the protection decreases very fast on the leeward side.
3. The ratio of height and width of a shelter belt should be roughly 1:10. Shelterbelts up to 50 m width are considered ideal under Indian condition.
4. Orientation of shelterbelts depends upon the direction and velocity of the prevailing winds. Rows of trees are established at right angles to the prevailing wind.
5. The minimum length of a shelterbelt should be about 25 m.
6. Tree species selected for shelterbelt establishment should have ability for wider adaptability to climatic conditions (drought, frost, extreme temperatures etc.), high growth rate, quick crown formation, developing a strong and deep root system (so that they do not compete for moisture and nutrients with agricultural crops), evergreen foliage, increased land productivity.

Benefits from Shelterbelts

Properly placed field shelterbelts provide agronomic and other benefits. The main agronomic benefits include the following:

1. **Reduces soil erosion by wind:** A shelterbelt modifies the microclimate, mostly in its leeward side. This modified microclimate includes reduced wind speed and, therefore, reduced soil erosion. A significant reduction of wind speed occurs on leeward side for a distance extending to approximately 20 times the height of the shelterbelt and also 3 to 5 times its height on the windward side. Therefore, a shelterbelt 5 m in height will provide a degree of protection for soils and crops for a total distance of up to 25 times its height i.e. 125 m. Since the zone of protection provided by a single shelterbelt is limited, a series of shelterbelts is required to protect the whole field. The shelterbelts must be planted perpendicular to the direction of the prevailing wind to provide more complete protection.
2. **Increases moisture for crop growth:** Shelterbelts reduces evaporation, thus providing more moisture for crop growth. It also protects the leeward areas from the desiccating effects of hot wind. Shelterbelts use moisture and nutrients from a greater depth than most annual crops.
3. **Reduced wind damage to crops:** Crops benefit from the reduced wind speeds in the protected zone. The crop plants are less likely to be twisted by the wind.
4. **Potential for increased farm productions:** Most of the research conducted around the world reports crop yield increases due to shelterbelts. However, crops vary in their yield response to shelterbelt

protection. Drought tolerant crops show the lowest response, forage crops are moderately responsive and weather-sensitive crops such as vegetables show the highest response. Besides, shelterbelts provide potential source of income for farmers (e.g. biomass, timber and non-timber products).

Soil Conservation Hedges

Trees and shrubs are planted on physical soil conservation works such as grass strips, bunds and terraces wherein they play two roles viz. i. to stabilize the soil conservation structure through the root system and ii. to make productive use of the land they occupy. The risers or terraces in steeply sloping landscapes are densely planted with multipurpose and/or fruit trees. The primary role of multipurpose/fruit trees and agricultural species is soil conservation and provision of various tree products. The important tree species used for soil conservation include *Grevillea robusta, Acacia catechu, Pinus roxburghii, Acacia modesta, Prosopis juliflora, Alnus nepalensis, Leucaena leucocephala* etc.

Silvipastopral System

Silvipasture as an agroforestry practice is specifically designed and managed for the production of trees, tree products, forage and livestock. Silvipasture results when forage crops are deliberately introduced or enhanced in a timber production system, or timber crops are deliberately introduced or enhanced in a forage production system. Integrating livestock production in the farming system promotes farm product diversification, improves food security and offers a diversified marketing opportunity that can stimulate rural economic development. The interactions among timber, forage and livestock are managed intensively to simultaneously produce timber commodities, a high quality forage resource and efficient livestock production. Overall, silvipastural systems can provide economic returns while creating a sustainable system with many environmental benefits.

Before new silvipastoral systems are established, implications of merging forestry and agricultural systems should be explored thoroughly for economic and environmental considerations. While making tree and forage crop selections potential markets, soil type, climatic conditions and species compatibility should be considered. The timber component should be marketable, high quality, fast growing, deep-rooted, drought tolerant, and capable of providing the desired products and environmental services. The forage component should be a perennial crop that is suitable for livestock grazing, compatible with the site (soil, temperature, precipitation), productive under partial shade and moisture stress, responsive to intensive management and tolerant of heavy utilization or grazing.

A successful silvipastural system requires understanding forage growth characteristics and managing the timing and duration of grazing to avoid browsing of young tree seedlings. Improper management of silvipastures can reduce desirable woody and herbaceous plants by over-grazing and soil compaction.

Benefits from Silvipastoral Systems

1. Economic risk is reduced because the system produces multiple products, most of which have an established market. Production costs are reduced and comprehensive land utilization in silvipastoral systems provides a relatively constant income from livestock sale and selective sale of trees and timber products. Well-managed forage production provides improved nutrition for livestock growth and production.
2. Grazing can enhance tree growth by controlling grass competition for moisture, nutrients and sunlight. Well managed grazing provides economical control of weeds. Fertilizer applied for forage is also used by trees. In addition, livestock manure recycles nutrients to trees and forage.
3. Some forage species tend to be lower in fiber and more digestible when grown in a tree-protected environment. Trees that provide shade or wind protection can have a climate-stabilizing effect to reduce heat stress of livestock. Protection from trees can cut the direct cold effect by 50 percent or more and reduce wind velocity by as much as 70 percent.
4. The forage protects the soil from water and wind erosion, while adding organic matter to improve soil properties. Some forage species fix nitrogen. Silvipastures provide an attractive landscape with an aesthetic value. It can also increase wildlife diversity.

Homegardens

This is one of the oldest agroforestry practices found extensively in the high rainfall areas in tropical south and south-east Asia. The word 'homegarden' has been used to describe diverse practices, from growing vegetables behind houses to complex multistoried systems. It is the intimate association of multipurpose trees and shrubs with seasonal and permanent arable crops and livestock within the compounds of individual houses. Mostly the whole system i.e. crop-tree-animal unit is managed by family labour. These systems are common in all ecological regions in the tropics and subtropics, especially in humid lowlands with high population density. The average size of a homegarden is usually much less than one hectare. In India, every homestead has around 0.2 to 0.5 ha land for personal production. In many parts of the world the fruit, vegetable and other foodstuff produced from homegardens provide a substantial part of the household food requirement. Food production is the primary function and role of most of the homegardens. The combination of crops with different production cycles results in a relatively uninterrupted supply of food products throughout the year. In most cases, animals and birds are kept in the homegardens. Fodder and legumes are widely grown to meet the daily fodder requirement of the animals. The waste materials from crops and homes are also used as fodder for animals and feed for birds. Cattle are mostly kept for diary products and land cultivation. Goats, chickens and fish are kept for household consumption. Products from animals or the animals themselves can also be sold in the market.

Structure of Homegardens

The layered configurations and combination of compatible species are the most important characteristics of all homegardens. The gardens are carefully structured systems where each component has a specific place and function. All homegardens usually consist of a herbaceous layer near the ground, a tree layer at upper levels, and intermediate layers in between. The lower layer is usually divided into two, with the lowermost (less than 1 m height) dominated by different vegetable and medicinal plants, and the second layer (1-3 m height) being composed of food plants such as banana, papaya, yam and so on. The upper tree layer is also partitioned into two, consisting of emergent, fully grown timber and fruit trees occupying the uppermost layer of over 25 m height, and medium-sized trees of 10-20 m occupying the next lower layer. The intermediate layer of 3-10 m height is dominated by various fruit trees.

Benefits of Home Gardens

1. Production is very diverse and continuous with less risk and there is a regular flow of products such as food, fuel, fodder, fruit, spices and timber.
2. The protective function of home gardens is very high with soil conservation, water retention and favourable micro-climate for humans and animals.
3. The use of labour for the farm is very efficient due to proximity of the garden to the house, within the walking distances.
4. Valuable crops or animals in need of protection can be given extra care by the farm family because of the short distance from the house.
5. Homegardens ensure a pleasant living environment, shade and provision of privacy.
6. They can also provide aesthetic values and open patches in the homegarden often serve as family or village gathering places.

Agri-horti-silvicultural System

In the agri-horti-silvicultural system, suitable arable crops are grown in inter-spaces of perennial fruit or multipurpose tree rows. In between two trees one fruit crop like mango, guava or pomegranate may be planted. When annual crop yield is substantially reduced due to canopy closure the system is converted to a horti-silvicultural system. With appropriate management practices this practice can give a sustainable production system.

Silvi-pastoral and Horti-pastoral System

In these systems, suitable fodder grasses like guinea (*Panicum maximum*), dinanath grass (*Pennisetum pedicellatum*), napier grass (*Pennisetum purpureum*), thin napier (*Panicum polystachion*), anjan grass (*Cenchrus ciliaris*) and fodder legumes like stylo (*Stylosanthes hamata* and *Stylosanthes scabra*), cowpea (*Vigna sinensis*) are grown in inter-spaces of perennial fruit or multipurpose tree rows. These systems are very effective to control soil erosion as the grasses give a permanent soil cover.

Aquaforestry

The aquaforestry system comprises composite fish culture in farm ponds, and various trees and shrubs, leaves of which are preferred by fish (Ex. *Leucaena leucocephala, Morus alba, Gliricidia sepium, Moringa olifera* etc.) are planted on the boundary and around fish ponds. Leaves of these trees are used as feed for fish. Inland fish such as catla, rohu, mrigal, common carp, silver carp and grass carp can be grown in the ponds. In the coastal regions farmers are cultivating fish and prawn in saline water and growing coconut and other trees on bunds of ponds. Now fish culture in the mangroves is also advocated, which form a rich source of nutrition to the aquatic life and breeding ground for juvenile fish, prawn and mussels. Other terms that have been used for this practice are silvipisciculture, agrisilviaquaculture and aquasilviculture. Some other modified aquaforestry systems are:

1. A well-balanced system of animal husbandry including goatery, poultry, duck farming, turtles and fishes in the small ponds in home gardens make a balanced system of high moisture, energy and nutrient use efficiency per unit area.
2. In paddy field, fish can easily be reared by planting trees on field bunds or boundary. This system can be practised in high rainfall areas.
3. Coconut plants can also be successfully planted on raised paddy field bunds with an alley space of 5 m width depression which is utilized for pisiculture purpose (Patra, *et. al.*, 2008).

Apisilviculture

In this system, various honey or nectar producing trees frequently visited by honeybees are planted on the boundary of the agricultural field. Bees benefit trees and trees in turn provide series of benefits to bees. The primary purpose of this system is to produce honey. Api-silviculture with *Eucalyptus, Gliricidia, Grevillea, Gmelina, Leuceana* and *Albizia* species were more remunerative and a good source of generating additional farm income. Fruit trees can also be integrated with apisilviculture for more profits.

Conservation Measures for Watershed Management

Various types of soil and water conservation measures have been recommended depending on the soil, topography, climate, size of the land holding.

1. **Contour cultivation:** Contour operations are done across the slope by cultivation of crops, trees on contour. The contour furrows created would form a multitude of mini barriers across the flow path of runoff. Contour cultivation remains the most effective on moderate slopes of 2-7%, besides in-situ conservation of moisture and water harvesting.
2. **Contour bunding:** This practice comprises of constructing narrow based bunds on contour to impound runoff water behind them, so that impounded water is absorbed gradually into the soil profile. The bunds should be constructed from the top of the catchment and preceded downwards.
3. **Graded bunding:** Graded bunds are constructed in relatively high rainfall areas. The excess water has to be removed out of the field to avoid water stagnation, especially in deep black soils. These bunds are outlets for safe removal of water. The channels of graded bunds are wide and shallow.
4. **Bench terracing:** Bench terracing involves converting the original ground into level step like fields constructed by half cutting and half filling, which reduces the degree of the slope. In hilly areas this approach of bench terracing for agroforestry models is gradually getting popular.
5. **Contour furrow:** Contour furrow is also called as strip farming. The cropping is usually intermittent on strips or in rows with catchment area left fallow. The principle is to collect runoff from catchment area to improve soil moisture on the cropped area, particularly on sloppy land with undulating topography.

Conclusion

The main principles of watershed management are based on resource conservation, resource generation and resource utilization. In watershed approach, development is not only confined to agricultural lands but also covers the area, starting from the highest point of the land to the outlet of the natural stream. Watershed management becomes increasingly important as a way to improve livelihood of people while conserving and regenerating their natural resources.

The primary objective of agroforestry systems in watershed areas is to maximise biomass production per unit area per unit time. The other major objectives of agroforestry systems in watershed areas include conservation of soil and water, soil improvement, moderation of microclimate and establishment of agro-based cottage industries. Agroforestry has both productive (like production of food, fuel wood, timber, fodder, fibre and other forest minor products) and protective functions (like providing shade, microclimate amelioration, reduction in wind speed, control of soil erosion, maintenance and improvement of soil fertility etc.).

Choice of suitable cropping system and appropriate agronomic management practices like selection of suitable crops and varieties, sowing time, seed rate, planting techniques, use of fertilizers etc. are the major biological considerations to tackle the problems of watershed areas. Similarly, engineering approaches like various types of soil and water conservation measures (contour cultivation, contour bunding, graded bunding, bench terracing, contour furrow etc.) have been recommended depending on the soil, topography, climate, size of the land holding. The agroforestry practices like alley cropping, boundary planting, homegardens, agri-horti-silvicultural, silvi-pastoral, horti-pastoral systems, aquaforestry, apisilviculture etc. can be adopted in watershed areas and the objectives of both watersheds and agroforestry can fully be achieved.

REFERENCES

Bene, J.G., Beall, H.W. and Cote, A. (1977): Trees, Food and People: Land Management in the Tropics, International Development Research Centre, Ottawa, Canada.

Garrity, D.P., and Agus, F. (1999): Natural Resource Management on a Watershed Scale: What can Agroforestry Contribute? pp. 165-193 (In): Lal, R. (ed.) Integrated Watershed Management in the Global Ecosystem, CRC Press, Washington, D.C.

http://agropedia.iitk.ac.in/content/watershed-management-dryland

http://en.wikipedia.org

http://forestry.about.com

http://www.agroforestry.co.uk

http://www.centerforagroforestry.org/practices

http://www.eoearth.org/article/agroforestry

http://www.fao.org/forestry

http://www.overstory.org

http://www.plant-trees.org

http://www.treesofstrength.org

http://www.worldagroforestry.org

http://www.worldagroforestry.org

Lundgren, B.O. and Raintree, J.B. (1982): Sustained agroforestry. (In): Nestel, B. (ed.). Agricultural Research for Development: Potentials and Challenges in Asia. International Service for National Agricultural Research, The Hague, Netherlands.

Mohapatra, A.K. and Patra, A.K. (2011): Importance of Agroforestry in Organic Farming. (In): Gulati, J.M.L. and Barik, T. (eds.). Recent Developments in Organic Farming. Department of Agronomy, OUAT, Bhubaneswar. pp. 366-374.

Nair, P.K.R. (2008): An Introduction to Agroforestry. Springer (India) Pvt. Ltd., New Delhi.

Patra, A.K. (2013): Alley cropping, *Science Horizon* 3(11): 6-10.

Patra, A.K. and Mohapatra, A.K., Gantayat, B.P. and Das, S. (2011): Evaluation of *Acacia nilotica* as Bund Plantation in Coastal Odisha, *Journal of Research, OUAT* Special Issue 1(1): 81-85.

Patra, A.K., Mohapatra, A.K., Gantayat, B.P. and Das, S. (2008): Performance of Coconut (*Cocos nucifera*) Based Agrihorticultural System in Coastal Orissa, *Journal of Research, OUAT* 26(2): 53-58.

Patra, A.K. (2013): Agroforestry: Theory & Practices. New India Publishing Agency, New Delhi. 242 pp.

Sharma, R., Jianchu, X. and Sharma, G. (2007): Traditional Agroforestry in the Eastern Himalayan Region: Land Management System Supporting Ecosystem Services. *Tropical Ecology* 48(2): 189-200.

Tideman, E.M. (2007): Watershed Management: Guidelines for Indian Conditions. Omega Scientific Publishers, New Delhi. 372 pp.

Young, A. (1988): Agroforestry and Its Potential to Contribute to Land Development in the Tropics. *Biogeography Journal* 15(1): 19-30.

Young, A. (1997): The Effectiveness of Contour Hedgerows for Soil and Water Conservation. *Agroforestry Forum* 8(1): 2-4.

Young, A. (2005): Agroforestry for Soil Management. CAB International, Walling Ford, U.K.

Water Management and Aquatic Ecosystem **Pages 68-115**
Edited by: Dr. Resham Bhalla & Dr. Pawan Kumar 'Bharti'
ISBN: 978-93-86841-96-4
Edition: 2019
Published by: Discovery Publishing House Pvt. Ltd., New Delhi (India)

5 Analysis Urbanization Pattern Around Major Water Bodies in Nagpur City, Maharashtra

[1]D. Nandi, [1]M Bhunia, [2]P.C Sahu, [1]B. Singh

ABSTRACT

Urban water body means Lakes and Rivers are important part of urban ecosystem. Remote Sensing (RS) and Geographical information system (GIS) can be effectively used for generating of information related to water bodies and hence an attempt has been made to map the urban area and urbanization pattern around major water bodies in city. Though relatively small in size, lakes perform significant environmental, social and economic functions, ranging from being a source of drinking water, recharging groundwater, acting as sponges to control flooding, supporting biodiversity and providing livelihoods. Nag River is main and important river in Nagpur City. This River is flowing middle parson in Nagpur City. Three approaches namely, visual interpretation, analysis urbanization pattern around water bodies, and identification of lake, rivers and other water bodies, comparison between water bodies and land use/land cover in this city. Highest area of vegetation and lowest area of recreational area around major water bodies (1 km buffer) were was observed through comparison approach followed by visual interpretation techniques. And other types of land use/land cover are built up area, agricultural land, road, waste land, open place, infrastructure area, railway around major water bodies (1 km buffer) in Nagpur city.

Keywords: RS, GIS, Land use pattern, water bodies.

Introduction

Urban areas are considered as the most dynamic portion on earth surface (National 2000). Urbanization refers to the population shift from rural to urban areas, "the gradual increase in the proportion of people living in urban areas", and the ways in which each society adapts to the change. It is predominantly the process by which towns and cities are formed and become larger as more people begin living and working in central areas. It is predicted that by 2050 about 64% of the developing world and 86% of the developed world will be

1 Department of Remote Sensing and GIS, North Orissa University, Baripada, Odisha, India
2 Department of Geology M.P.C Autonomous College, Baripada, Odisha, India

urbanized. That is equivalent to approximately 3 billion urbanites by 2050, much of which will occur in Africa and Asia. Notably, the United Nations has also recently projected that nearly all global population growth from 2017 to 2030 will be absorbed by cities, about 1.1 billion new urbanites over the next 13 years.

Urbanization is relevant to a range of disciplines, including geography, sociology, economics, urban planning and public health. The phenomenon has been closely linked to modernization, industrialization and the sociological process of rationalization. Urbanization can be seen as a specific condition at a set time (e.g. the proportion of total population or area in cities or towns) or as an increase in that condition over time. So urbanization can be quantified either in terms of, say, the level of urban development relative to the overall population, or as the rate at which the urban proportion of the population is increasing. Urbanization creates enormous social, economic and environmental changes, which provide an opportunity for sustainability with the-potential to use resources more efficiently, to create more sustainable land use and to protect the biodiversity of natural ecosystems.

Urbanization refers to the growth of towns and cities, often at the expense of rural areas, as people move to urban centres in search of jobs and what they hope will be a better life. In most countries the percentage of the total population living in urban areas is increasing.

One of the advantages of living in a city is the market potential of the population; that is, there is a much greater variety of shopping opportunities than in rural areas. This may result in lower prices and longer shopping hours. Most cities have shopping malls and big box centres with many different stores that stay open long hours, and that often include entertainment, food, recreation, and cultural activities to attract consumers. Many stores are owned by national and international chains, making it difficult for small independent businesses to succeed.

Urban centres are able to provide a variety of services that small rural centres cannot. These might include a public transportation system, water and sewage services, a greater variety of educational and recreational facilities, and larger and more specialized healthcare facilities. On the negative side, cities may experience traffic jams, infrastructure breakdowns such as water main breaks, lack of appropriate housing and jobs, and institutions that are so large that they become impersonal.

Urban centres also provide a great variety of accommodation for their citizens ranging from individually owned houses to high-density apartments and condominiums. Many new developments include open spaces for playgrounds, schools, and community centres. Many cities, however, also have areas where housing is poor and may even have a homeless population, often in downtown neighbourhoods. This may give rise to shelters for the homeless and soup kitchens for those down on their luck. Smaller communities are often able to provide more help because they are likely to know the individuals who need help and because there are fewer people in need.

The downtown areas of many large cities are facing problems such as old, rundown buildings, empty stores, and substandard housing for the inner-city population. This often leads to a variety of social problems, including vandalism, crime, unemployment, and poverty. Sometimes cities do not have the resources or political will to save heritage buildings or to improve life in their downtown areas.

Importance of Water Bodies in Urbanization

Water bodies, the aquatic systems on land, like lakes, reservoirs, tanks, ponds, act as storehouses for variety of wildlife, especially for avifauna, serving as breeding and nesting sites and often as flood controls. In the past, lakes and tanks were a very important source of water supply for the purposes of drinking and irrigation. The lakes and reservoirs across the country are in varying degrees of environmental degradation due to various anthropogenic activities like intensive urban growth, rapid industrial activities.

Urbanization has significantly altered both the quantity and quality of our water resources.

The concentration of people in urban areas has modified the natural landscape, bringing about water problems that strongly affect their daily lives.

Water is a vital resource for human activities. Its natural distribution is governed by climate and the physical character of the land surface. Urbanization, however, has altered this natural distribution as water has been utilized to supply man's needs and to carry away his wastes. Water is, in a sense, both artery and vein to urban life.

Lakes perform various important and indigenous functions in any urban area. Each of these water bodies is unique and has its own ecological character that is defined by the flora and fauna and, the urban ecosystem service it performs. However, some of the common predominant factors that characterize all urban water bodies are:

- Most urban lakes are manmade.
- Urban lakes are greener than non-urban lakes.
- They require high quality water treatment due to discharge of chemicals and oil into them.
- They show higher seasonal variations in turbidity levels, and
- Diagnostic sediment signature in them varies from place to place.

Urban water body means Lakes are important part of urban ecosystem. Though relatively small in size, lakes perform significant environmental, social and economic functions, ranging from being a source of drinking water, recharging groundwater, acting as sponges to control flooding, supporting biodiversity and providing livelihoods. Water in lakes is an easily available source of water for the needs of many sectors of economy such as agriculture, domestic and industrial. These water bodies, whether man-made or natural, fresh water or brackish play a very vital role in maintaining environmental sustainability particularly in urban environments especially in today's context when the cities are facing the challenges of unplanned rapid urbanization.

At present, in India, lakes and wetlands are in extremely bad shape and are in varying degrees of environmental degradation. Despite knowing their environmental, social and economic significance, city planners have wilfully neglected and destroyed these water bodies. Today these water bodies are encroached, full of sewage and garbage. Because of unplanned urbanization, much of the landscape around the lakes has been covered by impervious surfaces. As a result, instead of rainwater, it is the sewage and effluents that are filling up urban water bodies. Once the sponges of urban area, today urban lakes have turned into hazards that get choked even with low rainfall and overflow into the blocked canals during high rainfall causing floods in the city.

REMOTE SENSING AND GIS

Remote Sensing

Remote sensing is defined as 'the science and art of obtaining information about an object, area, or phenomenon through the analysis of data acquired by a device that is not in contact with the object, area or phenomenon under investigation' (Lillesand *et al.*, 2004).Remote sensing (RS) is the science and art of acquiring information (spectral, spatial, and temporal) about material object, area, or phenomenon, without coming into physical contract with the object or area, or phenomenon under investigation. In remote sensing, information transfer is accomplished by use of electromagnetic radiation (EMR) to sensor present at far away distance. EMR is a form of energy that reveals its presence by the observable effect is produces when it strikes the matter and is captured in different wavebands remote sensing is largely concern with the measurement of response of object to the electromagnetic radiation from the sun. Distinctive response of object different wave length when interacts with EMR captured is stored as a digital image and has different spatial, spectral and temporal regulation.

A digital image is defined as a matrix of digital unbars (DNs). Each digital number is the output of the process of analog-to-digital convention. This digital image cannot be use directly some processing has to be done on it and the process is known as digital image processing. It involves a serious of steps starting from processing, image enhancement, image transformation, image classification and analysis. Analysis of image is done by images by using a set of interpretation key. The interpretation keys are shape, size, pattern, tone, association, structure etc. applying these interpretation keys furthers analysis is done is various application fields. There is range of applications for remote sensing in forestry include terrain analysis, updating of existing forest inventories, forest cover type discrimination,the delineation of burned areas,mapping of cleared areas, stand height calculation, crown density estimation and much more. This renewed commitment to understanding forests at different scales and with a process – based perspective has helped generate demand for information about forest that is feasibly acquired only by remote sensing.

Remote sensing is the acquisition of data about an object or scene by a sensor that is far from the object (Colwell, 1983). Aerial photography, satellite imagery, and radar are all forms of remotely sensed data. Usually, remotely sensed data refer to data of the Earth collected from sensors on satellites or aircraft. Most of the images used as input to the ERDAS IMAGINE system are remotely sensed. However, you are not limited to remotely sensed data.

Geographic Information System (GIS)

Geographically referenced data (or geo data) is data that is connected to locations on the earth. The data may come in a variety of forms such as imagery (raster) datasets, vector (feature) datasets, terrain, LIDAR (point clouds), and others. That data might be based on a range of values, such as rainfall amounts or elevation above sea level, or it might deal with geographical features, such as lakes, city boundaries, land use zones, or road types. Geographic information puts geo data into a format that is meaningful for people but that can also be used and manipulated by computers.

Geographic Information is used by different organizations such as telecommunications companies; environmental management agencies; natural disaster management agencies; Earth observation companies; oil, gas, and utility companies; disaster and emergency management; and the military.

GIS generally refers to a description of the characteristics and tools used in the 3th organization and management of geography data. The term GIS is currently applied to computer storage, processing and retrieval system that has hardware and software spicily designed to cope with geographical referenced spatial data and corresponding informative attribute. Spatial data are commonly in the form of layers that may depict topography or environmental elements. Nowadays, GIS technology is becoming an essential tool for combining various map and satellite information source in modal that simulate the interaction of complex natural system.

Use of RS and GIS in Urban Planning

Urban Planning can be defined variously as: "the formulation of alternative patterns of urban settlement, the rational use of resources to alleviate urban problems, and the provision of city's physical and social infrastructure: transportation, utilities, housing, community facilities, and service". The urban planning application using R.S. and GIS tools is one of the many areas where such utilities can be used for managing planning activities. The planner can look for different options and choose the best suited for the end result. The automated process is not only faster but also can be monitored effectively at any eventuality.

Needs of the Study

Nagpur city and around area is covered with natural and manmade lakes. The significant lakes are Futala, Ambazari, Gandhisagar, Gorewada, Sonegaon, Sakhardara, Naik, Lendi, Surabardi, Mines of wadi, Wadi, Wakeshwar, and some tanks are Telhara, Dahegaon, and police line water pond. And mainly two surface water bodies such river Nag River and Pilli river. These lakes are being used for anthropogenic and recreational purpose. On the bank of these lakes, some of the slums are located, which are using lake water for washing, bathing and domestic activities. Nagpur Municipal Corporation (NMC) has taken steps to protect these lakes for being polluted due to local activities. Every year samples were collected from all these lakes and analyzed for physicochemical parameters to know the water quality status of these lakes. Water quality was observed that these lakes are exerting organic load in the form of BOD and COD due to manmade activities. The mineral contents are found to be high and increased every year with respect to dissolved solids, sulphates, hardness and chloride. Nutrient load in terms of nitrate and phosphate are found to be increased except Ambazari, futala, Gandhisagar and therefore these are on the verge of Eutrophication. The lakes are periodically deterioting and need attention. The heavy metals in some of the lakes are also found to be exceeded the permissible limits of drinking water.

The nag river flows through the major part of the city carrying mostly sewage generated from that particular areas. The Pilli river passing through mostly outskirts of city also carrying domestic sewage generated from the locality besides the river.

Objectives

Water bodies such as rivers and lakes play an important role in human development by providing drinking water and domestic use water for urban population in my study area Nagpur city, Maharashtra in India. Lake is an area of variable size filled with water, localized in a basin, that is surrounded by land, apart from any river or other outlet that serves to feed or drain the lake. Lakes lie on land and are not part of the ocean, and therefore are distinct from lagoons, and are also larger and deeper than ponds, though there are no official or scientific definitions. Lakes can be contrasted with rivers or streams, which are usually flowing. Most lakes are fed and drained by rivers and streams. Remote sensing(RS) and Geographic Information System(GIS) Can be effectively used for generating such information about water bodies has been made to map the study area.

The present study is conducted with following aim and objectives.

- To map the water bodies of Nagpur city and its surroundings.
- To map Land uses characteristics around 1 km major water bodies in Nagpur city.

Scope of the Study

The scope of the study is find out the land use pattern with in 1 km buffer of major water bodies.

Limitation

My project study has some limitation....

- Time is the first limitation in my project work because this project is 6 months.
- High resolution data using Bhutan portal has been used for my project work.

STUDY AREA

Location & Area

Nagpur city is located in Maharashtra state, between 21°45 north to 20°30 north latitude and 78°15 east to 79°45 east longitude. It can be said that Nagpur

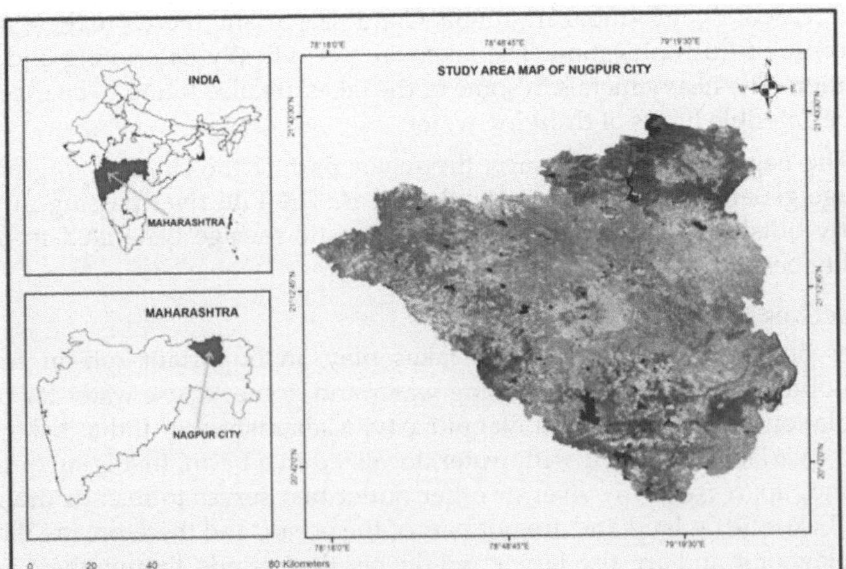

Fig. 5.1: Map of Nagpur City

falls in the Deccan plateau region. Nagpur is situated at a height of 312.42 meters above sea level. Nagpur is bordered by Amravati and Wardha in the west. Bhandara in the east and Chandrapur in the south. In the north, it shares its boundary with the state of Madhya Pradesh of which it was a capital till 1956. Nagpur city is at an advantageous position for the major highways like the NH-7 and NH-6 passes through this city of Maharashtra. The distance of Nagpur from the metropolitan cities like Delhi is 1094 km, from Mumbai is 837 km, From Kolkata 1140 km and from Chennai is 1092 km.

Climate

Nagpur has tropical savannah climate with dry conditions prevailing for most of the year. The city of Nagpur enjoys a very dry or semi humid climate throughout the year excepting the monsoon months of June and September. The climate of Nagpur can be broadly divided into three important seasons such as the summer season from March to June, the monsoon season from July to October & the winter season from November to February.

Temperature

In the summer seasons are extremely hot, lastly from March to June, with May being the hottest month. Winter lasts from November to January during which temperatures drop below 10°C. The highest recorded temperature in the city was 48°C on May 19, 2015, while the lowest was 3.9°C.

Rainfall

In the rainy season It receives about 163 mm of rainfall in June. The amount of rainfall is increased in July 294 mm. Gradual decreased of rainfall has been observed from July to August (278 mm) and September (160 mm).The highest recorded daily rainfall was 304 mm on 14 July 1994.

Land Use

Information of Land use is important for planning and management of the activities in study area. The Land use gives idea about the multifaceted use of land use and misuse of land as well as development process of the study area. The natural, social, Cultural, Historical, economical and political factors play a great role in the land use pattern of the study area. The Land use pattern of Nagpur city is divided in seven categories. There are vegetation, Agriculture Land, settlement Land, waste Land, Barren Land, communication land, recreational land.

Soil

The understanding rock type in the western and southern localities is Deccen Trap, the lava flows gave rise to flat topped and terraced features. The Eastern half covered by Crystalline Metamorphic Rock such as gneissis, schist and granites, In the Northern Part of the city, yellowish sand stones and clays of the lower Gondwana formations are found. In maximum part of the town, the under lying rock strata are covered with alluvial deposits resulting from the flood plain of the Kanhan river. In some places these gives rise to granular, sandy soils, but in many places, particularly in low lying, poorly drained areas, the soils are alluvial clays with poor permeability characteristics.

MATERIALS AND METHODS

Methodology

Data Used

To work out the Present study the following data were used.

- Resoursat–2, LISS–IV Data (2010)
- Cartosat–1 Panchromatic Data (2010)
- Survey of India (SOI) topographic maps on 1:50,000

The methodology for the present study is depicted in Figure 5.2.

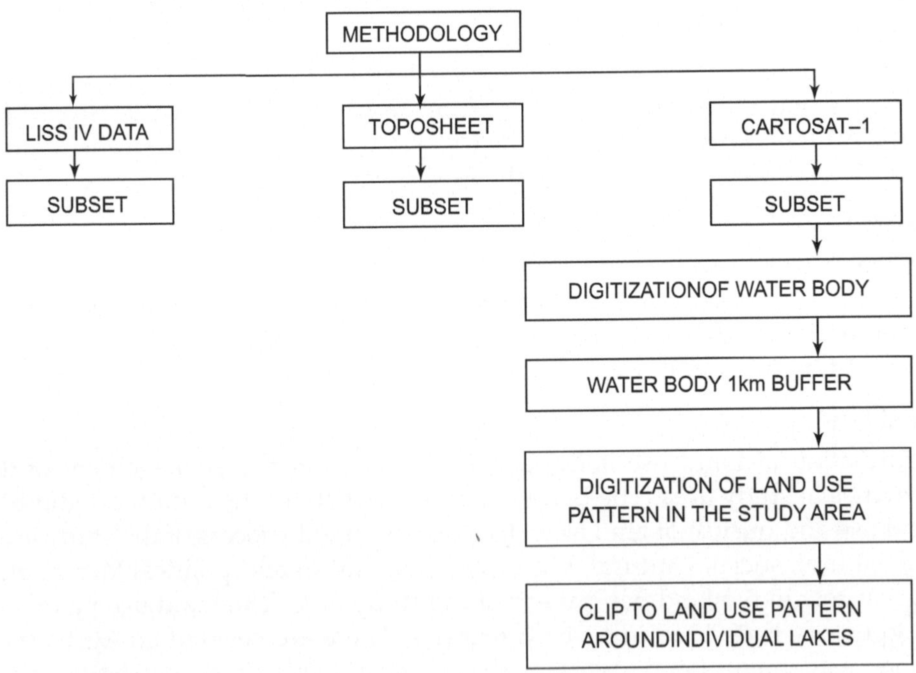

Fig. 5.2: Flowchart of Methodology

LISS-IV Data

The LISS-IV camera is a high resolution multi-spectral camera operating in three spectral bands. LISS-IV can be operated in either of the two modes. In the multi-spectral mode, a swath of 23km is covered in three bands, while in mono mode; the full swath of 70km can be covered in any one single band. The

LISS-IV camera can be tilted in the across track direction thereby providing a revisit period of 5 days (Figure 5.3).

Fig. 5.3: LISS-IV data of Nagpur city, Maharashtra, India

Cartosat Data

Cartisat-1 is a stereoscopic Earth observation satellite in a sun-synchronous orbit, and the first one of the Cartosat series of satellites. Cartosat-1 carries two state-of-the art panchromatic cameras that take black and white stereoscopic pictures of the earth in the visible region of the electromagnetic spectrum. The swath covered by these high resolution Pan cameras is 30km and their spatial resolution is 2.5 meters (Figure 5.4).

Resolution Merge

Higher resolution imagery is generally single band (for example Cartosat Panchromatic data), While multispectral imagery generally has the lower resolutions (for example LISS-IV data), these techniques are often used to produce high resolution multispectral imagery. This improves the interpretability of the data by having high resolution information which is also in colour (Figure 5.5).

This is three types of view **Multiplicative, Principal Components, and Brovey Transform.**

- **Multiplicative** is based on simple arithmetic integration of the two raster sets.
- **Principal Components** merge operates on PC-1 rather than the input raster image.

- **Brovey Transform** uses ratio algorithm to combine the images.

Working Process: Raster tab>Pan sharpen>Resolution Merge.

Software Used

To work out the present study the following data were used..

- Erdas15 and Arcgis9.3

Data Base Preparation

On the basis of above data, the following analysis/maps have prepared for find out urbanization pattern around 1 km buffer of major water bodies in Nagpur city.

- Pre-processing of LISS-IV imagery
- Pre-processing of CARTOSAT imagery
- Preparation of LISS-IV+ CARTOSAT merged imagery
- Visual interpretation of water body in Nagpur city
- Visual interpretation of urbanization pattern around 1 km buffer of individual major water body in Nagpur city.

Fig. 5.4: CARTOSAT data of Nagpur city, Maharashtra, India

Fig. 5.5: LISS-IV and CARTOSAT Merged data of Nagpur city, Maharashtra, India

On Screen Digitization

Digitization

Digitization is the process of converting information into a digital format. In this format, information is organized into discrete units of data that can be separately addressed (usually in multiple-bit groups called byte s). This is the binary data that computers and many devices with computing capacity (such as digital camera s and digital hearing aid s) can process.

Digitization is of crucial importance to data processing, storage and transmission, because it "allows information of all kinds in all formats to be carried with the same efficiency and also intermingled". Unlike analog data, which typically suffers some loss of quality each time it is copied or transmitted, digital data can, in theory, be propagated indefinitely with absolutely no degradation.

Processing

Subset

Subset refers to breaking out a portion of a large file into one or more smaller files. Often, image files contain areas much larger than a particular study area. In these cases, it is helpful to reduce the size of the image file to include only the area of interest (AOI). This not only eliminates the extraneous data in the file, but it speeds up processing due to the smaller amount of data to process. This can be important when dealing with multiband data.

Buffer

A buffer in GIS is a zone around a map feature measured in units of distance or time. A buffer is useful for proximity analysis. A buffer is an area defined by the bounding region determined by a set of points at a specified maximum distance from all nodes along segments of an object.

Clip

In GIS, to clip is to overlay a polygon on one or more target features (layers) and extract from the target feature (or features) only the target feature data that lies within the area outlined by the clip polygon. In other words, the boundaries of the second polygon are imposed on the first polygon. All other area is discarded and is no longer part of the first polygon feature. The clipped data becomes a new feature. This is analogous to a cookie cutter being used to cut a specific area out of a map create a new, smaller map.

Clipping to form a new feature class creates a study area or specific area of interest that is an important function when working in GIS. This becomes advantageous when an analyst only needs to work with a certain focus area; I can discard the unnecessary spatial information with no loss to my core data.

RESULTS AND DISCUSSIONS

Visual Interpretation

A visual interpretation of urbanization pattern was made using Cartosat data and supporting by LISS-IV data and Toposheet. Water bodies have been identified of Nagpur city through visual interpretation techniques using remote sensing images with Geodatabase in ARCMAP. Total water bodies are twenty, there are mainly two rivers Nag river, Pilli river and a sub river of Pilli river. There are tharteen lakes including Ambazari, Futala, Gandhisagar, Gorewada, Sonegaon, Naik, Lendi, Surobardi, Wadi, Wakeshwar, Mines of Wadi, Lake (21°14′42″N 79°5′24″E), Lake (21°15′33″N 79°5′44″E), Lake (21°9′42″N 78°55′18″E) and two tanks are Telhara, Dahegaon, and Police line water pond.

Table 5.1: Water Body of Nagpur City

No.	Name of the Lake	Area in Hector
1	Ambazari	154.68
2	Futala	42.39
3	Gandhisagar	18.73
4	Gorewada	149.27
5	Sonegaon	4.98
6	Naik	1.07
7	Lendi	1.17
8	Menis of wadi	1.42
9	Wadi	1.01
10	Surabardi	68.94
11	Wakeshwar	87.67
12	Lake(21°14′42″N 79°5′23″E)	22.90
13	Lake(21°15′33″N 79°5′44″E)	45.55
14	Lake(21°9′42″N 78°55′18″E)	4.89
No.	**Name of River**	**Area in Hactor**
1	Nag	55.29
2	Pilli	27.49
3	Tributary of Pilli	6.80
No.	**Name of Tank**	**Area in Hactor**
1	Dahegaon	18.63
2	Telhara	30.2
No.	**Name of Water Pond**	**Area in Hactor**
1	Police Line Water Pond	1.41

Fig 5.6: Water Body in Study area of Nagpur City, Maharashtra, India

4.1.1 Interpretation on Urbanization Pattern around Ambazari Lake

Show that urbanization pattern around Ambazari Lake of Nagpur city derived from Cartosat and LISS-IV data using ARCGIS ver. 9.3. Ambazari Lake is largest lake in Nagpur city. Land use pattern around this Lake have been given in (Table 5.2) and (Figure 5.7, 5.8). Total area around 1 km buffer of this Lake is 1226.56 hector, high density unplanned area is 44.14 hector, Medium density planned are is 12.79 hector, Medium density unplanned area is 223.61 hector, Low density unplanned area is 55.51 hector, Primary road is 17.54 hector, secondary road is 0.73 hector, Nag river is 1.67 hector, Ambazari lake area is 154.68 hector, Vegetation is 312.99 hector, Agricultural land is 4.49 hector, Built up area is 1.72 hector, Waste land is 19.80 hector, Open Place is 376.90 hector.

Table 5.2: Urbanization Pattern Around 1 km Buffer of Ambazari Lake

Land Use/Land Cover	Value(Area in Hector)	Percentage (%)	
High Density	Planned Area	–	–
	Unplanned Area	44.14	3.6
Medium Density	Planned Area	12.79	1.0
	Unplanned Area	223.61	18.2
Low Density	Planned Area	–	–
	Unplanned Area	55.51	4.5
Road	Primary	17.54	1.4
	Secondary	0.73	0.1
Water Body		1.67	0.1
Ambazari Lake		154.68	12.6
Vegetation		312.99	25.5
Agricultural Land		4.49	0.4

Built up area	1.72	0.1
Waste Land	19.80	1.6
Open Place	376.90	30.7
Total	1226.56	100.0

Area in %

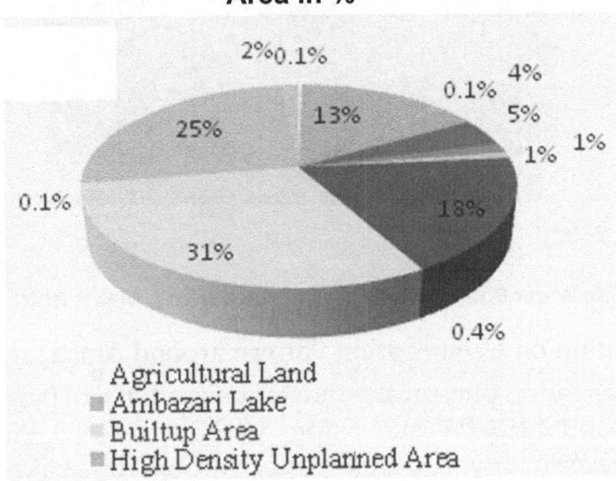

Fig. 5.7

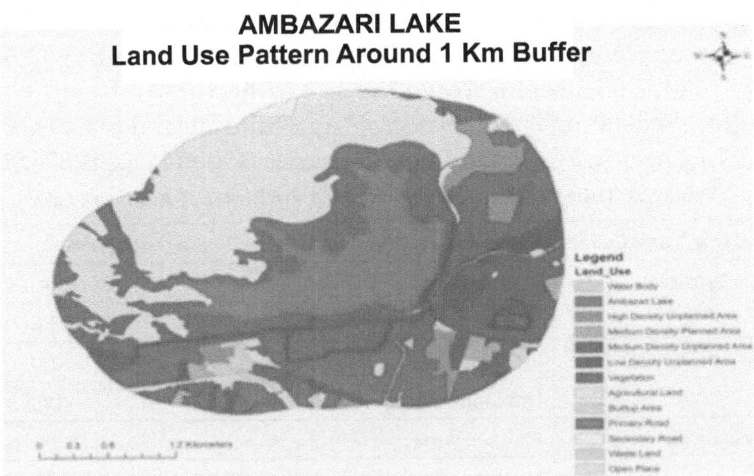

Fig. 5.8: Urbanization Pattern around Ambazari Lake in Nagpur City

Urbanization Pattern Around Futala Lake

Show that urbanization pattern around Futala Lake of Nagpur city derived from Cartosat and LISS-IV data using ARCGIS ver. 9.3. Futala Lake is nearest lake by Ambazari Lake. Land Use Pattern around this Lake has been identified (Table 5.3) and (Figure 5.9, 5.10). Total area around 1 km buffer of this Lake is

626.14 hector, high density unplanned area is 10.30 hector, Medium density planned are is 1.77 hector, Medium density unplanned area is 42.93 hector, Low Density planned are is 3.50 hector, Low density unplanned area is 55.51 hector, Primary road is 8.054 hector, secondary road is 1.45 hector, Futala lake area is 42.39 hector, Vegetation is 228.56 hector, Agricultural land is 90.41 hector, Waste land is 1.34 hector, Open Place is 61.80 hector.

Table 5.3: Urbanization Pattern Around 1 km Buffer of Futala Lake in Nagpur City, Maharashtra.

Land Use/Land Cover	Value (Area in Hector)	Percentage (%)	
High Density	Planned Area	–	–
	Unplanned Area	10.30	1.6
Medium Density	Planned Area	1.77	0.3
	Unplanned Area	42.93	6.9
Low Density	Planned Area	3.50	0.6
	Unplanned Area	55.51	4.5
Road	Primary	8.05	1.3
	Secondary	1.45	0.2
Futala Lake		42.39	6.8
Vegetation		228.56	36.5
Agricultural Land		90.41	14.4
Waste Land		1.34	0.2
Open Place		61.80	9.9
Total		626.14	100.0

Area in %

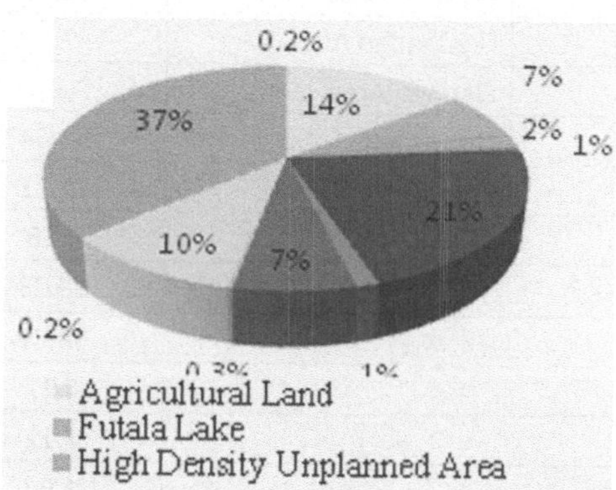

Fig. 5.9: Pattern of Urbanization around Futala Lake

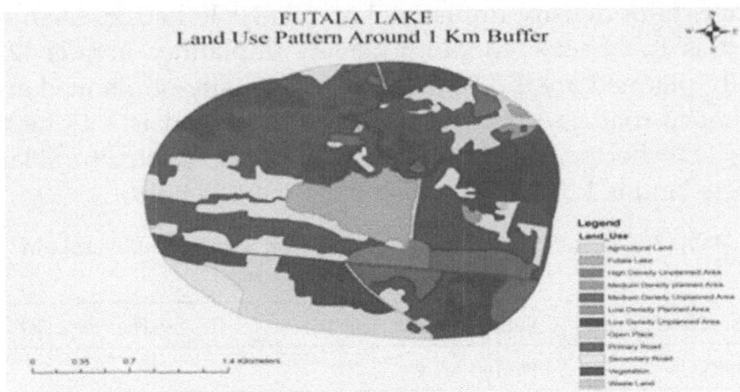

Fig. 5.10: Urbanization Pattern around Futala Lake in Nagpur City

Urbanization Pattern Around Gandhisagar Lake

Show that urbanization pattern around Gandhisagar Lake of Nagpur city derived from Cartosat and LISS-IV data using ARCGIS ver. 9.3. Land use pattern around this Lake have been identified (Table 5.4) and (Figure 5.11, 5.12). Total area around 1 km buffer of this Lake is 141.15 hector, high density unplanned area is 219.03 hector, Medium density planned are is 12.20 hector, Medium density unplanned area is 47.26 hector, Low density unplanned area is 67.63 hector, Primary road is 11.81 hector, secondary road is 5.86 hector, Gandhisagar lake area is 18.73 hector, Vegetation is 38.87 hector, Waste land is 4.94 hector, Open Place is 1.42 hector.

Table 5.4: Urbanization Pattern Around 1 km Buffer of Gandhisagar Lake in Nagpur City, Maharashtra.

Land Use/Land Cover	Value(Area in Hector)	Percentage (%)	
High Density	Planned Area	–	–
	Unplanned Area	219.03	49.06
Medium Density	Planned Area	12.20	2.8
	Unplanned Area	47.26	10.07
Low Density	Planned Area	–	–
	Unplanned Area	67.63	15.03
Road	Primary	11.81	2.7
	Secondary	5.86	1.3
Gandhi Sagar Lake		18.73	4.02
Vegetation		38.87	8.8
Railway		6.27	1.4
Built up area		7.12	1.6
Waste Land		4.94	1.1
Open Place		1.42	0.3
Total		141.15	100.0

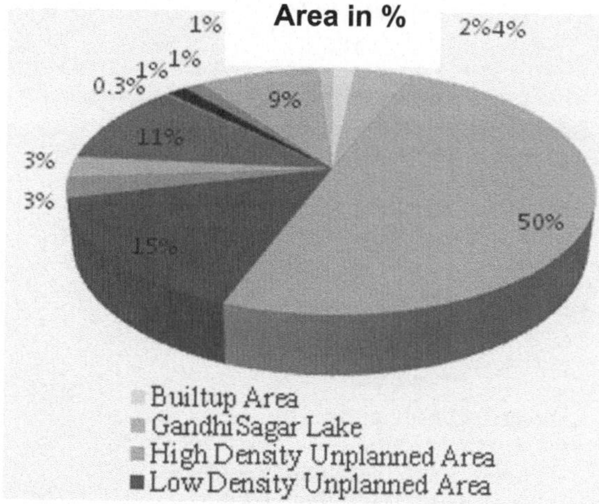

Fig. 5.11: Pattern of Urbanization around Gandhisagar Lake

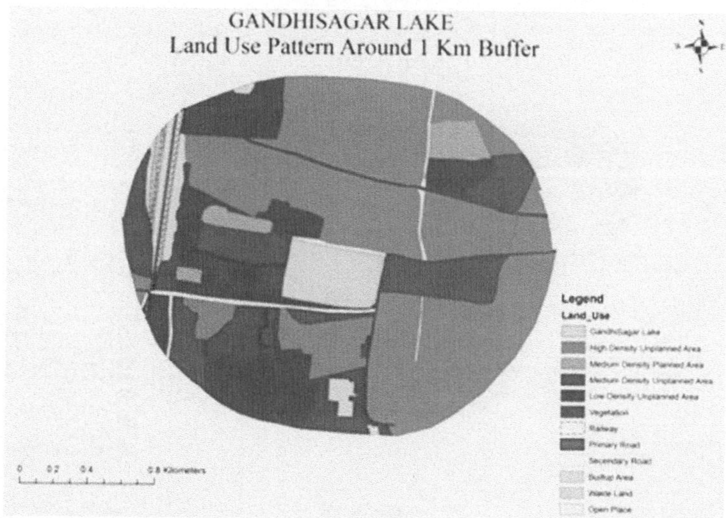

Fig. 5.12: Urbanization Pattern around Gandhisagar Lake in Nagpur City

Urbanization Pattern around Gorewada Lake

Show that urbanization pattern around Gorewada Lake of Nagpur city derived from Cartosat and LISS-IV data using ARCGIS ver. 9.3. Land use pattern around this Lake have been identified (Table 5.5) and (Figure 5.13, 5.14). Total area around 1km buffer of this Lake is 1330.80 hector, high density unplanned area is 13.06 hector, Medium density planned are is 0.95 hector, Medium density unplanned area is 27.50 hector, Low density unplanned area is 59.42 hector, Primary road is 1.68 hector, secondary road is 3.81 hector, Gorewada lake area is 149.27 hector, Vegetation is 974.71 hector, Agricultural Land is 54.46 hector, Waste land is 1.60 hector, Open Place is 44.34 hector.

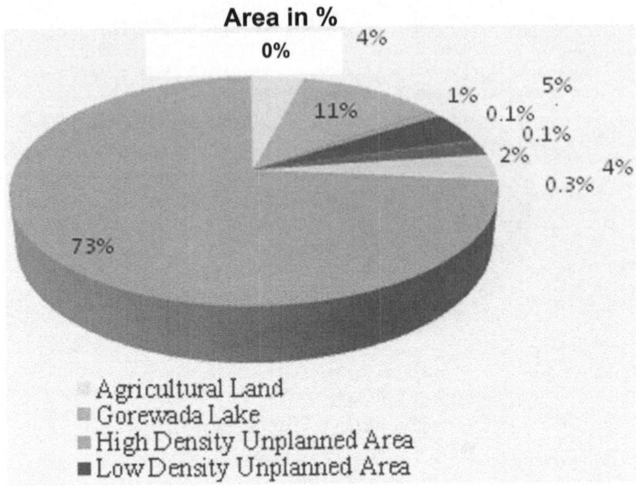

Fig. 5.13

Fig. 5.14

Table 5.5: Urbanization Pattern Around 1 km Buffer of Gorewada Lake in Nagpur City, Maharashtra.

Land Use/Land Cover	Value(Area in Hector)	Percentage (%)	
High Density	Planned Area	–	–
	Unplanned Area	13.06	1.0
Medium Density	Planned Area	0.95	0.1
	Unplanned Area	27.50	2.01
Low Density	Planned Area	–	–
	Unplanned Area	59.42	4.5

Road	Primary	1.68	0.1
	Secondary	3.81	0.3
Gorewada Lake		149.27	11.2
Vegetation		974.71	73.2
Agricultural Land		54.46	4.01
Waste Land		1.60	0.1
Open place		44.34	3.3
Total		1330.80	100.0

Urbanization Pattern around Sonegaon Lake

Show that urbanization pattern around Sonegaon Lake of Nagpur city derived from Cartosat and LISS-IV data using ARCGIS ver. 9.3. Land use pattern around this Lake have been identified (Table 5.6) and (Figure 5.15, 5.16). Total area around 1 km buffer of this Lake is 41.08 hector, high density unplanned area is 98.44 hector, Medium density planned are is 3.01 hector, Medium density unplanned area is 60.7 hector, Low Density planned are is 2.87 hector, Low density unplanned area is 35.30 hector, secondary road is 1.39 hector, Sonegaon lake area is 4.98 hector, Vegetation is 100.70 hector, Agricultural land is 0.84 hector, Infrastructural area is 17.56 hector, Built up area is 45.05 hector, Waste land is 0.97 hector, Open Place is 39.62 hector.

Table 5.6: Urbanization Pattern Around 1 km Buffer of Sonegaon Lake in Nagpur City, Maharashtra.

Land Use/Land Cover	Value(Area in Hector)	Percentage (%)	
High Density	Planned Area	–	–
	Unplanned Area	98.44	24.0
Medium Density	Planned Area	3.01	0.7
	Unplanned Area	60.7	14.6
Low Density	Planned Area	2.87	0.7
	Unplanned Area	35.30	8.6
Road	Primary	–	–
	Secondary	1.39	0.3
Sonegaon Lake		4.98	1.2
Vegetation		100.70	24.05
Agricultural Land		0.84	0.2
Infrastructural Area		17.56	4.3
Built up area		45.05	0.5
Waste Land		0.97	0.2
Open Place		39.62	9.6
Total		41.08	100.0

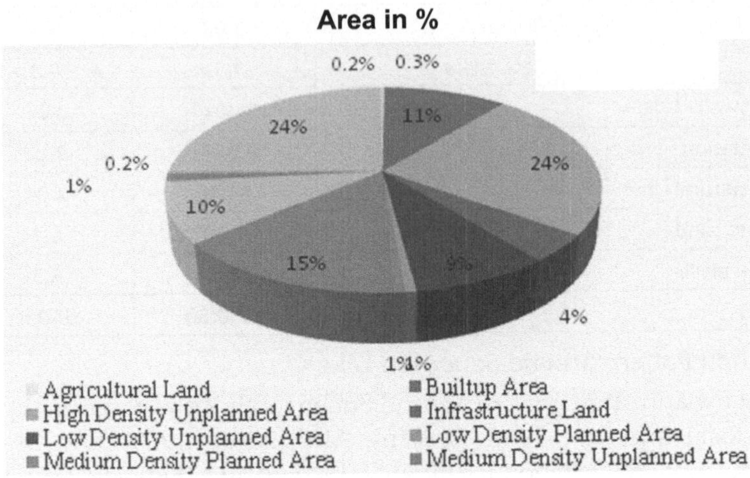

Fig. 5.15: Pattern of Urbanization around Sonegaon Lake

Fig. 5.16: Urbanization Pattern around Sonegaon Lake in Nagpur City

Urbanization Pattern Around Naik Lake

Show that urbanization pattern around Naik Lake of Nagpur city derived from Cartosat and LISS-IV data using ARCGIS ver. 9.3. Land use pattern around this Lake have been identified (Table 5.7) and (Figure 5.17, 5.18). Total area around 1 km buffer this Lake is 396.68 hector, high density unplanned area is 284.62 hector, Medium density planned are is 49.73 hector, Medium density unplanned area is 19.14 hector, Low density unplanned area is 6.95 hector, primary road is 5.91 hector, secondary road is 3.07 hector, Naik lake area is 1.07 hector, water body is 1.17hector, Vegetation is 9.19hector, Railway is 3.92

hector, Infrastructural area is 3.41 hector, Waste land is 3.94 hector, Open Place is 4.56 hector.

Table 5.7: Urbanization Pattern Around 1 km Buffer of Naik Lake in Nagpur City, Maharashtra.

Land Use/Land Cover	Value(Area in Hector)	Percentage (%)	
High Density	Planned Area	–	–
	Unplanned Area	284.62	71.75
Medium Density	Planned Area	49.73	12.54
	Unplanned Area	19.14	4.82
Low Density	Planned Area	–	–
	Unplanned Area	6.95	1.75
Road	Primary	5.91	1.49
	Secondary	3.07	0.77
Naik Lake		1.07	0.07
Water Body		1.17	0.30
Vegetation		9.19	2.32
Railway		3.92	0.99
Infrastructural Area		3.41	0.86
Waste Land		3.94	0.99
Open Place		4.56	1.15
Total		396.68	100.0

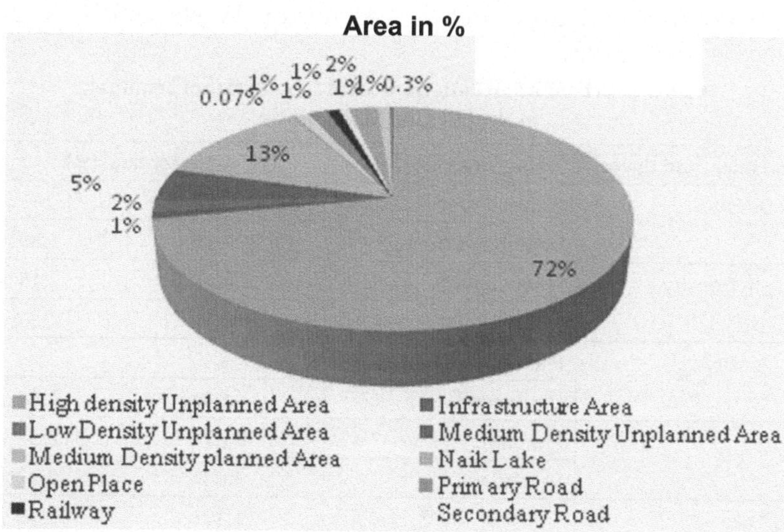

Fig. 5.17

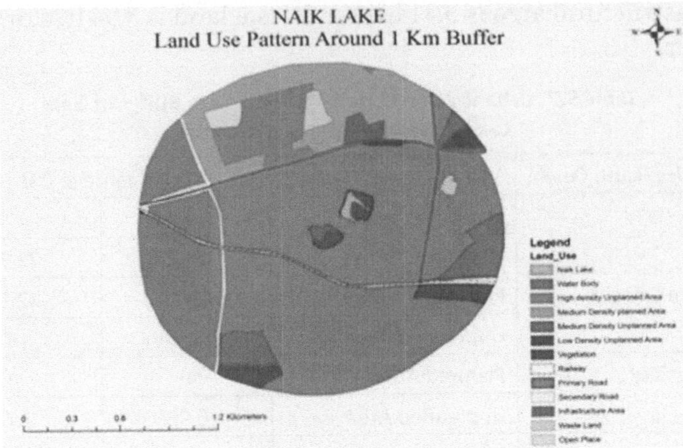

Fig. 5.18: Urbanization Pattern around Naik Lake in Nagpur City

Urbanization Pattern Around Lendi Lake

Show that urbanization pattern around Lendi Lake of Nagpur city derived from Cartosat and LISS-IV data using ARCGIS ver. 9.3. Land use Pattern around this Lake has been identified a (Table 5.8) and (Figure 5.19, 5.20). Total area around 1 km buffer of this Lake is 331.5 hector, high density unplanned area is 237.98 hector, Medium density planned are is 23.68 hector, Medium density unplanned area is 33.56 hector, Low density unplanned area is 4.00 hector, primary road is 7.67 hector, secondary road is 3.04 hector, Lendi lake area is 1.17 hector, water body is 1.08 hector, Vegetation is 9.15 hector, Railway is 0.76 hector, Infrastructural area is 3.41 hector, Waste land is 3.73 hector, Open Place is 1.82 hector.

Table 5.8: Urbanization Pattern Around 1 km Buffer of Lendi Lake in Nagpur City, Maharashtra.

Land Use/Land Cover	Value(Area in Hector)	Percentage (%)	
High Density	Planned Area	–	–
	Unplanned Area	237.98	1.89
Medium Density	Planned Area	23.68	7.15
	Unplanned Area	33.56	10.14
Low Density	Planned Area	–	–
	Unplanned Area	4.00	1.21
Road	Primary	7.67	2.32
	Secondary	3.04	0.92
Lendi Lake		1.17	0.35
Water Body		1.08	0.32
Vegetation		9.15	2.76

Railway	0.76	0.23
Infrastructural Area	3.41	1.03
Waste Land	3.73	1.13
Open Place	1.82	0.55
Total	331.5	Total

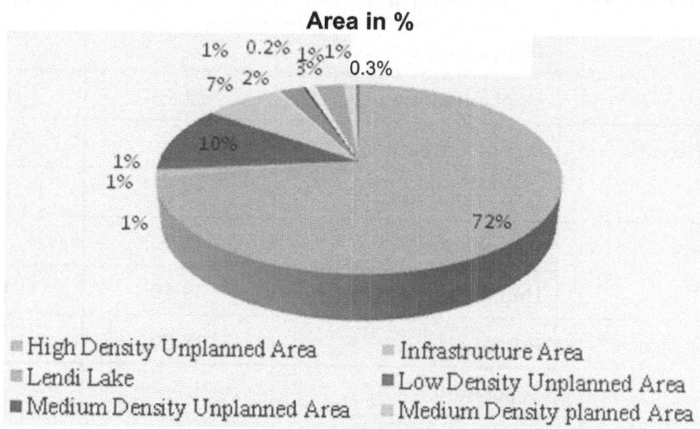

Fig. 5.19: Pattern of Urbanization around Lendi Lake

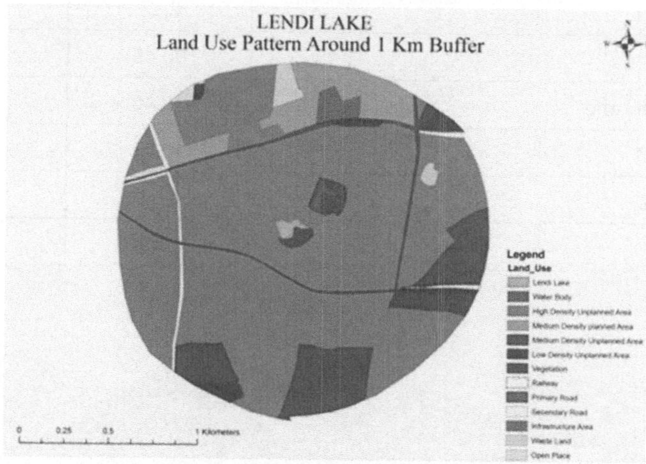

Fig. 5.20: Urbanization Pattern around Lendi Lake in Nagpur City

Urbanization Pattern Around Mines of Wadi Lake

Show that urbanization pattern around Mines of Wadi Lake of Nagpur city derived from Cartosat and LISS-IV data using ARCGIS ver. 9.3. Land use pattern around this Lake have been identified (Table 5.9) and (Figure 5.21, 5.22). Total area around 1 km buffer of this Lake is 381.27 hector, high density unplanned area is 72.96 hector, Medium density unplanned area is 93.31 hector, Low density planned area is 6.76 hector, Low density unplanned area is 69.19 hector, primary road is 12.00 hector, Mines of Wadi lake area is 1.42 hector, water body is 2.13 hector, Vegetation is 90.45 hector, Agricultural Land is 22.40 hector, Waste land is 10.42 hector, Open Place is 0.13 s.

Table 5.9: Urbanization Pattern Around 1 km Buffer of mines of Wadi Lake in Nagpur City, Maharashtra

Land Use/Land Cover	Value (Area in Hector)	Percentage (%)	
High Density	Planned Area	–	–
	Unplanned Area	72.96	19.1
Medium Density	Planned Area	–	–
	Unplanned Area	93.31	24.5
Low Density	Planned Area	6.76	1.8
	Unplanned Area	69.19	18.1
Road	Primary	12.00	3.1
	Secondary	–	–
Mines of Wadi Lake		1.42	0.4
Water Body		2.13	0.6
Vegetation		90.45	23.7
Agricultural Land		22.40	5.9
Waste Land		10.42	2.7
Open Place		0.13	0.6
Total		381.27	100

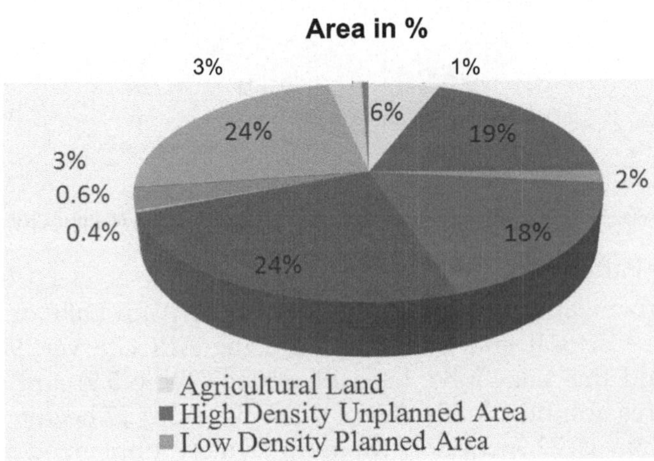

Fig. 5.21

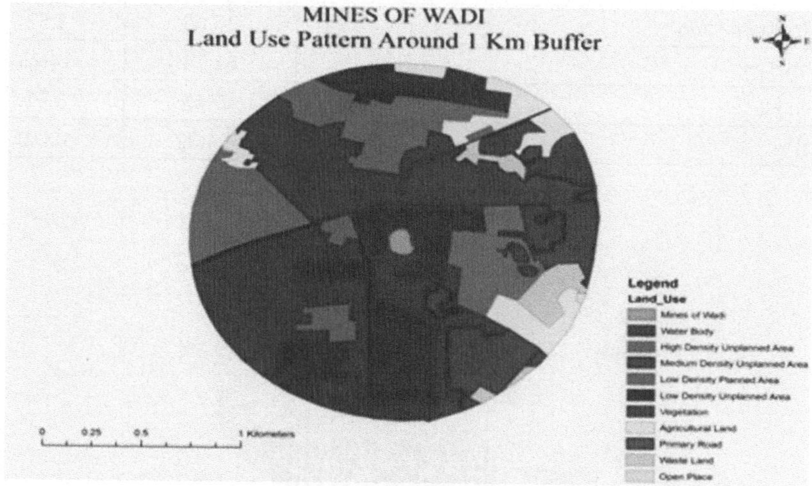

Fig. 5.22: Urbanization Pattern around Mines of Wadi Lake in Nagpur City

Urbanization Pattern Around Wadi Lake

Show that urbanization pattern around Mines of Wadi Lake of Nagpur city derived from Cartosat and LISS-IV data using ARCGIS ver. 9.3. Land use pattern around this Lake have been identified and applied (Table 5.10) and (Figure 5.23, 5.24). Total area around 1 km buffer of this Lake is 554.00 hector, high density unplanned area is 57.11 hector, Medium density unplanned area is 142.78 hector, Low density planned area is 0.77 hector, Low density unplanned area is 48.04 hector, primary road is 18.85 hector, Wadi lake area is 1.01 hector, water body is 2.54 hector, Vegetation is 151.03 hector, Agricultural Land is 30.66 hector, Waste land is 81.74 hector, Open Place is 19.47 hector.

Table 5.10: Urbanization Pattern Around 1 km Buffer of Wadi Lake in Nagpur City, Maharashtra

Land Use/Land Cover	Value(Area in Hector)	Percentage (%)	
High Density	Planned Area	–	–
	Unplanned Area	57.11	10.31
Medium Density	Planned Area	–	–
	Unplanned Area	142.78	25.77
Low Density	Planned Area	0.77	0.14
	Unplanned Area	48.04	8.67
Road	Primary	18.85	3.40
	Secondary	–	–
Wadi Lake		1.01	0.18
Water Body		2.54	0.46
Vegetation		151.03	27.26

Agricultural Land	30.66	5.53
Waste Land	81.74	14.75
Open Place	19.47	3.51
total	554.00	100.0

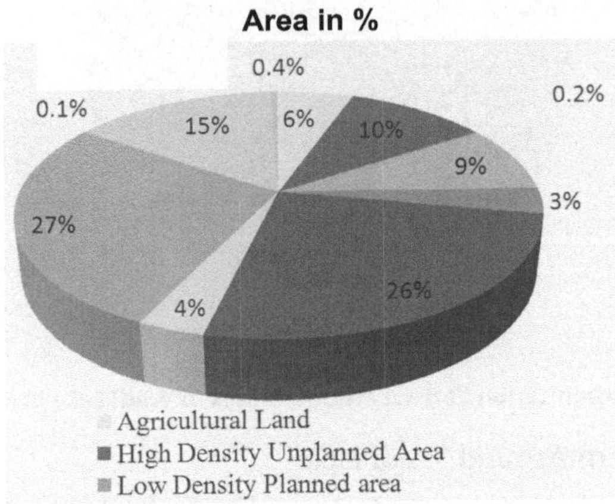

Fig. 5.23: Pattern of Urbanization around Wadi Lake

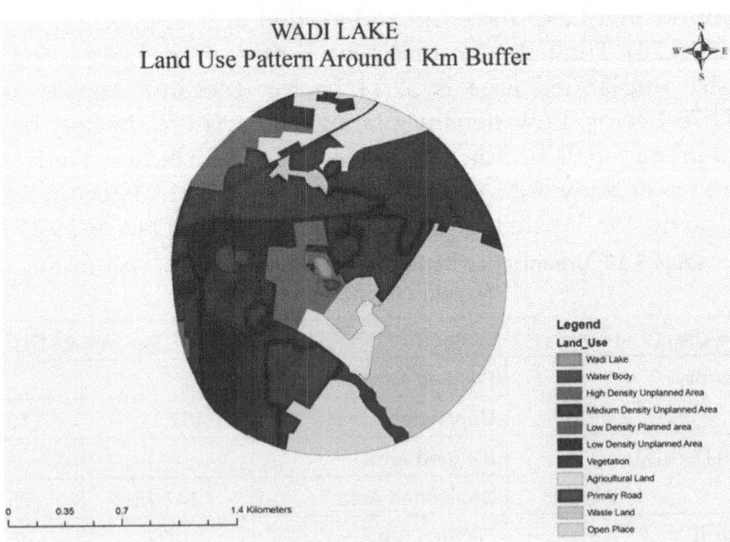

Fig. 5.24: Urbanization Pattern around Wadi Lake in Nagpur City

Urbanization Pattern Around Surabardi Lake

Show that urbanization pattern around Mines of surabardi Lake of Nagpur city derived from Cartosat and LISS-IV data using ARCGIS ver. 9.3. Land use pattern around this Lake have been identified (Table 5.11) and (Figure 5.25, 5.26). Total area around 1km buffer of this Lake is 785.7 hector, high density unplanned area is 3.83 hector, Medium density unplanned area is 2.60 hector, Low density planned area is 11.31 hector, Low density unplanned area is 10.73 hector, Surabardi lake area is 68.94 hector, Vegetation is 55.65 hector, Agricultural Land is 477.07 hector, Waste land is 152.69 hector, Open Place is 2.22 hector.

Table 5.11: Urbanization Pattern Around 1 km Buffer of Surabardi Lake in Nagpur City, Maharashtra

Land Use/Land Cover	Value (Area in Hector)	Percentage (%)	
High Density	Planned Area	–	–
	Unplanned Area	3.83	0.49
Medium Density	Planned Area	–	–
	Unplanned Area	2.60	0.33
Low Density	Planned Area	11.31	1.44
	Unplanned Area	10.73	1.37
Road	Primary	–	–
	Secondary	–	–
Surabardi Lake		68.94	8.78
Vegetation		55.65	7.09
Agricultural Land		477.10	60.77
Waste Land		152.69	19.45
Open Place		2.22	0.28
Total		785.7	100.0

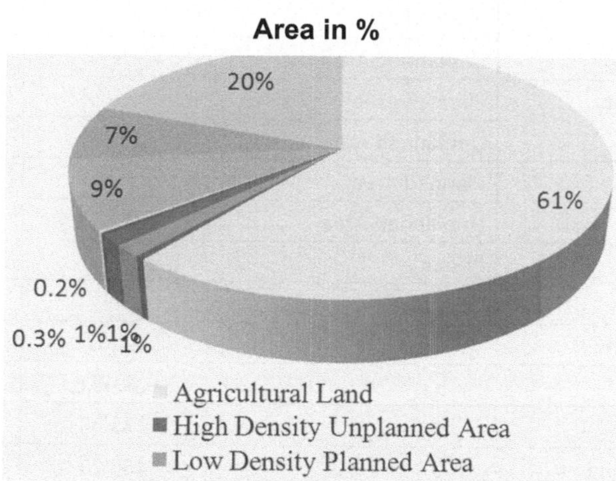

Fig. 5.25: Pattern of Urbanization around Surabardi Lake

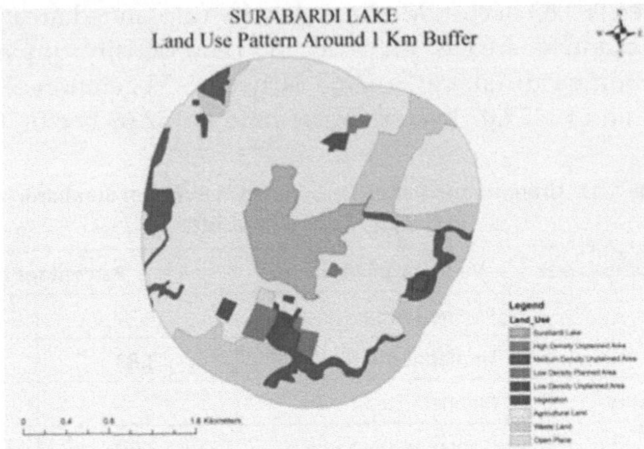

Fig. 5.26: Urbanization Pattern around Surabardi Lake in Nagpur City

Urbanization Pattern around Wakeshwar Lake

Show that urbanization pattern around Mines of Wakeshwar Lake of Nagpur city derived from Cartosat and LISS-IV data using ARCGIS9.3. Land use pattern around this Lake have been identified (Table 5.12) and (Figure 5.27, 5.28). Total area around 1 km buffer of this Lake is 837.35 hector, Medium density unplanned area is 13.34 hector, Low density unplanned area is 5.47 hector, Wakeshwar lake area is 87.67 hector, Vegetation is 223.62 hector, Agricultural Land is 460.25 hector, Waste land is 45.54 hector.

Table 5.12: Urbanization Pattern Around 1 km Buffer of Wakeshwar Lake in Nagpur City, Maharashtra

Land Use/Land Cover	Value (Area in Hector)	Percentage (%)	
High Density	Planned Area	–	–
	Unplanned Area	–	–
Medium Density	Planned Area	–	–
	Unplanned Area	13.34	1.59
Low Density	Planned Area	–	–
	Unplanned Area	5.47	0.65
Road	Primary	–	–
	Secondary	–	–
Wakeshwar Lake		87.67	10.37
Water Body		1.46	0.17
Vegetation		223.62	26.71
Agricultural Land		460.25	54.97
Waste Land		45.54	5.44
Total		837.35	100

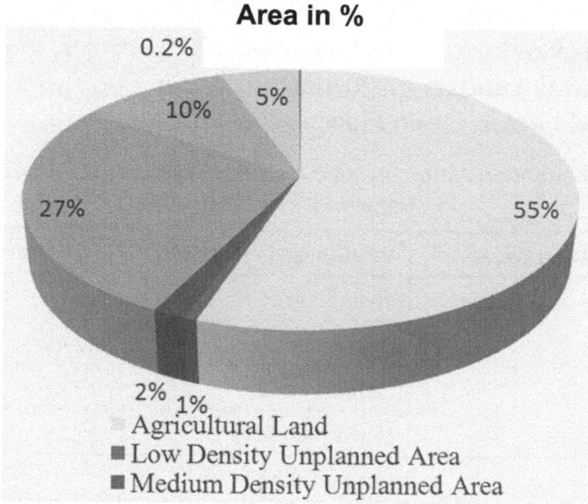

Fig. 5.27: Pattern of Urbanization Around Wakeshwar Lake

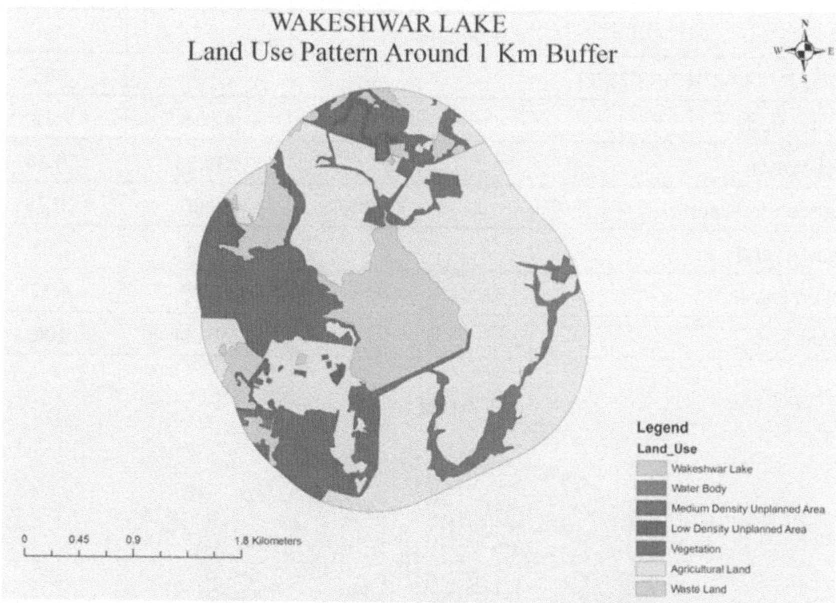

Fig. 5.28: Urbanization Pattern around Wakeshwar Lake in Nagpur City

Urbanization Pattern around Lake (21°14′42″N 79°5′23″E)

Show that urbanization pattern around Lake (21°14′42″N 79°5′23″E) of Nagpur city derived from Cartosat and LISS-IV data using ARCGIS ver. 9.3. Land use Pattern around this Lake have been identified (Table 5.13) and Land (Figure 5.29, 5.30). Total area around 1 km buffer of this Lake is 595.24 hector, High density unplanned area is 47.46 hector, Medium density Planned area is 12.27 hector, Medium density unplanned area is 12.25 hector, Low density unplanned area is 9.69 hector, this lake area is 22.90 hector, Vegetation is 299.56 hector, Agricultural Land is 63.90 hector, Water Body area is 42.38 hector, Waste land is 9.84 hector, Open Place is 26.89 hector.

Table 5.13: Urbanization Pattern Around 1 km Buffer of Lake (21°14’42”N 79°5’23”E) in Nagpur City, Maharashtra

Land Use/Land Cover	Value(Area in Hector)	Percentage (%)	
High Density	Planned Area	–	–
	Unplanned Area	47.46	7.97
Medium Density	Planned Area	12.27	2.6
	Unplanned Area	12.25	2.6
Low Density	Planned Area	–	–
	Unplanned Area	9.69	1.63
Road	Primary	48.10	8.08
	Secondary	–	–
Lake(21°14’42”N 79°5’23”E)		22.90	3.85
Water Body		42.38	7.12
Vegetation		299.56	50.33
Agricultural Land		63.90	10.73
Waste Land		9.84	1.65
Open Place		26.89	4.52
Total		595.24	100

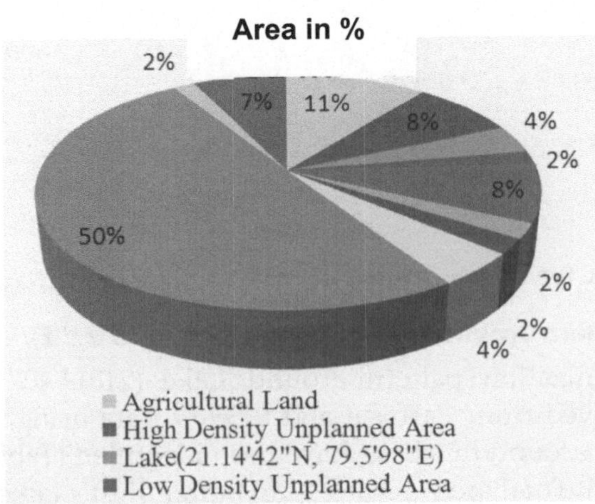

Fig. 5.29: Pattern of Urbanization around Lake (21°14’42”N, 79°5’98”N)

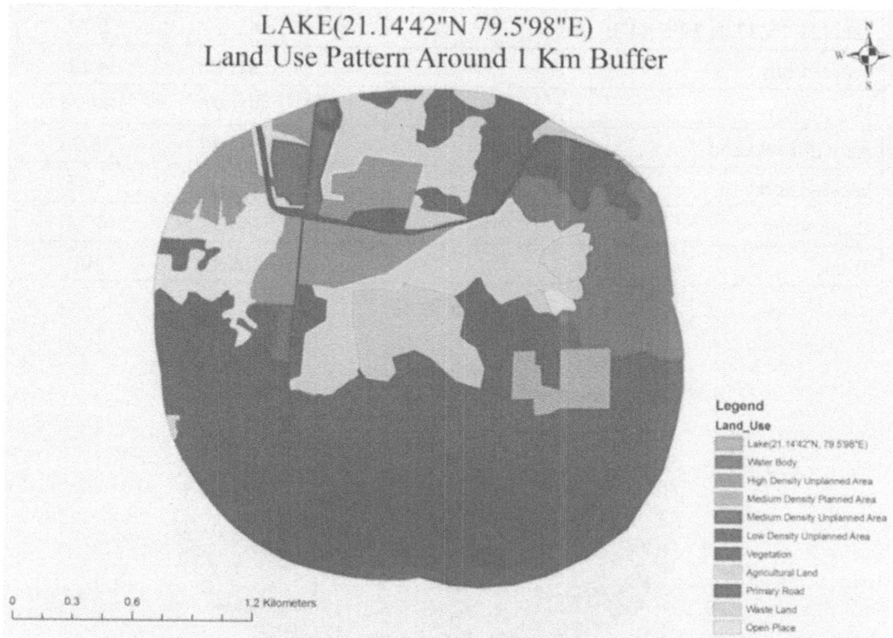

Fig. 5.30: Urbanization Pattern around Lake (21°14′42″N 79°5′23″E) in Nagpur City

Urbanization Pattern Around Lake (21°15′33″N 79°5′44″E)

Show that urbanization pattern around Lake (21°15′33″N 79°5′44″E) of Nagpur city derived from Cartosat and LISS-IV data using ARCGIS ver. 9.3. Land use pattern around this Lake have been identified (Table 5.14) and (Figure 5.31, 5.32). Total area around 1 km buffer of this Lake is 789.10 hector, High density unplanned area is 60.59 hector, Medium density unplanned area is 18.56 hector, Low density unplanned area is 12.82 hector, this lake area is 45.55 hector, Vegetation is 301.76 hector, Agricultural Land is 267.48 hector, Water Body area is 32.42 hector, Waste land is 35.16 hector, Open Place is 5.81 hector.

Table 5.14: Urbanization Pattern Around 1 km Buffer of Lake (21°15′33″N 79°5′44″E) in Nagpur City, Maharashtra

Land Use/Land Cover	Value(Area in Hector)	Percentage (%)	
High Density	Planned Area	–	–
	Unplanned Area	60.59	7.68
Medium Density	Planned Area	–	–
	Unplanned Area	18.56	2.35
Low Density	Planned Area	–	–
	Unplanned Area	12.82	1.63
Road	Primary	8.95	1.13
	Secondary	–	–

Lake(21°15’33”N 79°5’44”E)	45.55	5.77
Water Body	32.42	4.11
Vegetation	301.76	38.24
Agricultural Land	267.48	33.90
Waste Land	35.16	4.46
Open Place	5.81	0.74
Total	789.10	100

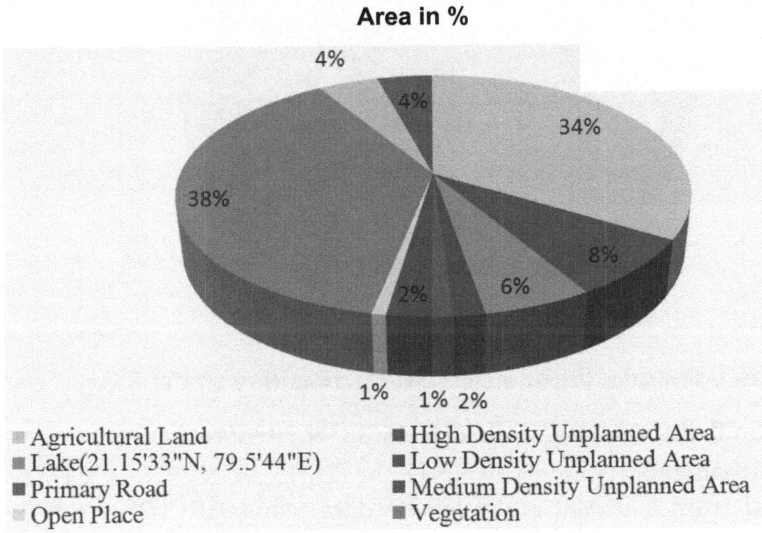

Fig. 5.31: Pattern of Urbanization around Lake (21°15’33”N, 79°5’44”N)

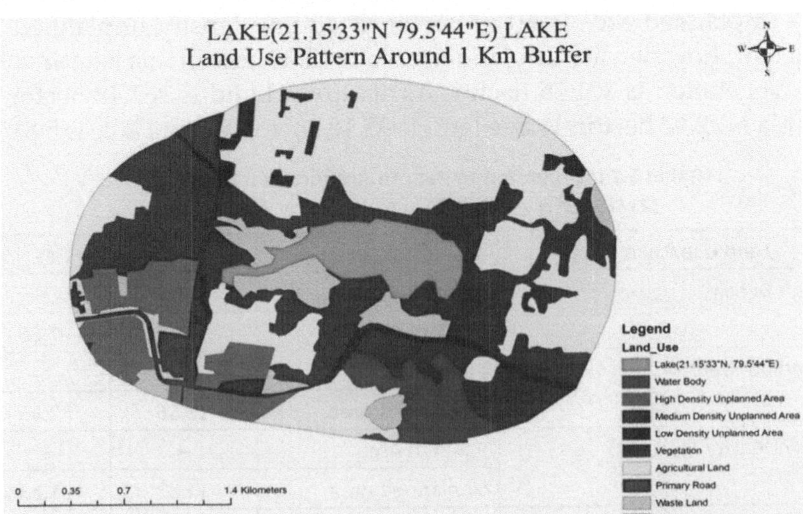

Fig. 5.32: Urbanization Pattern around Lake (21°15’33”N 79°5’44”E) in Nagpur City

Urbanization Pattern Around Lake (21°9′42″N 78°55′18″E)

Show that urbanization pattern around Lake (21°9′42″N 78°55′18″E) of Nagpur city derived from Cartosat and LISS-IV data using ARCGIS ver. 9.3. Land use Pattern around this Lake has been identified (Table 5.15). Land use pattern have been identified through visual interpretation techniques using ARCGIS Software (Figure 5.33, 5.34). Total area around 1 km buffer of this Lake is 413.04 hector, Low density unplanned area is 0.07 hector, this lake area is 4.89 hector, Vegetation is 145.03 hector, Agricultural Land is 126.45 hector, Waste land is 0.0 hector, Open Place is 136.61 hector.

Table 5.15: Urbanization Pattern Around 1 km Buffer of Lake (21°9′42″N 78°55′18″E) in Nagpur City, Maharashtra

Land Use/Land Cover	Value (Area in Hector)	Percentage (%)	
High Density	Planned Area	–	–
	Unplanned Area	–	–
Medium Density	Planned Area	–	–
	Unplanned Area	–	–
Low Density	Planned Area	–	–
	Unplanned Area	0.07	0.02
Road	Primary	–	–
	Secondary	–	–
(21°9′42″N 78°55′18″E) Lake		4.89	1.18
Vegetation		145.03	35.11
Agricultural Land		126.45	30.61
Waste Land		0.1	0.1
Open Place		136.61	33.1
Total		413.04	100

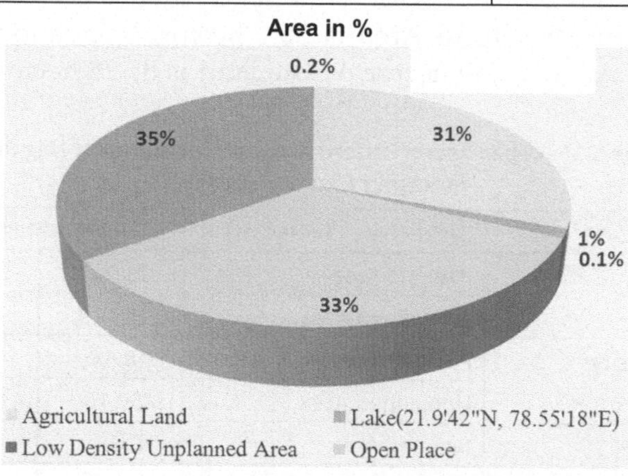

Fig. 5.33: Pattern of Urbanization around Lake (21°9′42″N, 78°5′18″N)

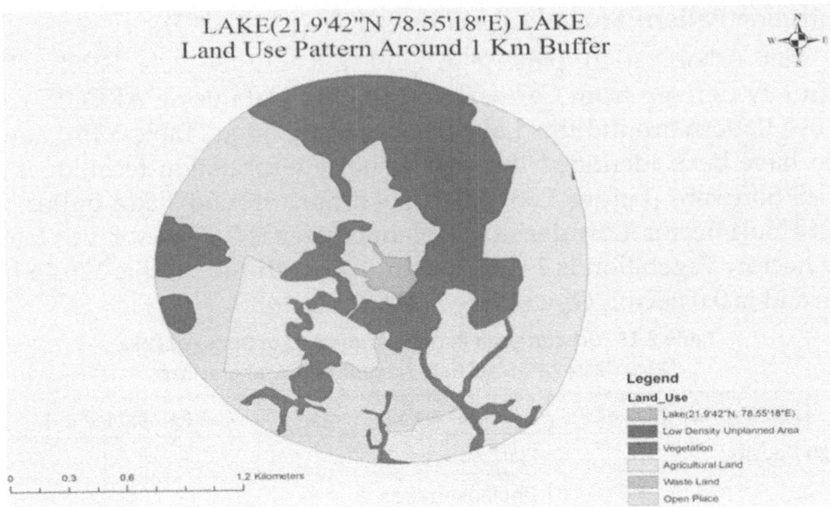

Fig. 5.34: Urbanization Pattern around Lake (21°9'42"N 78°55'18"E) in Nagpur City

Urbanization Pattern Around Nag River

Show that urbanization pattern around Nag River of Nagpur city derived from Cartosat and LISS-IV data using ARCGIS ver. 9.3. Land use pattern around this Lake have been identified (Table 5.16). Land use pattern have been identified through visual interpretation techniques using ARCGIS Software (Figure 5.35, 5.36). Total area around 1 km buffer of this river is 5815.92 hector, High density planned area is 18.72 hector, High density unplanned area is 1237.39 hector, Medium density Planned area is 48.56 hector, Medium density unplanned area is 857.75 hector, Low density Planned area is 0.88 hector, Low density unplanned area is 406.4 hector, this river area is 55.29 hector, Primary road is 73.80 hector, Secondary road is 43.0 hector, Vegetation is 421.43 hector, Agricultural Land is 2403.83 hector, Water Body area is 128.25 hector, Railway is 2.13 hector, Infrastructural Area is 6.21 hector, Recreational Area is 6.52 hector, Built up Area is 5.60 hector, Waste land is 85.28 hector, Open Place is 15.25 hector.

Table 5.16: Urbanization Pattern Around 1 km Buffer of Nag River in Nagpur City, Maharashtra

Land Use/Land Cover	Value (Area in Hector)	Percentage (%)	
High Density	Planned Area	18.72	0.3
	Unplanned Area	1237.39	21.3
Medium Density	Planned Area	48.56	0.8
	Unplanned Area	857.75	14.7
Low Density	Planned Area	0.88	0.1
	Unplanned Area	406.4	0.7

Road	Primary	73.80	1.3
	Secondary	43.0	0.7
Nag River		55.29	0.1
Water Body		128.25	2.2
Vegetation		421.43	7.2
Agricultural Land		2403.83	41.3
Railway		2.13	0.1
Infrastructural Area		6.21	0.1
Recreational Area		6.52	0.1
Built up Area		5.60	0.1
Waste Land		85.28	1.5
Open Place		15.25	0.3
Total		5815.92	100

Area in %

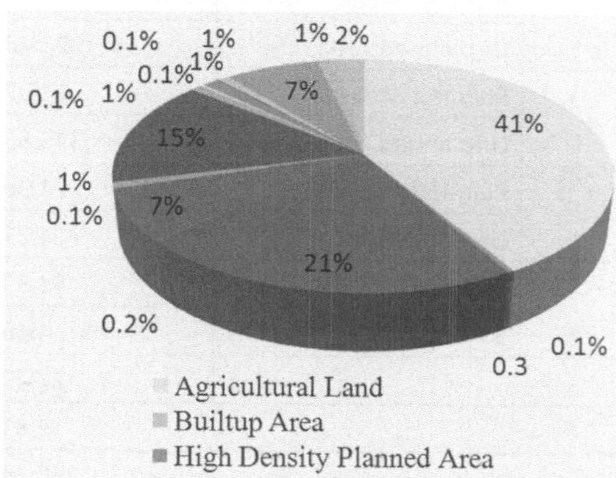

Fig. 5.35

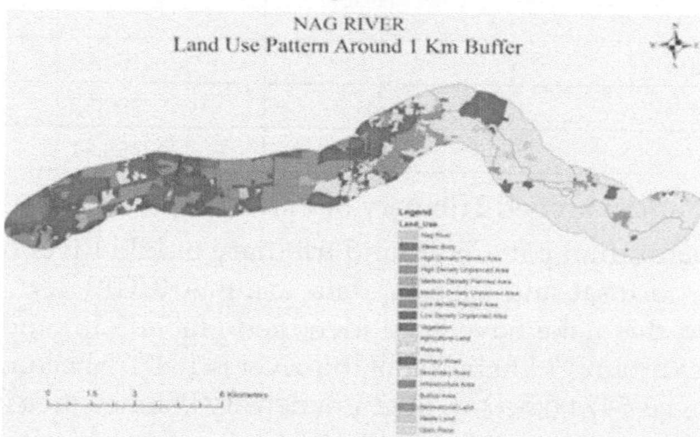

Fig. 5.36: Urbanization Pattern around nag River in Nagpur City

Urbanization Pattern Around Pilli River

Show that urbanization pattern around Pilli River of Nagpur city derived from Cartosat and LISS-IV data using ARCGIS ver. 9.3.. Land use pattern around this Lake have been identified (Table 5.17) and (Figure 5.37, 5.38). Total area around 1 km buffer of this river is 3458.81 hector, High density Unplanned area is 623.43 hector, Medium density Planned area is 15.07 hector, Medium density unplanned area is 346.83 hector, Low density Planned area is 24.96 hector, Low density unplanned area is 704.21 hector, Primary road is 43.39 hector, Secondary road is 4.46 hector, this river area is 55.29 hector, Vegetation is 296.84 hector, Agricultural Land is 2403.83 hector, Water Body area is 2.81 hector, Railway is 3.12 hector, Waste land is 64.99 hector, Open Place is 290.53 hector.

Table 5.17: Urbanization Pattern Around 1 km Buffer of Pilli River in Nagpur City, Maharashtra

Land Use/Land Cover	Value (Area in Hector)	Percentage (%)	
High Density	Planned Area	–	–
	Unplanned Area	623.43	17.45
Medium Density	Planned Area	15.07	0.44
	Unplanned Area	346.83	10.3
Low Density	Planned Area	24.96	0.72
	Unplanned Area	704.21	20.36
Road	Primary	43.39	1.25
	Secondary	4.46	0.13
Pilli River		27.49	0.79
Water Body		2.81	0.08
Vegetation		296.84	8.58
Agricultural Land		1030.68	29.80
Railway		3.12	0.9
Waste Land		64.99	0.8
Open Place		290.53	8.40
Total		3458.81	100

Urbanization Pattern around Tributary of Pilli River

Show that urbanization pattern around tributary of Pilli River of Nagpur city derived from Cartosat and LISS-IV data using ARCGIS ver. 9.3. Land use pattern around this Lake have been identified (Table 5.18) and (Figure 5.39, 5.40). Total area around 1 km buffer of this river is 1647.75 hector, High density Unplanned area is 547.00 hector, Medium density Planned area is 50.06 hector, Medium density unplanned area is 322.64 hector, Low density Planned area is 0.75 hector, Low density unplanned area is 0.5 hector, Primary road is 21.80

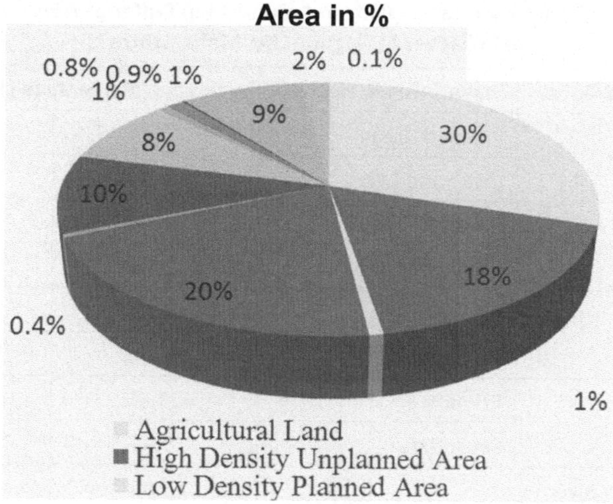

Fig. 5.37: Pattern of Urbanization around Pilli River

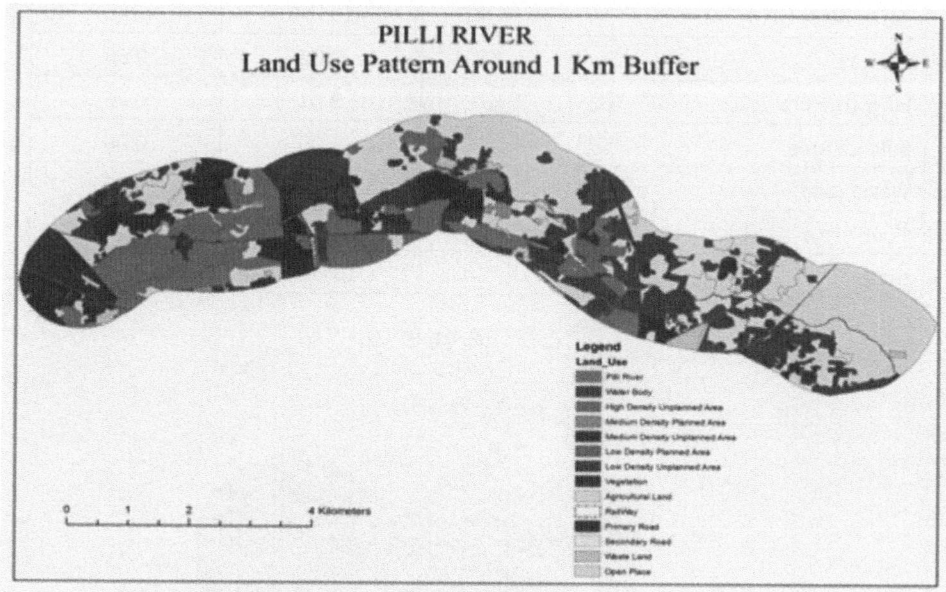

Fig. 5.38: Urbanization Pattern around Pilli River in Nagpur City

hector, Secondary road is 5.64 hector, this river area is 6.80 hector, Vegetation is 46.84 hector, Agricultural Land is 165.76 hector, Water Body area is 7.45 hector, Railway is 9.22 hector, Built up area is 1.00 hector, Waste land is 88.98 hector, Open Place is 0.77 hector.

Table 5.18: Urbanization Pattern Around 1 km Buffer of Tributary of Pilli River in Nagpur City, Maharashtra

Land Use/Land Cover	Value(Area in Hector)	Percentage (%)	
High Density	Planned Area	–	–
	Unplanned Area	547.00	33.20
Medium Density	Planned Area	50.06	3.04
	Unplanned Area	322.64	19.58
Low Density	Planned Area	0.75	0.5
	Unplanned Area	293.40	17.81
Road	Primary	21.80	1.32
	Secondary	5.64	0.34
Tributary of Pilli River		6.80	0.41
Water Body		7.45	0.45
Vegetation		46.84	2.84
Agricultural Land		165.76	10.6
Railway		9.22	0.56
Infrastructural Area		3.41	0.21
Built up Area		1.00	0.06
Waste Land		88.98	5.40
Open Place		0.77	4.67
Total		1647.75	100

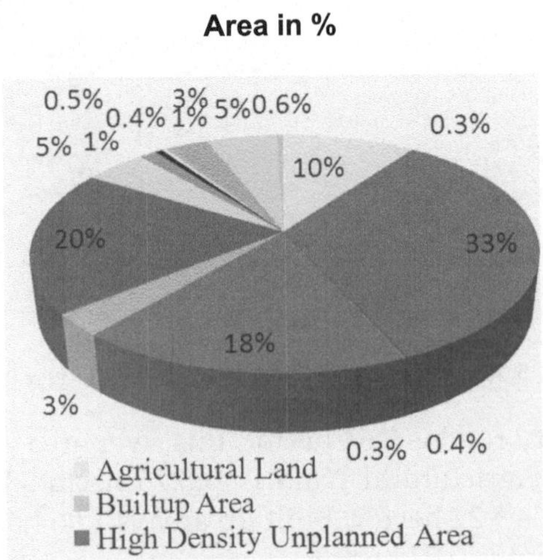

Fig. 5.39: Pattern of Urbanization around Tributary Pilli River

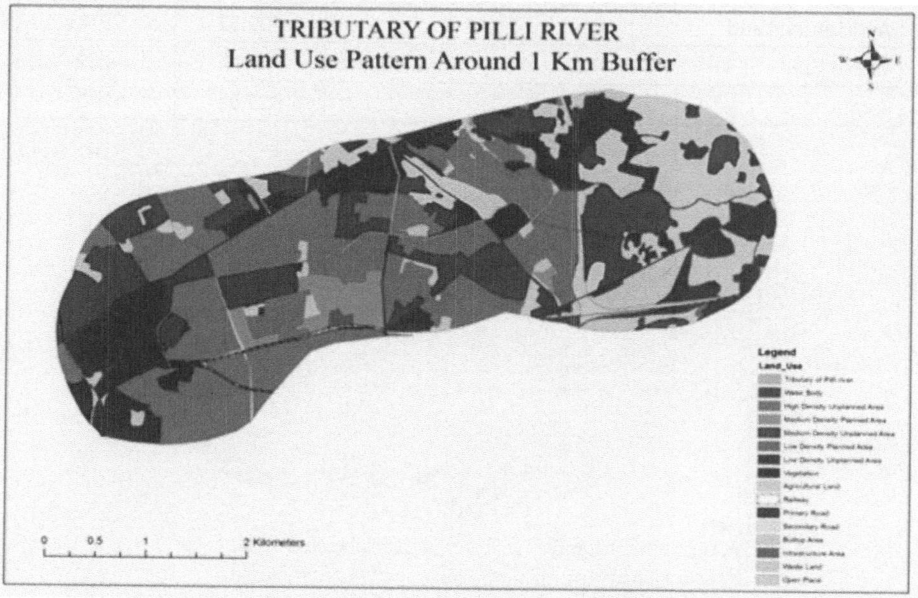

Fig. 5.40: Urbanization Pattern around Tributary of Pilli River in Nagpur City

Urbanization Pattern around Dahegaon Tank

Show that urbanization pattern around Dahegaon Lake of Nagpur city derived from Cartosat and LISS-IV data using ARCGIS ver. 9.3. Land use pattern around this Lake have been identified (Table 5.19) and (Figure 5.41, 5.42). Total area around 1 km buffer of this Lake is 515.54 hector, High density unplanned area is 2.14 hector, this lake area is 18.63 hector, Secondary road is 15.31, Vegetation is 24.50 hector, Agricultural Land is 409.52 hector, Waste land is 45.45 hector.

Table 5.19: Urbanization Pattern Around 1 km Buffer of Dahegaon Tank in Nagpur City, Maharashtra

Land Use/Land Cover	Value (Area in Hector)	Percentage (%)	
High Density	Planned Area	–	–
	Unplanned Area	2.14	0.41
Medium Density	Planned Area	–	–
	Unplanned Area	–	–
Low Density	Planned Area	–	–
	Unplanned Area	–	–
Road	Primary	–	–
	Secondary	15.31	2.97
Dahegaon Tank		18.63	3.61
Vegetation		24.50	4.75

Agricultural Land	409.52	79.43
Waste Land	45.45	8.82
Total	515.54	100

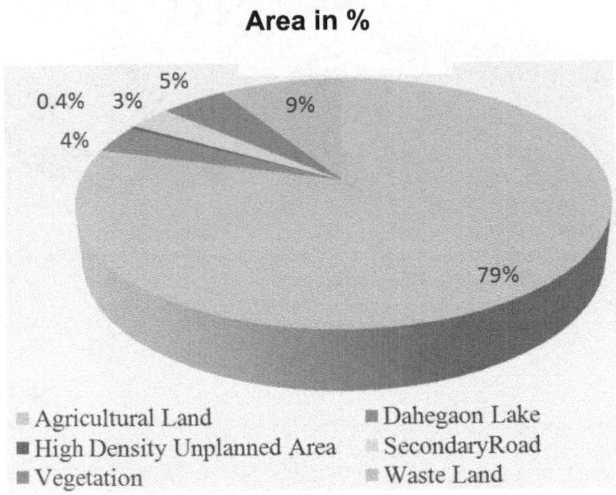

Fig. 5.41: Pattern of Urbanization around Dahegaon Tank

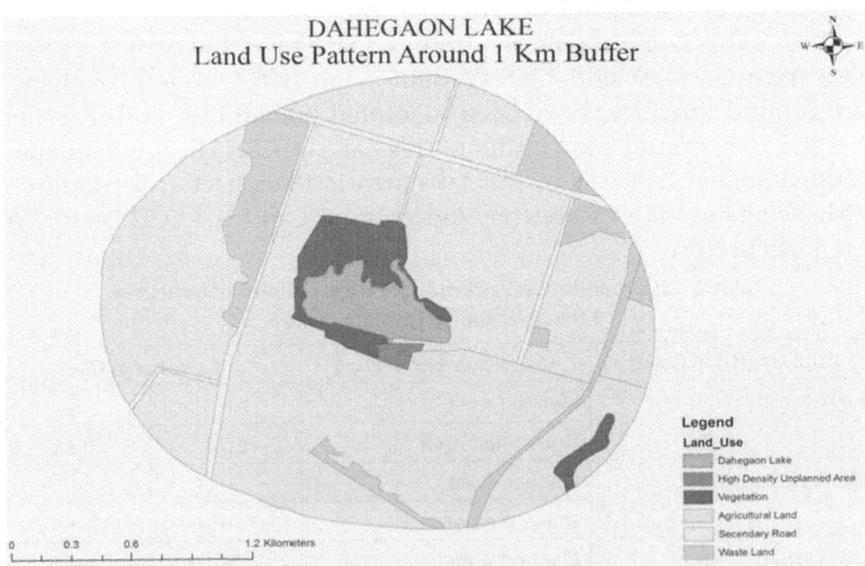

Fig. 5.42: Urbanization Pattern around Dahegaon Tank in Nagpur City

Urbanization Pattern Around Telhara Tank

Show that urbanization pattern around Telhara Lake of Nagpur city derived from Cartosat and LISS-IV data using ARCGIS ver. 9.3. Land use pattern around this Lake have been identified (Table 5.20) and (Figure 5.43, 5.44). Total area around 1 km buffer of this Lake is 552.11 hector, High density unplanned area is 2.94 hector, This lake area is 30.02 hector, Vegetation is 1.0 hector, Agricultural Land is 349.14 hector, Water Body area is 31.31 hector, Waste land is 112.40 hector, Open Place is 9.30 hector.

Table 5.20: Urbanization Pattern Around 1 km Buffer of Telhara Tank in Nagpur City, Maharashtra

Land Use/Land Cover	Value (Area in Hector)	Percentage (%)	
High Density	Planned Area	–	–
	Unplanned Area	2.94	0.5
Medium Density	Planned Area	–	–
	Unplanned Area	–	–
Low Density	Planned Area	–	–
	Unplanned Area	–	–
Road	Primary	–	–
	Secondary	16.00	2.9
Telhara Tank		30.02	5.1
Water Body		31.31	5.7
Vegetation		1.00	0.2
Agricultural Land		349.14	63.2
Waste Land		112.40	20.4
Open Place		9.30	1.7
Total		552.11	100

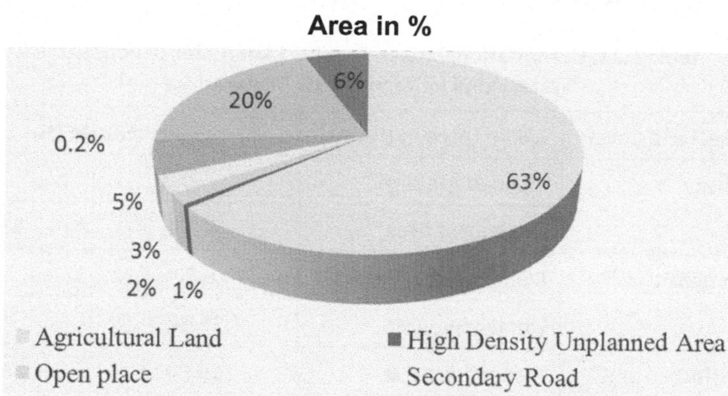

Fig. 5.43: Pattern of Urbanization around Telhara Tank

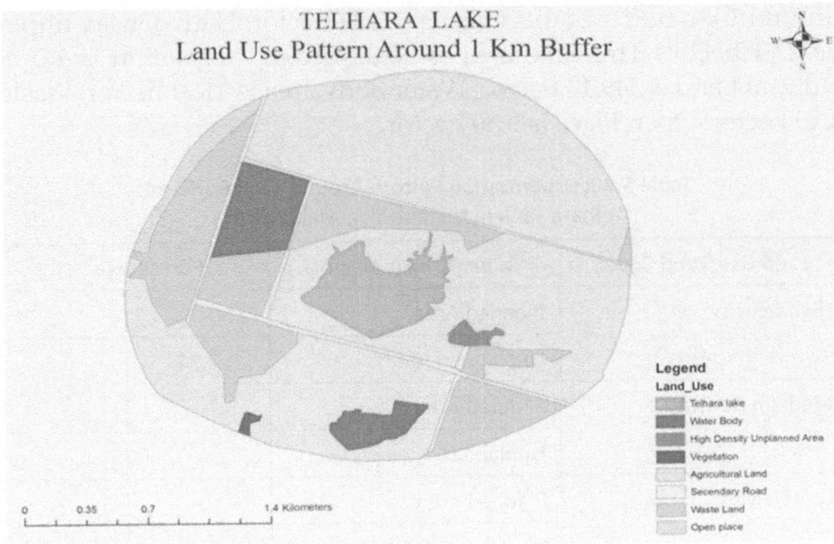

Fig. 5.44: Urbanization Pattern around Telhara Tank in Nagpur City

Urbanization Pattern Around Police Line Water Pond

Show that urbanization pattern around Police line water pond of Nagpur city derived from Cartosat and LISS-IV data using ARCGIS ver. 9.3. Land use pattern around this Lake have been identified (Table 5.21) and (Figure 5.45, 5.46). Total area around 1km buffer of this river is 373.04 hector, High density Unplanned area is 70.94 hector, Medium density Planned area is 6.80 hector, Medium density unplanned area is 15.37 hector, Low density Planned area is 10.00 hector, Low density unplanned area is 73.61 hector, Primary road is 4.22 hector, Secondary road is 6.32 hector, this pond area is 1.41 hector, Vegetation is 160.11 hector, Agricultural Land is 16.61 hector, Waste land is 5.87 hector, Open Place is 1.79 hector.

Table 5.21: Urbanization Pattern Around 1 km Buffer of Police Line Water Pond in Nagpur City, Maharashtra

Land Use/Land Cover	Value (Area in Hector)	Percentage (%)	
High Density	Planned Area	–	–
	Unplanned Area	70.94	19.0
Medium Density	Planned Area	6.80	1.8
	Unplanned Area	15.37	4.1
Low Density	Planned Area	10.00	2.7
	Unplanned Area	73.61	19.7

Road	Primary	4.22	1.1
	Secondary	6.32	1.7
Police line water pond		1.41	0.4
Vegetation		160.11	42.9
Agricultural Land		16.61	4.5
Waste Land		5.87	1.6
Open Place		1.79	0.5
Total		373.04	100

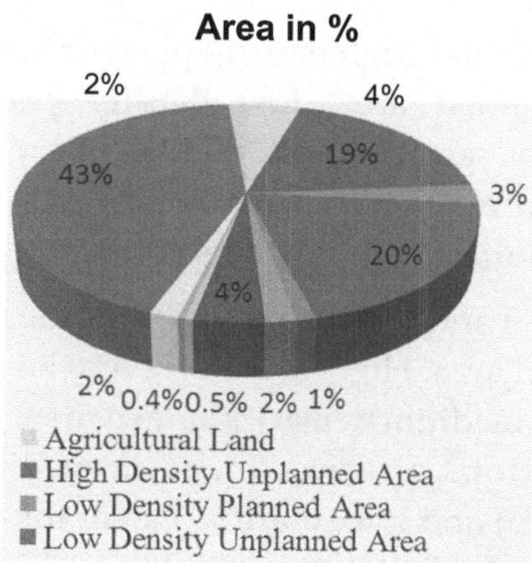

Fig. 5.45: Pattern of Urbanization around police Line Water Pond

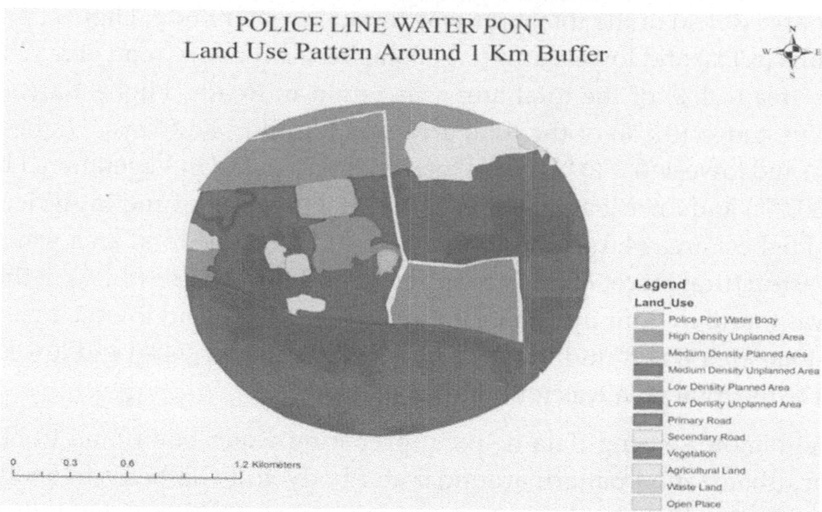

Fig. 5.46: Urbanization Pattern around Police Line Water pond in Nagpur City

Conclusion

Urbanization Pattern have been identified and estimated through remote sensing and GIS techniques. Three steps, namely, visual interpretation, identification of lake, rivers and other water bodies as well as analysis urbanization pattern around water bodies, and comparison between water bodies and land use/land cover in this city. The area around Nag River (1 km buffer) is 5815.92 ha. Land use patterns identification and estimation around major water bodies was validated with ground observation. The analysis of comparison of urbanization pattern is showing highest and lowest area around Water bodies. So, remote sensing and GIS is most important tools for identification of land use patterns in Nagpur city.

The land use patterns like high density planned/unplanned area, medium density planned/unplanned area, low density planned/unplanned area, vegetation, water body, agricultural land, primary and secondary road, railway, built up area, infrastructural area, recreational place, waste land, open place are found around major water bodies (1 km buffer) of Nagpur city.

Highest area (71.7%) and lowest are (0.4%) of the total area was found in high density unplanned area. Highest area (12.5%) and lowest area (0.1%) the total area was found in medium density planned area. Highest area (33%) and lowest area (1.6%) the total area was found in medium density unplanned area. Highest area (2.7%) and lowest are (2.1%) of the total area was found in low density planned area. Highest area (20.4%) and lowest area (0.7%) of the total area was found in low density unplanned area. Highest area (60%) and lowest area (0.1%) of the total area was found in water body. Highest primary road area (8.1%) and lowest area (0.1%), highest secondary road area (3%) and lowest area (0.1%) of the total area was found in Roads. Highest area (14%) and lowest area (0.2%) of the total area was found in Railways. Highest area (73.2%) and lowest (0.2%) %) of the total area was found in Vegetation. Highest area (60.8%) and lowest area (0.2%) of the total area was found in Agricultural Land. Highest area (4.3%) and lowest area (0.1%) of the total area was found in Infrastructural Place. Highest area (1.6%) and lowest area (0.1%) of the total area was found in Built up Area. Highest area (20.07%) and lowest area (0.2%) of the total area was found in Waste Land. Highest area (74%) and lowest area (0.3%) of the total area was found in Open Place.

The remote sensing data helps in preparing water body map in Nagpur city for urbanization pattern around water body and GIS helps in analysis of comparison land use/land cover around major water bodies (1 km buffer).

Comparison

Table 5.22: Comparison of Urbanization Pattern of Nagpur City

Category of Land Use/ Land Cover		Ambazari Lake	Futala Lake	Gandhisagar Lake	Gorewada Lake	Sonegaon Lake	Naik Lake	Lendi Lake	Mines of Wadi	Wadi Lake	Surabardi Lake	Wakeshwar Lake	Lake (21.14' 42"N 79.5' 23"E)	Lake (21.15' 33"N 79.5' 44"E)	Lake (21.9' 42" 78.55' 18"E)	Nag River	Pilli River	Tributary of Pilli River	Dahegaon Tank	Telhara Tank	Police Line Water Pond
High Density	Planned Area															0.3					
	Unplanned Area	3.6	1.6	49.6	1	24	71.7	1.9	19.1	10.3	49.0		7.9	7.8		21.3	17.3	33.2	0.4	0.5	19
Medium Density	Planned Area	1	0.3	2.8	0.1	0.7	12.5	7.1					2.6			0.8	0.4	0			1.8
	Unplanned Area	18.2	6.9	10.0	2.0	14.6	4.8	10.1	24.5	25.7	33.0	1.6	2.6	2.4		14.2	10.3	19.6			4.1
Low Density unplanned	Planned Area		0.6			0.7			1.8	0.1	1.4					0	0.7	0.5			2.7
	Unplanned Area	4.5	4.5	15	4.5	8.6	1.7	1.2	18.1	8.7	1.4	0.7	1.6	1.6	2.0	0.7	20.4	17.2			19.7
Road	Primary	1.4	1.3	2.7	0.1		1.5	2.3	3.1	3.4			8.1	1.1		1.3	1.3	1.3			1.1
	Secondary	0.1	0.2	1.3	0.3	0.3	0.8	0.9								0.7	0.1	0.3	3	3	1.7
Railway				1.4			1	0.2								0	0.9	0.6			
Water Body		0.1						0.3	60	46		17	7.1	4.1		2.2	0.1	0.5		5.7	
Vegetation		25.5	36.5	8.8	73.2	24.1	2.3	2.8	23.7	27.3	7.1	26.7	50.3	38.2	35.1	7.2	8.6	2.8	4.8	0.2	42.9
Agricultural Land		0.4	14.4		4.1	0.2			5.9	5.3	60.8	55	10.7	33.9	30.6	41.3	29.8	10.6	79.4	63.2	4.5
IlnInfrastructural Area						4.3	0.9	1								0.1		0.2			
Builtup Area		0.1		1.6		0.5										0.1		0			
Recreational Place																0.1					
Waste Land		1.6	0.2	1.1	0	0	1	1.1	2.7	14.8	19.5	5.4	1.7	4.5	0	1.5	0.8	5.4	8.8	20.4	1.6
Open Place		30.7	9.9	0.3	3.3	9.6	1.2	0.6	60	3.5	28		4.5	74	33	0.3	8.4	4.7		1.7	0.5

REFERENCES

Barney Cohen (2015). "Urbanization, City Growth, and the New United Nations Development Agenda". 3 (2). Cornerstone, The Official Journal of the World Coal Industry. pp. 4–7.

Bronstert, A.: Rainfall-runoff Modeling for Assessing Impacts of Climate and Land-use Change, Hydrol. Process, 18, 567–570, 2004.

Calder, I. R.: Hydrologic Effects of Land-use Change, in: Handbook of Hydrology, Edited by: Maidment, D. R., McGraw-Hill, New York, USA, 13.1-13.50, 1993.

Centre for Science and Environment 41, Tughlakabad Institutional Area New Delhi-110062 (Protection and Management of Urban Lakes in India)

Chowdary, V.M., Rao, N.M. and Sarma, P.B.S.,. GIS-based Decision Support System for Groundwater Assessment in Large Irrigation Project Areas. Agricultural Water Management 62 (2003) 229-252, 2003.

Deshpande Ajinkya*, Patel Dhruvi, Patel Drashti, Jadeja Jalpa and Desai Khushali "Chenge in the Land Use Pattern and Water Bodies of Vadodara City, INDIA with Respact to Recurring Severe Floods" Journal of Environmental Research and Development Vol. 10 No. 01, July-September 2015.

Environmental Impact Assessment of Urbanisation on Nagpur and Area Around, Nagpur District, Maharashtra Using Remote Sensing & GIS....Environmental Assessment PDF.

Gehrels, H., Peters, N. E., Hoehn, E., Jensen, K., Leibundgut, C., Griffioen, J., Webb, B., and Zaadnoordijk, W.-J. (Eds.): Impacts of Human Activity on Groundwater Dynamics, IAHS Publ. No 269, 2001.

https://www.edu.gov.mb.ca/k12/cur/socstud/frame_found_sr2/tns/tn-40.pdf Urbanization. TN. 40.

Kumar Rakesh, R.D. Singh and K.D. Sharma. "Water Resources of India", Current Sciences, vol. 89, No. 5, 2005.

Naiman,1992 "The Research Paper ans Lists of Recommendations for Improving the Quality Of Water of Umknrah River" The Publications Referred in the These are Listed in the References.

National Institute of Urban Affairs (NIUA) Urban Statistics – Handbook 2000.

NIUA (2000) National Institute of Urban Affairs. Waste Bengal Government First to Hold Elections to Kolkata Metropolitan Planning Committee (KMPC), Urban, Finance, 4(4), December.

P. J. Puri, M. K. N. Yenkie, S. P. Sangal, N. V. Gandhare, G.B. Sarote and D. B. Dhanorkar- "Surface Water (Lakes) quality Assessment in Nagpur City (India) Base on Water quqlity index(WQI)", Vol. 4, No. 1, 43-48(2011).

P.Rama Chandra Prasad *† K. S.Rajan † Vijaya Bhole ‡ and C.B.S.Dutt # IS Rapid Urbanization Leading to Loss of Water Bodies? Journal of Spatial Science (March 2009) Vol II (2): 43-52.

P.Rama Chandra Prasad., K. S.Rajan.,Vijaya Bhole and C.B.S.Dutt #Is Rapid Urbanization Leading to Loss of Water Bodies? Journal of Spatial Science (March 2009) Vol II (2): 43-52.

Patel V. Poverty, Inequality and Mental Health in Developing Countries. In: Leon D, Walt G, Editors. Poverty, Inequality and Health: An International Perspective. Oxford: Oxford University Press Inc; 2001. pp. 247–61.

Presentation on Environmental Status Report 2013-14 of Nagpur City Dr. D.G. Battalwar, Manager,Vidharbha Enviro Protection Ltd. Nagpur Municipal Corporation.

S, Chandra, A. Singh and P.K. Tomar "Assesment of Water Quality Values in Porur Lake Chennai, Hassain Sagar Hyedrabad and Vihar Lake Mumbi, India", Chem Sci Trans.,1(3), 508-515 2012.

S. P. Gorde1, M. V. Jadhav "Assessment of Water Quality Parameters" S. P. Gorde *et al.*, Int. Journal of Engineering Research and Applications www.ijera.com ISSN : 2248-9622, Vol. 3, Issue 6, Nov-Dec 2013, pp. 2029-2035 2029.

Sarfaraz Ahmad, Shahid Farooq, Zahoor-Ul-Islam, Md. Abdullah Khan, Wasi A. Zaidi1 and Huma Matloob "Impact of Urbanization on Hydrological Regime In Indian Cities." Journal of Environmental Research and Development, Vol. 2, No. 4, April-June, 2008.

Siddhartha Koduru and Swati Dutta "Urban Ecosystems: Preservation and Management of Urban Water Bodies".

Singh, R. B., 2001. Impact of Land-use Change on Groundwater in the Punjab-Haryana Plains, India. Impact of Human Activity on Groundwater Dynamics (Proceedings of a Symposium Held During the Sixth IAHS Scientific Assembly at Maastricht, The Netherlands, Jul(2001). IAHS Publ. no. 269, 2001.

Tang, Z., Engel, B. A., Pijanowski, B. C., and Lim, K. J.: Forecasting Land Use Change and Its Environmental Impact at a Watershed Scale, J. Environ. Manage., 76, 35- 45, 2005.

The Research and Lists of Recommendations for Improving the Quality of Water of Umkhrah River. The Publications Referred in the Thesis are Listed in the References. shodhganga. inflibnet.ac.in/bitstream/10603/5332/7/07_chapter%202.pdf

"Urban life: Open-air Computers". The Economist. 27 October 2012. Retrieved 20 March 2013.

"Urbanization in 2013". demographicpartitions.org/urbanization-2013/ Jan 28, 2014 - Urbanization in 2013 Demographic Partitions. Retrieved 8 July 2015.

"Urbanization". MeSH Browser. National Library of Medicine. Retrieved 5 November 2014. The Process Whereby a Society Changes from a Rural to an Urban Way of Life. It Refers also to the Gradual Increase in the Proportion of People Living in Urban Areas.

"Urbanization". UNFPA - United Nations Population Fund. www.unfpa.org/urbanization

Wang Genxu, Yang Lingyuan, Chen Lin and, Jumpei Kubota, 2005. Impacts of Land Use Changes on Groundwater Resources in the Heihe River Basin. Journal of Geographical Sciences 15, 4 (2005) 405-414.

William J. Schneider, David A. Rickert, and Andrew M. Spieker "Role of Water in Urban Planning and Management".

www.iasscore.in/samplenotes/Urban-Indian%20Society-1.pdf Urbanization in India.

Water Management and Aquatic Ecosystem **Pages 116-133**
Edited by: **Dr. Resham Bhalla & Dr. Pawan Kumar 'Bharti'**
ISBN: 978-93-86841-96-4
Edition: **2019**
Published by: **Discovery Publishing House Pvt. Ltd., New Delhi (India)**

6

Pollution and Aquatic Problems

[1]Hussein A. Kaoud

ABSTRACT

Aquatic systems are considered as suitable sites for disposal of and recycling the sewage and toxic wastes and drain off the excess to the sea. However, the increasing pollutant load and the over exploitation of the water resources for potable supplies, irrigation, industries and thermal power plants to meet the requirements of the ever-increasing population, significantly reduces their assimilative capacity.

The use of metals and chemicals in process industries has resulted in the generation of large quantities of effluent that contain high levels of toxic heavy metals, whereas mining and mineral processing operations also generate toxic liquid wastes. In recent years, the problem of marine environmental pollution with heavy metals (e.g. cadmium, lead, chromium, copper and zinc) has begun to raise a public attention.

The aquatic environment is more susceptible to the harmful effects of heavy metal pollution because aquatic organisms are in close and prolonged contact with the soluble metals. Increasing use of anti-microbial compounds poses the risk of release of the bio-active components into receiving waters. The toxic algae constitute major public-health hazards, besides causing mass mortality of fish and shellfish.

Keywords: Pollution, Aquatic Problems, Sources, Ecology.

Introduction

Pollution is the introduction of contaminants into an environment that causes instability, disorder, harm or discomfort to the ecosystem i.e. physical systems or living organisms. Pollution can take the form of chemical substances or energy Pollutants, the elements of pollution, can be foreign substances or energies, or naturally occurring; when naturally occurring, they are considered

[1] Department of Veterinary Hygiene and Environmental Pollution, Faculty of Veterinary Medicine, Cairo University, Egypt. Address: Faculty of Veterinary Medicine, Cairo University, Giza-Egypt, 12211.

contaminants when they exceed natural levels. The most important type of environmental pollution is Water pollution.

The world faces formidable challenges in meeting the increasing demand for potable water, as available supplies of freshwater are decreasing due to extended droughts, population growth, more stringent health-based regulations and competing demands from a variety of users. Increasing pollution of groundwater and surface water from a wide variety of industrial, municipal, and agricultural sources has additionally seriously tainted water quality in these sources, effectively reducing the supply of freshwater for human use.

Sources of Water Pollution

To understand the causes, effect and control of pollution, the sources of pollution should be clearly classified. The sources of water pollution with reference to fisheries can be classified into following categories:

- Domestic sewage.
- Soil erosion and sedimentation.
- Industrial organic and inorganic wastes.
- Agricultural wastes.
- Oil and oil dispersants.
- Radioactive wastes.
- Waste heat.
- Solid wastes.
- Acid rain.
- Algal toxins.

The use of metals and chemicals in process industries has resulted in the generation of large quantities of effluent that contain high levels of toxic heavy metals, whereas mining and mineral processing operations also generate toxic liquid wastes.

Moreover, groundwater is often contaminated by spills, agricultural practices, past waste disposal practices and leaking underground storage tanks. The presence of different organic and heavy metal contaminants in these, as well as other environmental water sources has a large environmental, public health and economic impact.

Most of the traditional technologies (Water Remediation) such as solvent extraction, activated carbon adsorption and common chemical oxidation, although effective, very often are costly and time consuming. The ability to remove toxic contaminants from these environments to a safe level and doing so rapidly, efficiently and within reasonable costs is thus important.

Industrial and municipal pollutants. While agriculture remains the biggest source of water pollution, wastes from industries and municipalities have increased enormously in recent decades. Between 200 and 400 major chemicals are estimated to contaminate the world's rivers. Industrial pollutants, such as wastes from chemical plants, are often dumped directly into waterways. Oils and salts are washed off city streets. Heavy metals and organochlorines are leached from municipal and industrial dump sites.

Fig. 6.1: Industrial and municipal pollutants

Furthermore, pollutants such as sulfur dioxide and oxides of nitrogen, which combine in the atmosphere to form acid rain, have had pervasive effects on both freshwater and land ecosystems. Acid rain lowers the pH of rivers and streams. Unless buffered by calcium (as contained in limestone), acidified waters kill many acid-sensitive fish, including salmon and trout. In the soil, acids can release heavy metals, such as lead, mercury, and cadmium, that then percolate into water ways.

Increasing use of anti-microbial compounds poses the risk of release of the bioactive components into receiving waters. Uptake of these with potable water supplies can lead to allergic reactions in humans. However, it has been observed that the use of oral medication leads to only negligible quantities of anti-microbial compounds being discharged through effluents from aquaculture facilities. Though the use of bath treatments can cause higher concentrations, all available evidence indicates that the discharge of anti-microbial compounds does not constitute a real environmental problem.

Experimental work has shown that degradation of the antibiotic oxytetracycline in seawater occurs within 128 and 168 hours at 5 and 15°C, respectively, under continual illumination, although in darkness the time increases to 190 and 234 hours, respectively. It has also been observed that most oxytetracycline gets bound to particulates and deposits at the bottom of the farm. In conditions where sedimentation is slow, the half-life of oxytetracycline has been reported to be 32 days. Biodegradation may be retarded by deposition of sediments over the antibiotic, and then the half-life may be doubled to 64 days. Antibiotic-containing sediments can affect fauna in the environment. The possible development of antibiotic-resistant microbial communities, as a result of antibiotic use in aquaculture farms.

Contamination by Trace Metals

Concerns regarding possible contamination of aquaculture products by trace metals and organochlorines have arisen because of the poisoning episodes in many parts of the world, and the identification of several trace metals, dioxins, dibenzofurans and coplanar PCBs as the causative contaminants in aquatic environments. However, most of these have not been found in aquaculture products, and those that are found in any appreciable concentrations are not considered to be of public health importance.

The trace elements that are of greatest concern are mercury and cadmium. The Minimata disease caused by mercury contamination from discharges from a chemical factory, identified for the first time from Minimata Bay in Japan, has received considerable attention all over the world. Subsequently, a number of other mercury poisoning episodes due to eating contaminated fish have been reported.

The median standard for mercury in fish is 0.5 $\mu g\ g^{-1}$ wet weight for fish and shellfish (with a range of 0.1–1.0 $\mu g\ g^{-1}$ wet weight).

Such accumulations do not appear to have been reported from aquaculture products so far. Though mercury is usually accumulated in lethal concentrations by only long-lived predatory species such as tuna and swordfish, the possibility of smaller farmed fish accumulating it in significant quantities in areas of excessive local contamination cannot be ruled out.

Cadmium is another trace metal that is highly toxic to mammals, but is not known to have caused any public health problems in humans.

However, there is significant concern about possible cadmium contamination due to the occurrence in Japan of the 'itai-itai' syndrome (an unusual disease of a rheumatic nature), believed to be caused by the discharge of cadmium-rich effluents from a zinc mine situated adjacent to a river about 50 km upstream from the affected area. The waters of the river were used for irrigation of rice fields, and consumption of rice from the affected area, containing high levels of cadmium, is thought to be the principal cause of the disease. The median standards laid down for cadmium in fish and shellfish are 0.3 and 1.0 $\mu g\ g^{-1}$ wet weight, respectively.

Another trace metal of concern as an environmental contaminant is lead, especially because of its possible effect on children. Concentrations of lead in seafood, however, are quite low and are unlikely to be a public health threat.

Copper and arsenic are also important contaminants of food products, but there appear to be no reports of any significant bioaccumulation of these in aquaculture products. Copper is of low toxicity to mammals and the arsenic found in most aquatic organisms is principally organic in nature. Concentrations of inorganic arsenic in aquatic species is very low (generally below 0.5 μg g^{-1} wet weight) and are thus of little toxicological effect.

Contamination by Organochlorines

While organochlorines are known to be toxic to aquatic organisms and terrestrial animals, their direct toxicity to humans is low and there are very few known instances of their public health impacts. The few groups of organochlorines that are hazardous to humans include dioxins, especially TCDD (2, 3, 7, 8-tetrachlorodibenzo-p-dioxins), dibenzofurans and certain polychlorinated biphenols (PCB). The well-known instances of contamination by dioxins, polychlorinated dibenzofurans and coplanar PCBs are the contamination of rice oil in Japan and Taiwan. The more widespread and disastrous environmental contamination that received international attention was the accidental emissions containing significant amounts of dioxin from a plant producing trichlorophenol in Seveso in northern Italy.

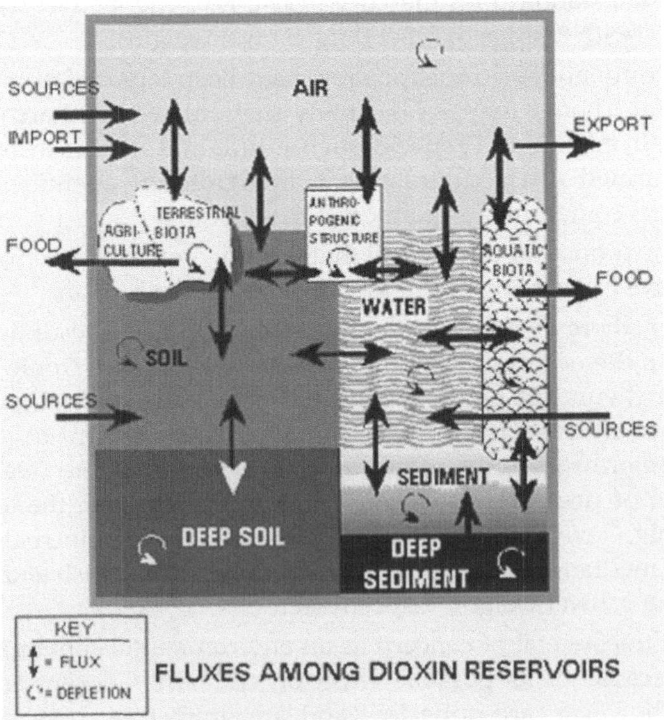

Fig. 6.2: Fluxes among dioxin reservoirs

Although dioxins are an environmental contaminant, exposure most often occurs through food by consumption of animal fats. Unfortunately, there are no safe and effective treatments to remove the dioxins now in humans. Dioxins metabolize slowly (over years), but reduction in exposure reduces dioxin levels over time. The best way to reduce an individual's dioxin level (and risk from dioxins) is to reduce exposure and intake of dioxins. Recently, the European Commission has assessed the dietary intake of dioxins and related PCBs by the populations of EU member states. Some Baltic fish had concentrations that concerned local authorities and there is apprehension that fishmeal prepared from these species could bioaccumulate in animals fed with feeds incorporating these fishmeal products. From 1995 to 1999, the average concentrations of dioxins and related PCBs in UK salmon Baltic wild salmon and farmed salmon were 0.71, 7.04 and 1.47 (in pg TEQ g^{-1} product as toxic equivalents of 2,3,7,8-TCDD), respectively.

Contamination by Algal Toxins

The occurrence of red tides or algal blooms and their impact on aquaculture. These blooms can be toxic, rendering filter-feeding shellfish toxic almost overnight, or noxious, clogging the gills of filter-feeding fish and other animals, or cause oxygen depletion through decay and thereby anoxia. The toxic algae constitute major public-health hazards, besides causing mass mortality of fish and shellfish. Worldwide occurrence of toxic algal blooms has been reviewed by Shum way (1990).

Though historically the most common algal blooms were of dinoflagellates, more recently blooms of other species such as *Dinophysis*, *Aureococcus* and *Gymnodinium* have also become common. The toxins associated with these algae are highly potent, and shellfish feeding on them accumulate the toxins, becoming vectors of various forms of shellfish poisoning, such as paralytic shellfish poisoning (PSP), diarrhoeal shellfish poisoning (DSP) and neurotoxic shellfish poisoning (NSP). Consumers of affected shellfish become poisoned and, therefore, marketing of shellfish is generally prohibited.

Fig. 6.3: Red tide.

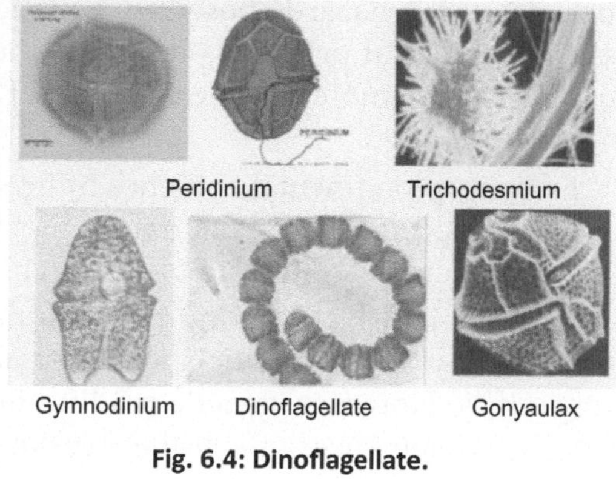

Fig. 6.4: Dinoflagellate.

The dinoflagellate *Protogonyaulax tamarensis* is the species that has caused PSP in many parts of the world, although other species have also been reported from Europe and the northwest Pacific. As crustaceans do not accumulate these toxins, they are safe to eat even during intense blooms.

NSP, which has milder symptoms similar to PSP and is caused by *Ptychodiscus* (*Gymnodinium*) *breve*, has been reported to occur annually along the coasts of Florida and Texas in the USA. DSP has symptoms very similar to gastroenteritis associated with eating shellfish and can, therefore, go unidentified.

Toxins associated with DSP include okadaic acid dinophysistoxin-1 and dinophysistoxin-3, which are lipid-soluble. Recent research has demonstrated multiple toxin profiles associated with DSP.

While *Dinophysis acuminata* is considered to be the main source of DSP in Europe, *D. norvegica* and *D. acuta* are reported to be the most likely organisms that cause DSP in Norway. *D. fortii* is also believed to be implicated in DSP occurrence in Japan, and the benthic dinoflagellate *Prorocentrum lima* in Spain.

Algal toxins persist for many months after the blooms have disappeared and can, therefore, cause major economic damage to shellfish culture industries, besides causing public-health problems.

Aquatic Pollution

Aquatic systems are considered as suitable sites for disposal of and recycling the sewage and toxic wastes and drain off the excess to the sea. However, the increasing pollutant load and the over exploitation of the water resources for potable supplies, irrigation, industries and thermal power plants to meet the requirements of the ever-increasing population, significantly reduces their assimilative capacity. Thus, the dual stress exerted on the watercourses is ultimately faced by the biological communities inhabiting them. Of this fish is the most important aquatic community concerning the man.

Hazards Posed by Aquatic GMOs

Concerns about hazards posed by aquatic GMOs have been inferred on the basis of ecological principles however, the totality of the impact and how it might occur are more complex than what is presented in these papers based on principles.

Existing experimental evidence indicates that most transgenics pose little ecological risk and a subset of transgenics may pose a potential risk, although these data were derived from models in highly artificial situations.

Transgenic fish, assuming they are derived from domestic strains, may not have any more genetic impact on natural populations than domestic conspecifics. However, genetic modifications that would allow expansion of a species' range – essentially the development of an exotic species – would probably have the greatest ecological impact. For instance, the development of a cold-resistant tilapia or a cold-resistant salmon with antifreeze protein would allow these fish to expand their geographical range. As an exotic species, they would interact with local biota and have the potential for ecological impact, as alterations in species composition are considered detrimental.

The genetic impact of genetically improved aquaculture fish could have neutral, positive or negative effects on wild populations, in the short term or long term. Transgenic fish could escape and the transgene become part of the gene pool. This could add genetic diversity to the population, lower or raise fitness or have no phenotypic or ecological effect. If there is a lowering of fitness, it should be temporary as the transgene should be selected against. The mixing of the gene pools might enhance genetic resources, increase genetic variation or result in heterosis, all potentially positive results.

The wild fish may out compete and eliminate the domestic fish or the domestic fish may have no long-term impact on the performance of the population – neutral or non-effects. Negative impacts could result from out breeding depression, which would theoretically be temporary, or from the elimination of wild genotypes through competition.

Problem of Heavy Metals and Pesticides

In recent years, the problem of marine environmental pollution with heavy metals and pesticides has begun to raise a public attention especially in coastal areas. Dumping wastes into marine environments contribute to the larger problem of aquatic pollution, which can seriously damage the marine environment and cause health hazards to people in some areas. Although several adverse health effects of heavy metals and pesticides have been known for a long time, the exposure to these elements continues; moreover, it is even increasing in some parts of world, in particular in the less developed countries, though emissions have declined in most developed countries over the last 100 years. Owing to their toxicity persistence and tendency to accumulate in water and sediment, heavy metals, metalloids and pesticides when occurring in higher concentrations, become severe poisons for all living organisms.

The bioaccumulation of heavy metals and some pesticides in the different fish tissues has been studied by several investigators. Bioaccumulation of metals may lead to high mortality rate or cause many biochemical and histological alterations in the survived fish.

The bioaccumulation factor (BAF) is the ratio between the accumulated concentration of a given pollutant in any organ and its dissolved concentration in water:

$$\text{Bioaccumulation factor (BAF)} = \frac{\text{pollutant concentration in fish organ (mg/kg)}}{\text{pollutation water (mg/l)}}$$

A. Sources of Metals and Pesticides Contamination

Significant amounts of heavy metals and pesticides are eventually carried into fresh, marine, estuarine and coastal water systems. The biota concentrates many heavy metals and pesticides relative to their environment. The invertebrates appear to have a particularly high capacity for concentrating metals from the environment when they filter plankton during feeding. Because of the ability of many metals to form complexes with organic substances, there is a tendency for them to be fixed in the tissue and not to be excreted and they may be passed up the food chain to higher organisms including man.

They enter aquatic systems via natural and anthropogenic sources, including industrial, agricultural, and mining activities. The aquatic environment is more susceptible to the harmful effects of heavy metal pollution because aquatic organisms are in close and prolonged contact with the soluble metals. What's more, unlike toxic organic compounds, metals cannot be degraded but undergo bioaccumulation through the food chain.

Human activities can increase metal concentrations to higher than background levels. Anthropogenic sources of metals include industrial and municipal waste products, urban and agricultural runoff, fine sediments eroded from catchments, atmospheric deposition, CCA treated wood walkways antifouling paints from ships (mainly tin and copper), metals from pipes in sewage treatment plants and drainage from acid sulfate soils and mine sites. Mine drainage, in particular, can significantly increase the concentrations of some metals. Metal contamination tends to be localized to areas situated in close proximity to mine sites, industrial installations and large cities.

Agricultural use of pesticides is a subset of the larger spectrum of industrial chemicals used in modern society. The American Chemical Society database indicates that there were some 13 million chemicals identified in 1993 with some 500 000 new compounds being added annually.

Because the environmental burden of toxic chemicals includes both agriculture and non-agricultural compounds, it is difficult to separate the ecological and human health effects of pesticides from those of industrial compounds that are intentionally or accidentally released into the environment. However, there is overwhelming evidence that agricultural use of pesticides has a major impact on water quality and leads to serious environmental consequences.

B. Environmental Significance and the Ecological Effects

Metals tend to accumulate in animals and plants including mangrove vegetation and sea grasses. They enter aquatic organisms through body and respiratory surfaces, and by ingestion of particulate matter and water. Toxicity manifests as impairment of metabolic function, with possible changes to the distribution and abundance of populations. Sublethal effects may include changes in morphology, physiology, biochemistry, behavior and reproduction. Massive fish kills can occur when aluminum and iron are mobilized with drainage from acid sulfate soils. The extent of metal uptake, toxicity and bioaccumulation varies depending on the organism, and can be modified by temperature, pH, turbidity, dissolved oxygen and the concentrations of other metals in solution. Accumulation of metals by aquatic organisms *e.g.* bivalves and crabs can be a useful indicator of the presence of metals in biologically available forms. If metal levels in organisms are too high for human consumption, shell fishing waters are closed.

Ecological effects of pesticides extend beyond individual organisms and can extend to ecosystems. Swedish work indicates that application of pesticides is thought to be one of the most significant factors affecting biodiversity. Pesticides are included in a broad range of organic micro pollutants that have ecological impacts. Different categories of pesticides have different types of effects on living organisms, therefore generalization is difficult. Although terrestrial impacts by pesticides do occur, the principal pathway that causes ecological impacts is that of water contaminated by pesticide runoff. The two principal mechanisms are bioconcentration and biomagnification.

Persistent Organic Pollutants (POPs) and Organochlorine pesticides (OCPs) are capable of persisting in the environment, transporting between phase media and accumulating to high levels, implying that they could pose a risk of causing adverse effects to human health and the environment. Consequently, most OCPs are designated as persistent organic pollutants (POPs) and even as endocrine disrupting chemicals (EDCs). POPs, including aldrin, chlordane, chlordecone, DDT, dieldrin, endrin, heptachlor, hexachlorobenzene, α/β-hexachlorocyclohexanes, lindane, mirex, pentachlorobenzene, and toxaphene.

The ecological effects of pesticides (and other organic contaminants) are varied and are often inter-related. Effects at the organism or ecological level are usually considered to be an early warning indicator of potential human health impacts.

EFFECT OF HEAVY METALS AND PESTICIDES ON FISH

Heavy Metals

Heavy metals, such as cadmium, lead, arsenic, chromium, mercury and copper, are among the most dangerous and abundant inorganic environmental pollutants, arising from industrial discharges and mining practices.

When fish are exposed to elevated levels of metals in a polluted aquatic ecosystem, they tend to take these metals up from their direct environment. Heavy metal contamination may have devastating effects on the ecological balance of the recipient environment and the diversity of aquatic organisms.

Transport of metals in fish occurs through the blood where the ions are usually bound to proteins. The metals are brought into contact with the organs and tissues of the fish and consequently accumulate to a different extent in different organs and tissues of the fish. Heavy metals are non-biodegradable and once they enter the environment, bioconcentration occurs in the fish tissue in the case of aquatic environment, by means of metabolic and biosorption processes. The presence of heavy metals has been associated with decreased fertility and other reproductive abnormalities in birds, fish, shellfish and mammals, as well as altered immune function. Heavy metals like mercury and cadmium are known to accumulate in marine organisms, and cause rapid genetic changes. It is also possible that may increase the susceptibility of aquatic animals to various diseases by interfering with the normal functioning of their immune, reproductive and developmental processes.

Prolonged exposure to water pollutants even in very low concentrations have been reported to induce morphological, histological and biochemical alterations in the tissues which may critically influence fish quality. It was reported that aquatic organisms showed high capability to accumulate heavy metals.

Cadmium (Cd) has been reported to exert deleterious effects in terms of nephrotoxic, cytotoxic, genotoxic, immunotoxic and carcinogenic. Long exposure of cadmium produces a wide variety of acute and chronic effects in aquatic animals. Its prime site is kidney (kidney damage: renal tubular damage). Cd may exert immunosuppressive effects in both fishes and crustaceans. Recent reports suggest that cell mediated immunity is most affected and phagocytosis, natural killer cell activity and host resistance towards experimental infections are markedly impaired in cadmium toxicity. Cadmium in high doses induce structural and function alterations in various vital organs including liver, kidney, gill and intestine of fishes. Cd accumulates in liver of fishes in high concentrations. It also induces various pathological changes in liver tissues including engorgement of blood vessels, congestion, vacuolar degeneration of hepatocytes, necrosis of pancreatic cells and fatty changes in the peripancreatic hepatocytes. Gills are also reported to act as storehouse of cadmium in experimental studies.

Gills of Tilapia, Oreochromis *mossambicus,* have morphological and biochemical changes after experimental Cd exposure. In scanning electron microscopic studies, observed an augmentation of microbridges in pavement cells and an increase in the apical membrane of chloride cells.

Lead (Pb) is not necessary for the biological functions of animals even at low concentrations. It is being discharged to aquatic systems mainly from petroleum, chemistry, dye and mining industries, which has toxic effects and can cause mortality to aquatic animals. Chronic lead poisoning has similar toxic effects in fish as in mammals. These include hematological and neural disorders and tetanic spasms together with some morphological changes such as darkening in caudal fin, deformation of vertebrate, anomalies in pigment formation and covering of the gills by a mucus layer. The main mechanisms of lead toxicity are the activation of cellular functions due to this metal's calcium mimicking effect, and the inhibition of the activity of different proteins through its binding to sulfhydryl groups. Lead has high affinity for sulfhydryl groups and can inactivate enzymes, especially those involved in heme synthesis, such as aminolevulinic acid dehydratsase and ferrochelatase. On the other hand, lead has a higher affinity than calcium for calmodulin and can activate some calmodulin-dependent processes, inhibit the calcium bombs (calcium–ATPase, sodium–potassium) and channels and replace calcium in several of its receptors. This interaction between lead and calcium has been identified in numerous papers, which show that lead absorption is inversely related to dietary calcium; thus it seems that a low dietary intake of calcium can lead to higher levels of lead in blood.

Arsenicals. Recently, the anthropogenic activities such as treatment of agricultural land with arsenical pesticides, treating of wood using chromated copper arsenate, burning of coal in thermal plants power stations and the operations of gold-mining have increased the environmental pervasiveness of arsenic and its rate of discharge into freshwater habitat. Furthermore, arsenic is used broadly as sodium arsenite to control submerged aquatic vegetation in freshwater ponds and lakes. 1.5-3.8 mg arsenite /L are effective and considered safe for fish. Many species of fish that live in arsenic polluted water contain arsenic between 1 - 10 g/g. At the bottom, arsenic levels in fish are reported to be higher than 100 μg/g. The liver cells were found to lose their regular shape due to partial precipitation of both cytoplasmic and nuclear material, resulting shape deformation, vacuolization, necrosis and even cell damage. Also, the gill hyperplasia was found the most induced branchial changes due to arsenic exposure (The DTC values recorded for the liver of arsenic exposed fish were significantly higher than those recorded for the control group, mg/L) than those subjected to arsenate only 56 mg/L.

Chromium. Acute exposure to hexavalent chromium proved to be highly toxic to *Labeo rohita* and induced cumulative deleterious effects at various vital functional sites like metabolic rate, hematological indices and biochemical profiles. The metal induced decrease in the total protein content could possibly affect the enzyme mediated bio-defense mechanisms of the fish, which pose a serious threat to human beings by secondary poisoning through food chain. Three-week exposure of rainbow trout to 2.0 mg/l of hexavalent chromium increased the levels of haemoglobin and haematocrit in their blood. Long-term exposure (30 days) to low concentrations of chromium (1.9 and 2.9 mg/L) increased the erythrocyte count, concentration of haemoglobin, and per cent of haematocrit in the blood of freshwater barbus, and rainbow trout, *Salmo gairdneri*. An increase in these indices was observed in the blood of various fish species after 15-day exposure to 10 mg/L of hexavalent chromium. Earlier works reported a fall in RBC count, hemoglobin percent and packed cell volume and decrease in MCH, MCHC and MCV in freshwater fishes exposed to cadmium, zinc and nickel indicating anemia, erythropenia and leucopoiesis. The TEC, hemoglobin per cent and mean cell hemoglobin (MCH) were appreciably declined in *Labeo rohita* exposed to chromium reflecting the anemic state of the fish which could be possibly due to iron deficiency and its consequent decreased utilization for hemoglobin synthesis. Anemia in fish is an early manifestation of acute and chronic intoxication of chromium.

Mercury is a highly volatile element with a long atmospheric half-life. As result of these physical properties, it is ubiquitous in the environment and exposure is not an isolated concern but rather a global threat to human health. In recent years, research has revealed that even chronic exposure to very low concentrations of exposure has the ability to cause long-lasting neurological and kidney impairment. Hg is one of the most toxic heavy metals in our environment including the lithosphere, hydrosphere, atmosphere and biosphere.

Mercury's volatile nature and long atmospheric residence time (approximately one year) have resulted in the global cycling of Hg and its deposition in land, marine, freshwater, and wetland ecosystems in regions of the world remote from the source. Inorganic mercury deposited from the atmosphere may be converted by microorganisms in aquatic ecosystems into the highly toxic methylmercury (MeHg) which can bioaccumulate within organisms and biomagnify more than a million-fold in aquatic foodwebs. Consequently, current ecosystem and human health concerns stem from the ubiquitous distribution of Hg in the environment and the health effects associated with high concentrations of MeHg in top predators, including humans.

Copper (Cu) is an essential trace metal in small concentrations for several fish metabolic functions. Essentiality of copper arises from its specific incorporation into a variety of enzymes which play important roles in physiological processes (e.g. enzymes involved in cellular respiration, free radical defense, neurotransmitter function, connective tissue biosyntheses and other functions), as well as, into some structural proteins. Although the crucial role of Cu in several enzymatic processes, this heavy metal can exert adverse toxicological effects, when present in high concentrations in water. In fact, it is potentially toxic when the internal available concentration exceeds the capacity of physiological detoxification processes. Increasing agricultural production has resulted in increasing number of freshwater systems being impacted by the contaminants present in wastewater releases. In Portugal Cu has been used in viticulture to control fungal diseases in vineyard plants. High concentrations of this heavy metal were detected in some aquatic ecosystems collecting vineyard runoff water and it is also highly concentrated in ground water. There are also anthropogenic sources of environmental contamination by Cu including mining, smelting, foundries, municipal waste incinerators, burning of coal for power generation and a variety of copper-based products used in building and construction. When exposed to toxic concentrations, organs of aquatic animals may accumulate copper, which can lead to redox reactions generating free radicals and, therefore, may cause biochemical and morphological alterations. Gills are the first target of waterborne pollutants due to the constant contact with the external environment, as well as the main place for copper uptake. It is well known that changes in fish gill are among the most commonly recognized responses to environmental pollutants. Copper salts (copper hydroxide, copper carbonate and copper sulphate) are widely used in agriculture as fungicide, algaecide and nutritional supplement in fertilizers. They are also used in veterinary practices and industrial applications. Copper sulphate is released to water as a result of natural weathering of soil and discharge from industries, sewage treatment plants and agricultural runoff. Copper sulphate is also intensively introduced in water reservoirs to kill algae. Thus excessive amount of copper accumulates in water bodies and cause toxicity to aquatic fauna and flora and ultimately to man. Copper and its compounds have been designated as priority pollutants.

Pesticides

Exposure of fish to pesticides-water-pollutants even in very low concentrations has been reported to induce:

Hematological effect: The most common blood parameters monitored include total erythrocyte count, total leucocyte count, and haemoglobin and haematocrit conten. Several workers recorded increased lymphocyte, leucocyte and erythrocyte counts, packed cell volume and hemoglobin in several species of fishes challenged with cypermethrin, deltamethrin and fenvalerate. Jayaprakash and Shettu observed a decrease in hemoglobin content, total erythrocyte count, packed cell volume, mean corpuscular volume, and mean corpuscular hemoglobin concentration and an increase in total leukocyte count, mean corpuscular volume, erythrocyte sedimentation rate and clotting time values in the snakehead, *Channa punctatus,* exposed to deltamethrin. Other biochemical variables such as total serum protein, albumin, and globulin contents, albumin-globulin ratio, plasma glucose, alanine aminotransferase, and cholinesterase were reduced in fishes exposed to cypermethrin and deltamethrin.

Hyperglycemia: Reduction in hepatic glycogen accompanied by a rise in blood glucose is a common reaction of fish against xenobiotic insult. Depletion of hepatic glycogen due to cypermethrin treatment has been observed in

Tilapia mossambica and *Clarias batrachus*. Glycogen depletion is a regulatory step against xenobiotic insult. It increases intermediary metabolism resulting in the protection of the hepatocytes. Increase in the activity of lactate dehydrogenase (LDH), an enzyme responsible for conversion of pyruvate to lactate in fish exposed to sublethal concentration of cypermethrin and ë-cyhalothrin, is an indication of such metabolism.

Enzymatic effect: The enzymes of energy metabolism have also been found to have the potential to be used as biomarkers of type II pyrethroid toxicity in fish. Total adenosine triphosphatase, sodium-potassium adenosine triphosphatase, and magnesium adenosine triphosphatase activities in the gills of *Catla catla* were significantly reduced when exposed to sublethal concentrations of cypermethrin. Liver alkaline phosphatase is also known to play a role in glycogen metabolism. The enzyme is capable of inactivating phosphorylase enzymes and promotes glycogen synthesis. Inhibition of alkaline phosphatase activity in the liver is thus related to the breakdown of glycogen to meet the energy demand under stress or decrease in the rate of transphosphorylation or uncoupling of oxidative phosphorylation. There are reports that alkaline phosphatase activity of fish increases after exposure to cypermethrin. Higher activities of lactate dehydrogenase (LDH) and acid and alkaline phosphatases were also observed in *Channa punctatus* exposed to cypermethrin and ë-cyhalothrin. Necrosis of liver and subsequent leakage of alkaline phosphatase into blood stream might be responsible for an increase of the enzyme in blood.

Oxidative stress: Lipid peroxidation, induced by reactive oxygen species (ROS), is a common oxidative stress biomarker of toxicants. Lipid peroxides are capable of modifying the properties of biological membranes, eventually resulting in damage of cellular membrane. The most widely used assay for lipid peroxidation is malondialdehyde (MDA), a secondary product of lipid peroxidation caused by free radicals. Fish, like other organisms, have evolved defense systems comprising both enzymatic and non-enzymatic processes to minimize cell damage by lipid peroxides. Catalase (CAT), an enzymatic antioxidant, scavenges ROS and converts them to less reactive species thereby preventing lipid peroxidation. Fish exposed to deltamethrin showed a tendency towards increase in the level of MDA and reduction in the activity of CAT, although cadmium pre-exposure at low concentrations appeared to modulate deltamethrin-induced oxidative stress. *Channa punctatus* exposed to alphamethrin also showed a decrease in the activity of CAT. Enzymes of nitrogen metabolism. Increased activities of enzymes of nitrogen metabolism such as aspartate aminotransferase (AST), alanine aminotransferase (ALT), glutamate dehydrogenase, and glutamine synthetase in response to cypermethrin and λ-cyhalothrin exposure served as useful biomarkers. Increase in the activities of ALT, AST and transaminases appeared as specific reaction of type II pyrethroids. Alanine aminotransferase (ALT) and aspartate aminotransferase (AST) activities increased in response to cypermethrin in *Orecochromis niloticus*. Marked increase in the activities of transaminases in *Clarias batrachus* and an increase in the activities of aspartate and alanine aminotransferase in *Prochilodus lineatus* have also been reported in response to cypermethrin, a type II pyrethroid.

Acetylcholinesterase (AChE) Activity: AChE activity has been established as a potent biomarker for organophosphorus and carbamate pesticides, while unequivocal evidence is lacking for organochlorines. The activity of the AChE was not inhibited by deltamethrin in three species of fishes. Similarly, esfenvalerate exposure had no effect on AChE activity.

Effects on Biodiversity

It is now well established that there are anthropogenic chemicals released to the environment that can disrupt the endocrine systems of a wide range of wildlife species. The reproductive hormone-receptor systems appear to be especially vulnerable. Indeed, changes in sperm counts, genital tract malformations, infertility, an increased frequency of mammary, prostate and testicular tumors, feminization of male individuals of diverse vertebrate species and altered reproductive behaviors, have all been reported. With regard to environmental management, the problem of endocrine disrupting chemicals is extremely difficult to address. Basic research is required to strengthen the scientific foundation for risk assessment: e.g., baseline studies on endocrine dysfunction across classes of animals to reduce the uncertainty associated with species extrapolations.

An extensive list of chemicals which are thought to be capable of disrupting the reproductive endocrine systems of animals has been assembled. They fall into the following categories:

1. Environmental oestrogens (oestrogen receptor mediated) (e.g., methoxychlor, bis¬phenolic compounds);
2. Environmental antioestrogens (e.g., Dioxin, Endosulphan);
3. Environmental antiandrogens (e.g., Vinclozolin, DDE, Kraft mill effluent);
4. Toxicants that reduce steroid hormone levels (e.g., Fenarimol and other fungicides; endosulphan);
5. Toxicants that affect reproduction primarily through effects on the CNS (e.g., dithiocarbamate pesticides, methanol); and
6. Other toxicants that affect hormonal status (e.g., cadmium, benzidine-based dyes).

Threats to Aquatic Biodiversity

Human activities are causing species to disappear at an alarming rate. Aquatic species are at a higher risk of extinction than mammals and birds. Losses of this magnitude impact the entire ecosystem, depriving valuable resources used to provide food, medicines, and industrial materials to human beings. Runoff from agricultural and urban areas, the invasion of exotic species, and the creation of dams and water diversion have been identified as the greatest challenges to freshwater environments. Over exploitation of aquatic organisms for various purposes is the greatest threat to marine environments, thus the need for sustainable exploitation has been identified by the Environmental Defense Fund as the key priority in preserving marine biodiversity. Other threats to aquatic biodiversity include urban development and resource-based industries, such as mining and forestry that destroy or reduce natural habitats. In addition, air and water pollution, sedimentation and erosion, and climate change also pose threats to aquatic biodiversity.

Population Growth

Increasing population leads to increasing pressure on aquatic resources.

The impact of development and human changes to aquatic landscapes has caused massive reductions in aquatic species biodiversity. Certain fish, snails, mussels, crayfish, and other aquatic creatures have completely disappeared. Others have been substantially and continually reduced in numbers over the years. Tragically, many species are lost before we even know that they existed.

1. Humans live near water sources for a variety of reasons
2. Transportation
3. Drinking water supply
4. Recreation.

Climate Change

1. Some forests in some coastal habitats vulnerable to changes in sea levels.
2. During the past 100 years, sea levels have risen by 4-8 inches.

Air and Water Pollution

Air and water pollution are widespread threats that can directly poison threatened and endangered species, reduce their numbers, and diminish their available habitat. Acid rain is poisoning and global warming is heating our surface waters, resulting in dramatic declines in aquatic biodiversity.

REFERENCES

Coetser, S.E., Heath, R.G., and Ndombe, N. (2007) Diffuse Pollution Associated with the Mining Sectors in South Africa: A First–Order Assessment. Water Sci. Technol. 55 9–16.

Lee J.S. et al. (1988) Diarrhetic Shellfish Toxins in Norwegian Mussels. Nippon Suisan Gakkaishi, 54, 1953–7.

Moe, C.L., and Rheitigans, R.D. (2006) Global Challenges in Water, Sanitation and Health. J. Water Health. 4 41–57.

Savage, N., and Diallo, M.S. (2005) Nanomaterials and Water Purification: Opportunities and Challenges. J. Nanopart. Res. 7 331–342.

Sharmaa, Y. C., Srivastava, V., Singh, V. K., Kaul, S. N. and Weng, C. H. (2009). Nano-Adsorbents for the Removal of Metallic Pollutants from Water and Wastewater. Environ. Technol., 30: 583–609.

Shumway S.E. (1990) A Review of the Effects of Algal Blooms on Shellfish and Aquaculture. J. World Aquacult. Soc., 21(2), 65–104.

Tchobanoglous, G., Burton, F.L., and Stensel, H.D. (2003). Wastewater Engineering (Treatment Disposal Reuse) / Metcalf & Eddy, Inc. (4th ed.). McGraw-Hill Book Company.

Tewari G and Bisht A.(2012): Aquatic Biodiversity: Threats and Conservation. Aquatic Fish Database. Est. 2012 Ascot International.

The Health and Environment Linkages Initiative (HELI). "Vector-borne Disease". Geneva, Switzerland: World Health Organization. Retrieved 7 April 2014.

Tsai, Kan-Jen (2008). "Bacterial Heavy Metal Resistance". Osaka Biology. Retrieved 2008-05-11.

van der Bruggen, B., Manttari, M. and Nystrom, M. (2008). Drawbacks of Applying Nanofiltration and How to Avoid Them: a Review. Separat. Purificat. Technol., 63: 251–263.

Vickers, Amy (2002). Water Use and Conservation. Amherst, MA: Water Plows Press. p. 434.

Water Reuse: Potential for Expanding the Nation's Water Supply through Reuse of Municipal Wastewater. National Research Council. 2012.

Water Saver Technologies Aqus Uses Sink Greywater for Toilet. Treehugger.com. October 7, 2006. Retrieved May 22, 2007.

WordNet Search 3.1. Vector". Princeton University. Retrieved 7 April 2014.

"Water - Use It Wisely."(2010) U.S. Multi-city Public Outreach Program. Park & Co., Phoenix, AZ. Accessed 2010-02-02.

Zemlyn S, Wilson WW, Hellweg PA (1981). "A Caution on Iodine Water Purification". Western Journal of Medicine 135 (2): 166–7

Zhang, W. (2005). "Nanotechnology for Water Purification and Waste Treatment". In Frontiers in Nanotechnology, Washington, DC: U.S. EPA Millennium Lecture Series.

Water Management and Aquatic Ecosystem **Pages 134-141**
Edited by: Dr. Resham Bhalla & Dr. Pawan Kumar 'Bharti'
ISBN: 978-93-86841-96-4
Edition: 2019
Published by: Discovery Publishing House Pvt. Ltd., New Delhi (India)

7

Assessment of Water Quality variables of Kirung Ri River at Nganglam, Pemagatshel, Bhutan

[1]Dr. Pawan Kumar 'Bharti' and [2]P. Kumar

ABSTRACT

The project site is surrounded by hills and mountains at high elevation near Nganglam in Eastern Himalayas. The project site is located at about 4.5 km north of Nganglam and 10 km from indo-Bhutan border. The assessment of water quality has been carried out to estimate the effect of any anthropogenic activities on the environment of the study area and to formulate mitigation measures to prevent the surface water bodies and stream water from further pollution.

Heavy Metals like Cadmium, copper, iron, manganese, lead and zinc were not found in high concentration at both sites during any season. Cadmium, manganese and copper was absolutely absent in all seasons, while lead concentrations were also found below detection limit in maximum samples. The concentration of iron was maximum observed 0.1 mg/l during the entire study. Zinc concentration was also found below the standards limit.

The present study deals with the preliminary physico-chemical characteristics of the river water and exhibits the natural quality of water with minimum anthropogenic activities, which contribute in pollution load of an ecosystem.

Key words: Physico-chemical characteristics, Water quality, Heavy Metals, Pollution status

Introduction

Bhutan is blessed with enormous water resources as a result of the many glaciers and glacial lakes, vast forest cover and high precipitation. Royal government of Bhutan (RGoB) appointed the National Environment Commission (NEC) as the apex body for coordinating the water resources management in the country. The topography is rugged and characterized by swift flowing of rivers. The climate of Bhutan is dominated by monsoon, which sweeps in from the way of Bengal during June, is intense during July and August and finally peters out during September. The period from November to January is

[1,2] Antarctica Laboratory, R & D Division, Shriram Institute for Industrial Research, 19, University Road, Delhi-110 007, India

normally dry. During April and May pre-monsoon showers occur often with substantial rainfall along the southern border with India. The major rivers of the country flow north to south, with their source in the alpine zone and flowing right down to the tropical zone on the border with India. The rivers of Bhutan generally have steep gradients and narrow steep-sided valleys, which occasionally open up to give small areas of flat land for cultivation. Bhutan has abundant water resources, but these resources will face new, complex and pervasive challenges caused by population growth, climate change and socio-economic development.

Water resources in the study area may be classified in to two major categories, (1) stream/ spring water, and (2) surface water. The villagers use mostly spring water as their principal source for domestic consumption. In some villages the spring water is collected in a tank and supplied by pipelines to different houses as protected water supply for both drinking and cooking purpose. Assessment of background quality of water in the area was carried out once in every season. Water quality study of water resources with reference to quantity and quality depicts impacts of anthropogenic activities.

To assess the water quality of study area two number of river water samples from different stations were drawn and analyzed for various physico-chemical parameters, Heavy Metals and biological parameters. The assessment has been carried out to estimate the effect of any anthropogenic activities on the environment of the study area and to formulate mitigation measures to prevent the surface water bodies and stream water from further pollution. There are no lake and ponds and even no well and borewell were found in the study area. In most part of the study area, the water streams are moving from north to south direction. Kirung Ri river flows from Nganglam towards Chenkari entrance bridge and Dungsam Cement Corporation Limited (DCCL) project site. Kirung Ri river passes adjacent to DCCL project site at a distance of 0.1 Km. Kirung Ri river meets the Manas river which is a major tributary of Brahmaputra after traveling around 36 Km after confluence point of Kirung and Kurung rivers.

The present study reveals to characteristics the water nutrient chemistry, influenced by anthropogenic activity & quarrying of the geologically sediment environments and to determine the nature and degree of anthropogenic impacts on quantitative variations in nutrients in relation to physico-chemical parameters and Heavy Metals of river water.

Study Area

Bhutan is situated in the Eastern Himalayas. The DCCL project site is located at Lower Chenkari village of Nganglam, Pemagatsel Dzonkhag (district) in Eastern Bhutan. The project site is surrounded by hills and mountains at high elevation. The project site is located at about 4.5 Km north of Nganglam and

10 km from indo-Bhutan border. The topography of surrounding area of DCCL project site has an undulating terrain with hills, covered by thick vegetation. Towards west there are some agriculture fields along with some rocks and hilly terrain. The geo-co-ordinates of the study area is 26°52′ to 26°55′ N Latitude and 91°12′ to 91°14′ E Longitude. The average sea level is 1588 meter. The maximum temperature in summer is 32°C and minimum 5°C in winters. There are no industrial activities exist in the area. Nganglam's economy is mainly based on agriculture and animal husbandry. The study area has no transport linkage at present. The villages spread over different hillocks.

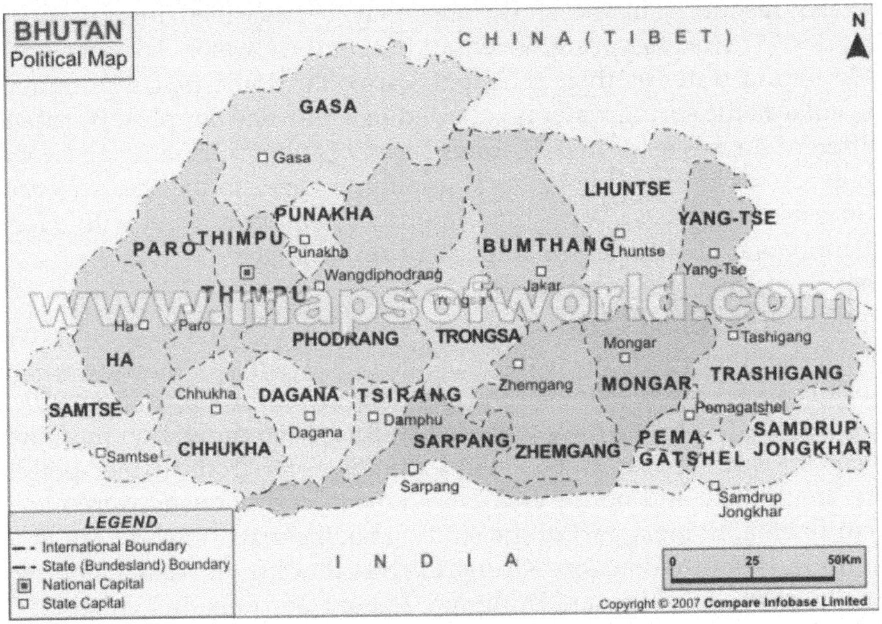

Map-1: showing the districts of Bhutan including Pemagatshel

Materials and Methods

Grab water samples were collected in 5 litre plastic jerry canes and 250 ml sterilized clean glass/ pet bottles for physico-chemical parameters and bacteriological test respectively from selected sampling locations. Water quality parameters were analyzed as per standard procedures/ method given in IS:3025 (revised part) and APHA (1998).

The water samples were collected from Kirung Ri River upstream (U/S sampling site A) Near Military camp and downstream (D/S sampling site B) near DCCL project site according to the analytical requirement in morning period 9:00 Hrs. to 10:00 Hrs. The samples for physico-chemical parameters and Heavy Metals were collected by using rinsed Borosil glassware, and analyzed with the help of the procedure described by APHA (1995) and Trivedi and Goel (1984). Colour, odour, turbidity, velocity, temperature and Dissolved oxygen were analysed on sampling sites. Samples were collected from selected sites and immediately preserved in ice boxes, and transfer to the lab for further analysis. Water samples were digested and Heavy Metals were detected using Atomic absorption spectrophotometer.

Results and Discussion

Kirung Ri river is flowing throughout a valley of hills chain near the Indo-Bhutan Border, enriched with limestone and lignite rocks, which affect the water quality of stream according to the locations. Nutrients concentration and related physico-chemical parameters from selected sites are depicted in tables. Kirung Ri river has the spatio-temporal variations of water parameters, which play a vital role in all physico-biochemical reactions and self-purification power of aquatic system (Badola & Singh, 1981). Turbidity is striking characteristic of the physical status of the water bodies. Although in Kirung Ri river water is clear because there is no more pollution, siltation was the main source of turbidity in tributaries. Detritus and other non-organic material being added to water mass due to rainfall and anthropogenic activities (Camron, 1996). Maximum turbidity was recorded 2 NTU during rainy season at upstream and 4 NTU in monsoon season at downstream. Turbidity reduce the transparency and minimize the photic zone and always obstructs into light penetration in a aquatic ecosystem. The maximum depth of photic zone provides the better biological production for all aquatic organisms (Malik and Bharti, 2005b). Total dissolved solids were found in the range of 65 mg/l in to 110 mg/l at upstream and 97-135 mg/l at downstream, due to the gradual increases in velocity of river which favoured effective sedimentation (Subramanian, 1979), (Malik and Bharti, 2005c).

The pH of natural water was controlled in a great extent by the interaction of hydroxyl ions arising from the hydrolysis of bicarbonate (Sharma, 1986). The pH of river water was recorded slightly alkaline (7.8 – 8.2) at upstream and (7.9-8.4) at downstream. Total hardness is mainly due to percentage of calcium and magnesium salts of bicarbonates, carbonates, sulphates and chlorides, while the value of alkalinity occured due to presence of bicarbonates. The concentration of hardness was analyzed 48-92 mg/l at upstream and 75-110 mg/l at downstream during the study. Alkalinity was also found 40-99 mg/l with a small fluctuation. A positive relationship between hardness and alkalinity was recorded in river Ganga at Rishikesh (Chopra and Patric, 1994). Chloride concentration was recorded (3-7 mg/l) at upstream and (4-6 mg/l) at downstream. Chloride and hardness showed a positive relationship (Chopra and Patric, 1994). Chloride was found in the form of chloride ion, and one of the major inorganic anion present in natural water (Malik and Bharti, 2009).

Calcium and magnesium the dominant cations, and these represent the main weathering products, but significant hydro-chemical differences between the two sampling sites associated with the bedrock geology exist (Jenkins *et al.*, 1995) Calcium is one of the essential nutrients, which plays an important role in biological system. Calcium concentration was recorded (11-26 mg/l) at upstream and (20-28 mg/l) at downstream. Magnesium is also an essential element but it is toxic at higher concentration. The concentration of magnesium in river was found maximum (11 mg/l) and minimum (5 mg/l). During the summer season nutrients concentration in rivers and hill-streams became more. Miller *et al.*, (1997) described the nutrients availability in selected environmental settings of the Potomac River and Cameron (1996) showed the similar type of fluctuation in Fraser river of British Columbia. Bond (1979) described similar nutrients concentration pattern in a stream draining a mountain ecosystem in Utah.

Heavy Metals like Cadmium, copper, iron, manganese, lead and zinc were not found in high concentration at both sites during any season. Cadmium, manganese and copper was absolutely absent in all seasons, while lead concentrations were also found below detection limit in maximum samples. The concentration of iron was maximum observed 0.1 mg/l during the entire study. Zinc concentration was also found below the standards limit. Malik *et al.*, (2009) described the role of Heavy Metals in the surface water of north India. The results of Bharti *et al.*, (2010) were also indicated the relation of Heavy Metals and phytoplankton in a north Indian water body.

The present results conclude that significant differences in river water nutrient concentrations exist among different environmental settings within the two subunits. The environmental setting with the highest potential by more soluble nutrients, fluctuations in nutrient concentrations were the land use and carbonate bedrock that was predominated in the Bhutanese valley. The spatial variations in TDS are attributed to climatic and lithological control over the ionic concentrations. Absence or low concentration of Heavy Metals shows that the water is still industrial pollution free. Heavy Metals were found almost nil or in very low concentrations at both selected site. The present study deals with the preliminary physico-chemical characteristics of the river water and exhibits the natural quality of water with minimum anthropogenic activities, which contribute in pollution load of an ecosystem. However, the Indian standards are not so strict (Bharti, 2007), but Heavy Metals never cross the limits during the study period. On the basis of nutrients and Heavy Metals, the water may be considered for drinking and other purposes.

Analysis of the water has been conducted at both sampling locations on the river basins. The natural water quality of Kirung Ri River can be characterized as highly oxygenated, slightly alkaline with low conductivity and no salinity was recorded. The mountain streams and rivers are free of salinity and suitable for irrigation.

Table 7.1: Physical Characteristics of Kirung Ri River Water

S. No.	Parameters	Unit	Kirung Ri Upstream				Kirung Ri Downstream				Desirable Limit
			Winter	Summer	Monsoon	Post-monsoon	Winter	Summer	Monsoon	Post-monsoon	
1.	Colour	-	Clear	Clear	Clear	Clear	Clear	Clear	Clear	Clear	-
2.	Odour	-	Nil	Nil	Nil	Nil	Nil	Nil	Nil	Nil	-
3.	Turbidity	NTU	2	1	1	1	4	2	3	1	5
4.	Velocity	m/s	0.9	0.8	1.0	0.8	0.7	0.6	0.8	0.8	-
5.	TDS	Mg/l	90	65	110	85	120	97	135	115	500

Table 7.2: Chemical Characteristics of Kirung Ri River Water

S. No.	Parameters	Unit	Kirung Ri Upstream				Kirung Ri Downstream				Desirable Limit
			Winter	Summer	Monsoon	Post-monsoon	Winter	Summer	Monsoon	Post-monsoon	
1.	pH	-	8.2	8.1	8.1	7.8	8.3	8.4	7.9	7.9	6.5-8.5
2.	Alkalinity	Mg/l	65	84	40	55	85	99	78	75	200
3.	Total Hardness	Mg/l	70	92	48	64	96	110	75	105	300
4.	Calcium	Mg/l	15	26	11	14	25	28	20	24	75
5.	Magnesium	Mg/l	7	8	5	7	8	10	6	11	30
6.	Chlorides	Mg/l	3	4	7	6	4	4	5	6	250

Table 7.3: Heavy Metals in Kirung Ri River Water

S. No.	Parameters	Unit	Kirung Ri Upstream				Kirung Ri Downstream				Desirable Limit
			Winter	Summer	Monsoon	Post-monsoon	Winter	Summer	Monsoon	Post-monsoon	
1.	Cadmium	Mg/l	BDL	BDL	BDL	BDL	BDL	BDL	BDL	BDL	0.01
2.	Copper	Mg/l	BDL	BDL	BDL	BDL	BDL	BDL	BDL	BDL	0.05
3.	Iron	Mg/l	BDL	0.1	BDL	0.05	0.1	0.1	0.08	BDL	0.3
4.	Lead	Mg/l	BDL	0.02	BDL	BDL	BDL	0.02	BDL	BDL	0.05
5.	Manganese	Mg/l	BDL	BDL	BDL	BDL	BDL	BDL	BDL	BDL	0.1
6.	Zinc	Mg/l	BDL	0.03	BDL	0.04	0.02	0.02	0.02	BDL	5.0

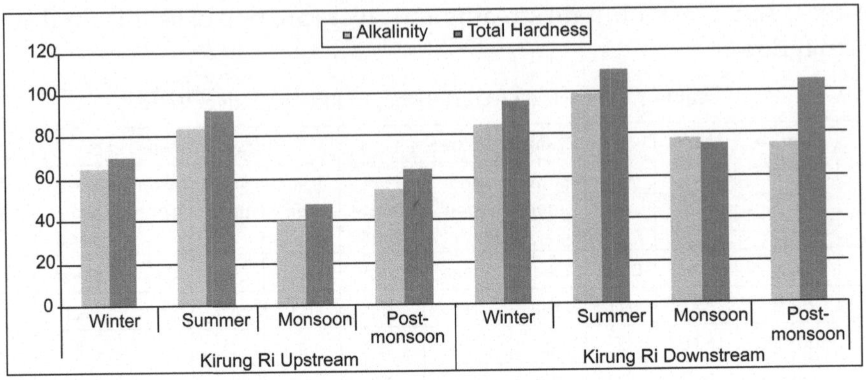

Fig. 7.1: Total hardness and Alkalinity trend of Kirung Ri river water.

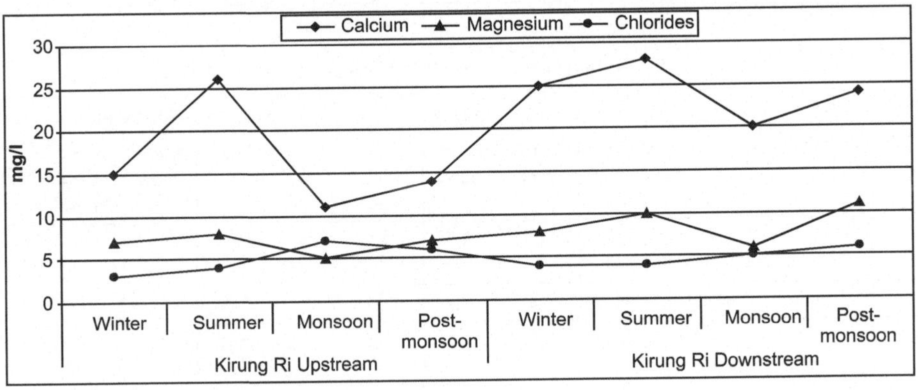

Fig. 7.2 : Showing the nutrients concentration in Kirung Ri river during the study period.

REFERENCES

APHA (1995): Standard Methods for Examination of Water and Waste Water. *American Public Health Association, 19th edition. Inc, New York.* pp. 1970.

Badola, S.P. and Singh, H.R. (1981) Hydrobiology of the River Alaknanda of Garhwal Himalaya. *Indian J. Ecol.*, 8(2): 269-276.

Baron, J. & Bricker, O.P. (1990) Hydrological and Chemical Flux in Loch Vale Watershed, Rocky Mountain National Park. In: Biogeochemistry of Major Rivers. SCOPE 42. Wiley and Sons, New York, USA.

Bharti, P.K. (2007): Why Indian Standards are not so Strict?, *Current Science,* 93(9): 1202.

Bharti, P.K., Malik, D.S. and Rashmi Yadav (2010): Influence of Heavy Metals on Abundance of Cyanophyceae Members in Three Spring-fed Lake in Kempty, Dehradun, In: 'Advances in Aquatic Ecology, Vol-III' ed. by V.B. Sakhare, *Daya Publishing House, New Delhi,* pp. 107-111.

Bond, H. B. (1979): Nutrient Concentrations Patterns in a Stream Draining a Montane Ecosystem in Utah. *Ecology.* 60(6): 1184-1196.

Cameron, E. M. (1996): Hydrogeo-chemistry of the Fraser River British Columbia: Seasonal Variation in Major and Minor Components. *J. Hydrol.* 182(1-4): 209-255.

Chopra, A. K. and Patrick, N. J. (1994): Effect of Domestic Sewage on Self-purification of Ganga Water at Rishikesh. *A. Bio. Science.* 13(11): 75-82.

Jenkins, A., Sloan W.T. & Cosby, B.J. (1995) Stream Chemistry is the Middle Hills and High Mountain of the Himalaya, Nepal. *Journal of Hydrology.* Vol. 166, No-1-4: 61-79.

Khanna, D.R and Singh. R.K. (2000). Seasonal Fluctuations in the Plankton of Suswa River at Raiwala Dehradun. *Env. Conservations J.* 1(2 & 3): 89-92.

Malik, D. S. and Bharti, P. K. (2005b): Fluctuation in Planktonic Population of Sahastradhara Hill-stream at Dehradun (Uttaranchal), *Aquacult.* 6 (2): 191-198.

Malik, D. S. and Bharti, P. K. (2005c): Primary Production Efficiency of Sahstradhara Hill-stream, Dehradun, *Env. Cons. J.* 6 (3): 117-121.

Malik, D. S. and Bharti, P. K. (2009): Ecology of Sahastradhara Hill-stream at Dehradun (Uttaranchal), In: 'Advances in Aquatic Ecology, Vol-I' ed. by V.B. Sakhare, *Daya Publishing House, New Delhi,* pp: 1-11.

Malik, D. S. and Bharti, P. K., Negi, K.S. and Rashmi Yadav (2009): Distribution of Metals in Water of an Artificial Lake at Mussoorie, Uttarakhand, In: 'Aquatic Biology and Aquaculture' Edited by V.B. Sakhare, Ambajoagi, MS, *Manglam Publication, New Delhi,* pp. 77-95.

Malik, D. S. and Bharti, Pawan K. (2005a): Nutrient Dynamics in Rhithron Zone of Shivalik Himalayan Stream Sahastradhara, Dehradun (Uttaranchal), *Env. Cons. J.* 6 (2): 63-68.

Miller, C. V.; Denis, J. M.; Ator, S. W. and Brakebill, J. W. (1997): Nutrients in Stream during Baseflow in Selected Environmental Settings of the Potomac River Basin. *J. American Wat. Resour. Association.* 33(6): 1155-1171.

Odum, E. P. (1971): Fundamentals of Ecology. New York. W. B. *Saunders and Co.* pp. 1-344.

Psenner, R. (1989). Chemistry of High Mountain Lakes in Siliceous Catchments of Central Alps. *Aquatic Sci.* 51: 108-128.

Shrama, R.C. (1986). Effect of Physico-chemical Factors on Benthic Fauna of Bhagirathi River Garhwal Himalaya. *Indian. J.Ecol.* 13(1): 133-137.

Subramanian, V. (1979) Chemical and Suspended Sediment Characteristics of River of India. *J. Hydrol,* 44: 37-55.

Trivedi, R. K. and Goel, P. K. (1984): Chemical and Biological Methods for Water Pollution Studies. Karad. Environmental Publication. pp. 1-25.

Xue, H.B. and Schooner, J.L. (1994) Acid Deposition and Lake Chemistry in Southwest China. *Wat. Air, Soil Pollut.* 75: 61-78.

Water Management and Aquatic Ecosystem **Pages 142-171**
Edited by: Dr. Resham Bhalla & Dr. Pawan Kumar 'Bharti'
ISBN: 978-93-86841-96-4
Edition: 2019
Published by: Discovery Publishing House Pvt. Ltd., New Delhi (India)

8

Aquatic Ecosystems

Significance for Living Organisms

[1]Syed Sana Mehraj, [2]Azra N Kamili, [3]Ruqeya Nazir and [4]Henah M Balkhi

Introduction

An ecosystem is a natural unit of living and nonliving parts that interact to produce a stable system. Ecology is the study of ecosystems, or how living things relate to the environment and to one another. Understanding this relationship is important because living things and non-living things depend upon and impact each other. Ecosystems operate from day to day by exchanging energy.

Fig. 8.1: Types of ecosystems

Source: www.tutorvista.com

[1,4]Centre of research for development and Department of Biotechnology, University of Kashmir, Hazratbal, Srinagar, Jammu and Kashmir 190006, India

The energy exchanged within an ecosystem is recycled between the physical and biological components. The plants within an ecosystem convert the sun's energy into food, and are in turn grazed upon by animals, which are consumed by predators. Microorganisms within an ecosystem, such as fungi and bacteria, also exchange energy within the ecosystem by breaking down waste material to substances that can be used by plants for food. In this way, each element within the ecosystem depends on the others for survival. Ecosystems are of various types depending on habitat as described in (Figure 8.1).

Aquatic ecosystems include lakes, rivers, streams, ponds, oceans and estuaries. Within these aquatic ecosystems are living things that depend on the water for survival, such as fish, plants, and microorganisms. These ecosystems are very fragile and can be easily disturbed by pollution.

Aquatic Ecosystems

An aquatic ecosystem is an ecosystem in a body of water. They are collectively the wet parts of the environment. They can be rivers, streams, swamps, lakes, estuaries, marine systems, and underground aquifers. They have biodiversity values as well as resource values and provide many services to the environment and humankind. The two main types of aquatic ecosystems are marine ecosystems and freshwater ecosystems.

Fresh Water Ecosystems

A fresh water ecosystem is an aquatic system that contains drinkable water or water of almost no salty content. It has habitats classified by different factors, including temperature, light penetration, and vegetation. Its resources include lakes, ponds, rivers, streams, reservoirs, wetlands as well as groundwater. Very small proportion of earth's area that is only 0.8 percent of the earth's surface is covered by them. Primary production in a fresh-water ecosystem is controlled by light and nutrient availability. Fresh water can be defined as the water that contains a relatively small amount of dissolved chemical compounds. It includes standing water like lakes & ponds and moving water bodies like rivers & streams.

Standing Water: Standing water ecosystems are known as Lentic ecosystems such as lakes and ponds. The organisms in lentic ecosystem includes algae, rooted and floating-leaved plants, invertebrates such as crabs, shrimps, crayfish, clams etc, amphibians such as frogs and salamanders and reptiles like alligators and water snakes.

Moving Water: Flowing water ecosystems are known as lotic ecosystems with water flowing in uniform direction and in a unidirectional way such as rivers and streams, which harbor several species of insects and fishes. Crustaceans like crayfish and crabs and mollusks such as clams and limpets.

(I) Pond as an Aquatic Ecosystem

Ecosystem is the basic functional unit with which ecology deals since it includes both the organisms and non-living environment, each influencing the properties of the other and both necessary for the maintenance of life on earth.

Fig. 8.2: A view of pond ecosystem

Source: www.texasponds.com

A pond ecosystem (Figure 8.2) refers to fresh water ecosystem where there are communities of organism dependent on each other with the prevailing water environment for their nutrients and survival. Usually ponds are shallow water bodies with a depth of 12-15 feet in which the sun rays can penetrate to the bottom permitting the growth of plants there. The functional components of a pond ecosystem are:

Abiotic Components

The abiotic components of pond ecosystem are formed as a result of the mixture of some organic and inorganic materials. The basic components are water, oxygen, carbon dioxide, salts of calcium and nitrogen etc. Only a small amount of these elements are present in soluble state in pond water, but a large amount is held in reserve solid form in the bottom sediments as well as within the organisms. Various organisms get their nourishment from these abiotic substances. The rate of release of reserve nutrients, the solar input and the cycle of temperature, day length and other climatic conditions regulate the function of the pond ecosystem.

Biotic Components

The biotic components of pond ecosystem consists of -

Producers: The producers are of two types, larger rooted and floating vegetation together termed macrophytes and phytoplanktons which are microscopic floating algae. Phytoplanktons are available upto the depth of water where light penetrates. The phytoplanktons are filamentous alga like Ulothrix, Oedogonium, Spirogyra, Anabena, Oscillatoria and minute floating plants like Microcystis, Gloeotrichina, volvox etc. The macrophytes include marginal emergent plants like Typha, Acerus, Ipomea, submerged plants like Hydrilla, Utricularia, Trapa, Nymphea etc surface floating plants like Pistea, Lemna, Wolffia, Eichhornia, Salvinia etc.

Consumers: Consumers of pond ecosystem are heterotrophs which depend for their nutrition on other organisms. Zooplanktons form primary consumers, include Brachionus, Asplanchna, Lechane, (all rotifers) Colops, Dilepteus, Cyclops, Stenocypris (crustacean), who feed on phytoplankton. Nectic animals like insects, beetles, fishes form secondary consumers as they feed on zooplanktons. Benthic animals like snakes, big fishes live on nectic animals and are termed tertiary consumers.

Decomposers: Most of the decomposers of pond ecosystem are saprophytes but some parasites are also found. Bacteria, fungi like Aspergillus, Cladosporium, Rhizopus, Alternaria, Fusarium, and Saprolegnia etc. are decomposers. Generally the decomposers either live in the soil layer beneath water or in the mud. They act on dead and decayed organic matter of plants and animals and supply raw materials to the producers.

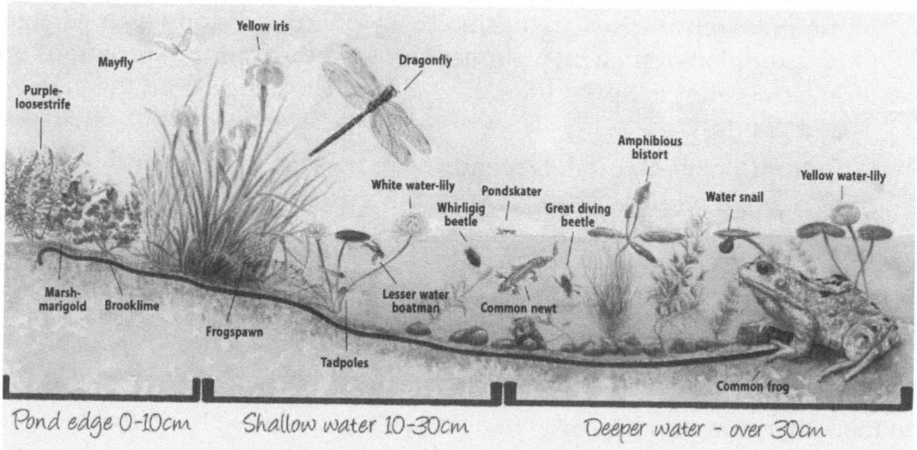

Fig. 8.3: A view of pond ecosystem

Source: www.texasponds.com

Energy Flow in Pond Ecosystem

Phytoplanktons are the producers of pond ecosystem along with other floating plants. The energy produced by the autotrophs is passed through "eat and being eaten chain". In pond the larvae of insects consume autotrophs as food. So according to law of energy flow the larvae assimilate energy from autotrophs. So larvae are primary consumers. These primary consumers are taken as food by prawns, small carnivorous fishes etc and so they collect energy from larvae. They are, therefore secondary consumers. Large fishes consume secondary consumers, and are tertiary consumers, so flows the energy from one level to another.

Habitats in a Pond Ecosystem

There are mainly four habitats in pond ecosystem, namely, shore, surface film, open water and bottom water habitats.

1. **Shore Habitat:** The organisms inhabiting shore habitat vary depending upon whether the shore is rocky, sandy, or muddy. In case of rocky shores, plants might not be able to grow, whereas in muddy or sandy or mixed type, plants like grasses, algae can be present along with organisms such as earthworms, protozoa, snails, insects, small fish and microorganisms.
2. **Surface Film Habitat:** Surface film habitat, implies to the surface of the pond. In general, insects like water striders and marsh traders, organisms that are free-floating and those that can walk on the surface of water inhabit the surface habitat. They feed on the floating plants, dead insects and sometimes, feed on each other.
3. **Open Water Habitat:** Open water habitat is inhabited by fish and the plankton or tiny organisms. Both phytoplankton (such as algae) and zooplankton (such as insect larvae, rotifers, tiny crustaceans and invertebrates) are present in this habitat. The fish feed on the plankton and plants.
4. **Bottom Water Habitat:** Depending upon whether the pond is shallow or deep, the bottom habitat varies. For example, if a pond is shallow and has a sandy bottom, organisms like earthworms, snails and insects inhabit the bottom. On the other hand, if the pond is deep and has a muddy bottom, microorganisms, flatworm, rat-tailed maggot and nymphs of dragonflies mostly inhabit the bottom habitat.

Food Chain and Food Web in Pond Ecosystem

The food chains in pond ecosystem are divided into three basic trophic levels - the first, second and third trophic levels for example a simple food chain in pond water is Algae (producer) ! Insect (herbivore / primary consumer) ! Fish (carnivore/secondary consumer) combination of various food chains ultimately form complex food webs which can be best explained in (Figure 8.4).

For Better Understanding, the Three Trophic Levels are Explained Below

The first level is represented by the producers or the autotrophs, for example, phytoplankton and plants. They prepare their own food with the help of energy from sunlight through the process of photosynthesis. The second trophic level

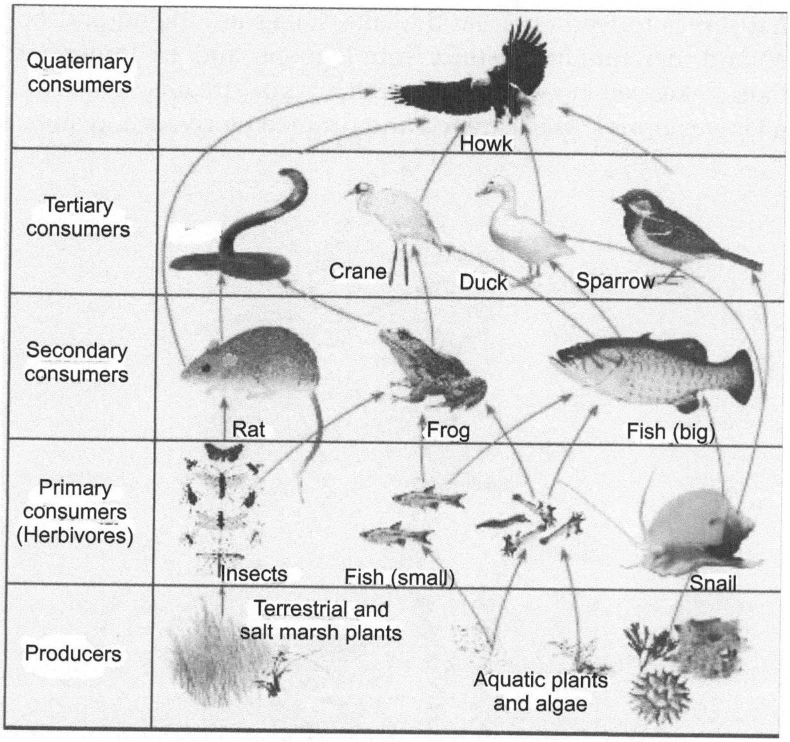

Fig. 8.4: Food chains and food webs in a pond ecosystem

Source: Biology.tutorvista.com

is characterized by presence of herbivores such as insects, crustaceans and invertebrates inhabiting the pond. Organisms in this level consume the plants or producers. The third and the topmost trophic level comprise the carnivores, especially the fish species, which can feed on both plants and the herbivores of the first trophic level and second trophic level respectively. In addition to the three trophic levels as shown in (Figure 8.5), there are saprotrophic organisms, commonly known as decomposers, which are located at the bottom of the food chain. Decomposers, mostly the bacteria and fungi, are very important in the nutrient cycle. They convert all the organic matter from the dead and decayed organisms into carbon dioxide and nutrients such as nitrogen, phosphorus and magnesium. These nutrients are generated in such a way that they can be readily used by algae and plants for production of food, which is again consumed by the herbivores. Furthermore, the carnivores feed on the producers and herbivores. Thus, the flow of energy is maintained in an ecosystem.

(II) Lake as an Aquatic Ecosystem

A lake is a body of relatively still water of considerable size, localized in a basin that is surrounded by land apart from a river, stream, or other form of moving water that serves to feed or drain the lake. Lakes are inland and not part of the ocean and therefore are distinct from lagoons, and are larger and deeper than ponds. Lakes can be contrasted with rivers or streams, which are usually flowing. However most lakes are fed and drained by rivers and streams.

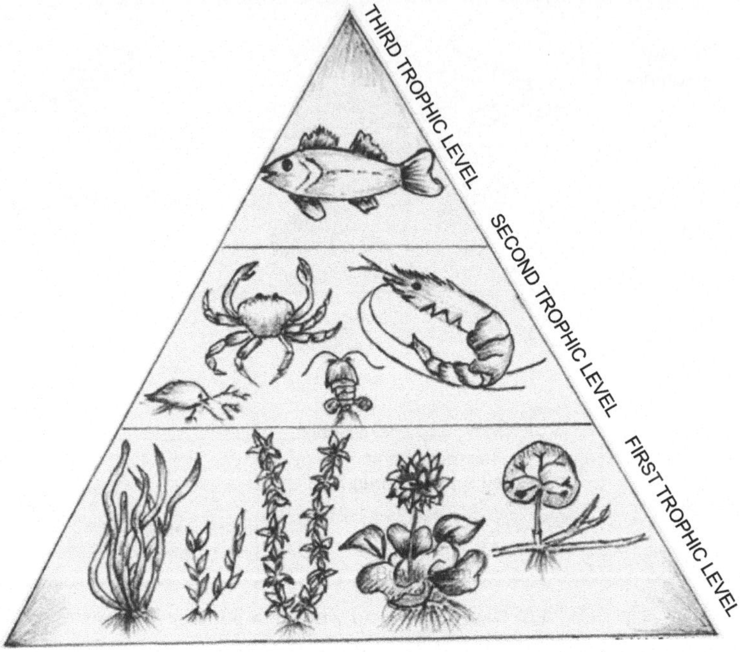

Fig. 8.5: Pond-ecosystem Pyramid

Source: www.buzzle.com

A lake has an open-water zone away from shore, as far down as sunlight reaches. Most large fish spend most of their time in this zone, swimming into the shoreline zone and then to feed or spawn. In the deep-water zone, below the open-water zone, light does not reaches the bottom for plants to grow. This makes the deep-water zone oxygen poor and not much lives there. Dead organic matter sinks to the lake bottom, where bacteria and other decomposers break it down.

The ecosystem of a lake includes biotic (living) plants, animals and micro-organisms, as well as abiotic (nonliving) physical and chemical interactions which are defined below:

Biotic Components in Lake Ecosystem

Nearly 6% of total known species are supported by freshwater systems. Moreover, some of the world's oldest lakes contain a high diversity of endemic species that have evolved through the process of adaptive radiation. In lakes, much of the species diversity is concentrated in the littoral zone, near the shore, where algae and plants thrive in the abundant light needed for photosynthesis. Living within the plant matter is a cornucopia of animals including snails, amphibians, crustaceans, insects, and fish. Beyond the littoral zone is the limnetic zone. This is the zone of open water where light is still able to penetrate and support photosynthetic algae (i.e., photic zone). Consumers in this zone include zooplankton, which feed on the algae, some insects, and fish. Finally, the benthic zone is the bottom sediment (e.g., mud, sand, rock) of the habitat, which is dominated by invertebrate species.

Producers

Primary producers are broadly divided into three groups, periphyton, phytoplankton, and macrophytes. Periphyton grows on substrates such as mud, sand, rocks, and leaf litter where it appears as a green or brown film. This is an important resource for a diversity of herbivores including macro invertebrates (e.g., snails) and amphibian larvae. Phytoplankton is algae suspended in the water column. Phytoplankton is divided into several groups (cyanobacteria, diatoms, chrysophytes, dinoflagellates, desmids) that tend to dominate at different levels of lake productivity. Herbivores such as zooplankton are common consumers of phytoplankton. Macrophytes are generally the most visible group of primary producers in lakes. Macrophyte species possess a diversity of growth forms. Emergent macrophytes undergo photosynthesis above the water and are typically found close to the shoreline. As depth increases, submerged macrophytes that undergo photosynthesis under the water, dominate. Macrophytes provide resources for many herbivores as well as important refuge from predators.

Consumers

The consumer species found in lentic habitats include worms, snails, amphibians, crustaceans, insects, reptiles, fish and birds. Herbivorous groups such as snails, amphibian larvae, and crustaceans play an important role in controlling primary productivity and algal blooms. Additionally, these groups are a critical resource for predators. By integrating primary producers, herbivores, and predators together, a food web is formed where species interact both directly and indirectly with each other.

Abiotic Factors

Light

Light provides the solar energy required to drive the process of photosynthesis, the major energy source of lentic systems. The amount of light received depends upon a combination of several factors. Once light has penetrated the surface, it is scattered by particles suspended in the water column. This scattering decreases the total amount of light as depth increases. Lakes are divided into photic and aphotic regions, the prior receiving sunlight and latter being below the depths of light penetration, making it void of photosynthetic capacity. In relation to Lake Zonation, the pelagic and benthic zones are considered to lie within the photic region, while the Profundal zone is in the aphotic region.

Temperature

Temperature is an important abiotic factor in lentic ecosystems because most of the biota is poikilolthermic, where internal body temperatures are defined by the surrounding system. Water can be heated or cooled through radiation at the surface and conduction to or from the air and surrounding substrate. Shallow lakes often have a continuous temperature gradient from warmer waters at the surface to cooler waters at the bottom. In addition, temperature fluctuations can be very great in these systems, both diurnally and seasonally.

Temperature regimes are very different in large lakes. In temperate regions, as shown in (Figure 8.6), as air temperatures increase, the icy layer formed on the surface of the lake breaks up, leaving the water at approximately 4 °C. This is the temperature at which water has the highest density. As the season progresses, the warmer air temperatures heat the surface waters, making them less dense. The deeper waters remain cool and dense due to reduced light penetration. As the summer begins, two distinct layers become established, with such a large temperature difference between them that they remain stratified. The lowest zone in the lake is the coldest and is called the hypolimnion. The upper warm zone is called the epilimnion. Between these zones is a band of rapid temperature change called the thermocline. During the colder fall season, heat is lost at the surface and the epilimnion cools. When the temperatures of the two zones are close enough, the waters begin to mix again to create a uniform temperature, an event termed lake turnover. In the winter, inverse stratification occurs as water near the surface cools freezes, while warmer, but denser water remains near the bottom. A thermocline is established, and the cycle repeats.

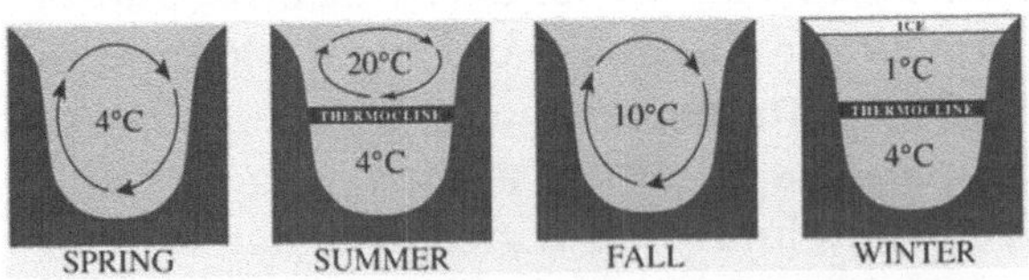

Fig. 8.6: Seasonal stratification in temperate lakes

Source: en.wikipedia.org

Oxygen

Oxygen is essential for organism's respiration. The amount of oxygen present in standing waters depends upon various factors as:

1. The area of transparent water exposed to the air.
2. The circulation of water within the system and
3. The amount of oxygen generated and used by organisms present.

Phosphorus

Phosphorus is not found in large quantities in freshwater systems, thus limiting photosynthesis in primary producers, making it the main determinant of lentic system production. Phosphorus mainly enters a lake through runoff from the watershed or by atmospheric deposition. Upon entering the system, a reactive form of phosphorus is usually taken up by algae and macrophytes, which release a non-reactive phosphorus compound as a byproduct of photosynthesis. This phosphorus can drift downwards and become part of the benthic or profundal sediment, or it can be remineralized to the reactive form by microbes in the water column. Similarly, non-reactive phosphorus in the sediment can be remineralized into the reactive form. Sediments are generally richer in phosphorus than lake water, however, indicating that this nutrient may have a long residency time there before it is remineralized and re-introduced to the system.

Food Webs in Lake Ecosystem

The lake biota is linked in complex web of trophic relationships. These organisms can be considered to loosely be associated with specific trophic groups (primary producers, herbivores, primary carnivores, secondary carnivores, etc.) (Figure 8.7) Several theories have been developed in order

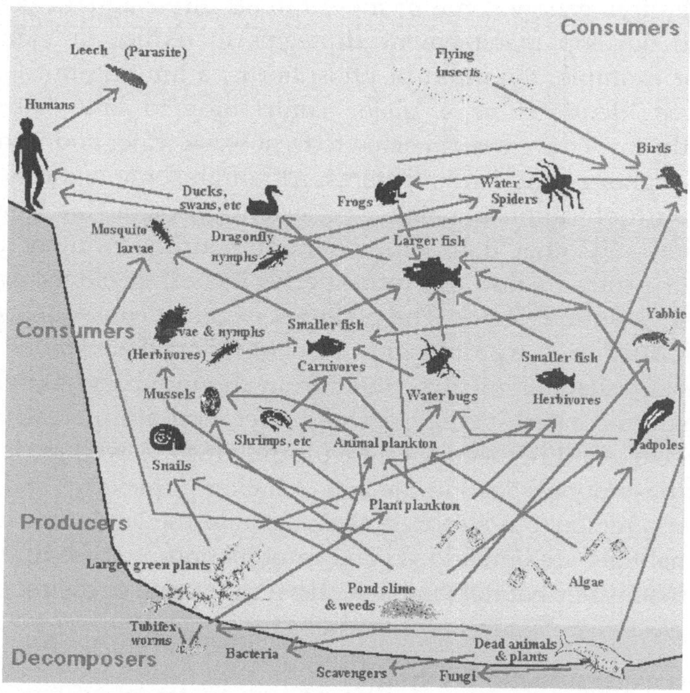

Fig. 8.7: Food chains and Food webs in Lake Ecosystem

Source: Josh K., hodnettbiomeproject.wikispaces.com

to understand the mechanisms that control the abundance and diversity within these groups. Generally, top-down processes dictate that the abundance of prey taxa is dependent upon the actions of consumers from higher trophic levels. Typically, these processes operate only between two trophic levels, with no effect on the others. In some cases, however, aquatic systems experience a trophic cascade; for example, this might occur if primary producers experience less grazing by herbivores because these herbivores are suppressed by carnivores. Bottom-up processes are functioning when the abundance or diversity of members of higher trophic levels is dependent upon the availability or quality of resources from lower levels. Finally, a combined regulating theory, bottom-up: top-down, combines the predicted influences of consumers and resource availability. It predicts that trophic levels close to the lowest trophic levels will be most influenced by bottom-up forces, while top-down effects should be strongest at top levels.

Threats to Lake Ecosystem

The biodiversity of freshwater habitats is increasingly threatened by human activities. Habitat loss, eutrophication, acidification, chemical contamination, global warming, and exotic species are just some of the factors that have directly or indirectly impacted lentic systems. Substantial progress has been made in identifying how some of these threats affect aquatic communities, and how to develop management strategies to reduce or eliminate their impacts. For example, the input of phosphorus, a limiting nutrient in lentic systems, was identified as a major contributor to lake eutrophication. Consequently, laws have been enacted to treat wastewater and reduce sewage input of phosphorus into lentic systems. Although some lentic systems have recovered, eutrophication remains a persistent problem due to agricultural intensification and other non-point pollution sources. Another challenging problem is the introduction of exotic species including plants, animals, and pathogens into lentic systems. The potential negative consequences of exotic species introduction is well recognized, controlling their spread is difficult and, once established, eliminating them from communities has been difficult. Lastly, human-mediated habitat loss and alteration are increasing concerns driven by the expanding need for agricultural lands as well as development. These activities not only lead to the loss of habitat for species and vital water resources for a region, but also fragment and alter the landscape in which the remaining habitats are embedded. The combination of these threats and the scarcity of freshwater habitats make lentic systems one of the most imperiled on the planet.

(III) Streams as an Aquatic Ecosystem

A stream (Figure 8.8) is a body of water with a current, confined within a bed and stream banks. Depending on its locale or certain characteristics, a stream may be referred to as a branch, brook, beck, burn, creek, "crick", gill, kill, lick, mill race, rill, river, rivulet, wash or runnel.

Streams are important as conduits in the water cycle, instruments in groundwater recharge, and corridors for fish and wildlife migration. The biological habitat in the immediate vicinity of a stream is called a riparian zone. Streams play an important corridor role in connecting fragmented habitats and thus in conserving biodiversity. The study of streams and waterways in general is known as surface hydrology and is a core element of environmental geography.

Fig. 8.8: A view of Stream

Source: fullstreamahead.com

Types of Streams

- **Brook:** A stream smaller than a creek, especially one that is fed by a spring or seep. It is usually small and easily forded. A brook is characterized by its shallowness and its bed being composed primarily of rocks.
- **Creek:** A small to medium sized natural stream. Sometimes navigable by motor craft and may be intermittent. A tidal inlet, typically in a salt marsh or mangrove swamp, or between enclosed and drained former salt marshes or swamps. In these cases, the stream is the tidal stream, the course of the sea water through the creek channel at low and high tide.
- **River:** A large natural stream, which may be a waterway.
- **Runnel:** The linear channel between the parallel ridges or bars on a shoreline beach or river floodplain, or between a bar and the shore. Runnel is also called a swale.
- **Tributary:** A contributory stream, or a stream which does not reach the sea but joins another river (a parent river). Sometimes also known as branch or fork.

The Water Balance in Stream

The amount of water in a stream will affect the stream flora and fauna. An increase in water volume will cool the stream off; while a decrease in water flow will warm it up. The various sources of stream water are best described in Figure 8.9:

WATER BALANCE FOR A SMALL STREAM OR RIVER

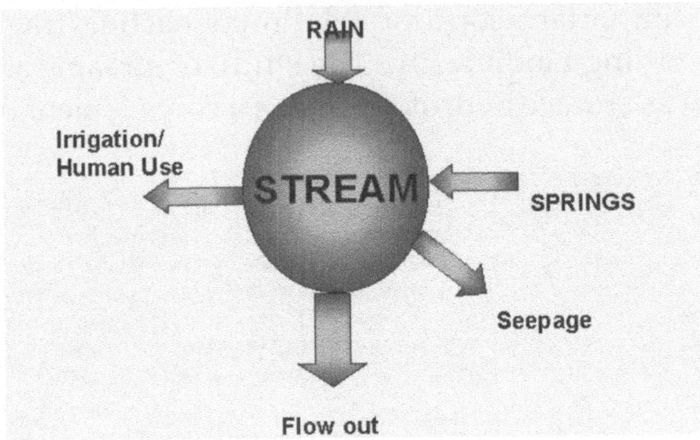

Fig. 8.9: Water balance for a small stream

Source: www.combat-fishing.com

Food Chain and Food Webs in Stream Ecosystem

The food web for a stream has essentially 6 levels as given in figure: 10 (each level mainly eats the one below it, and may be two below it. Level 5 may eat

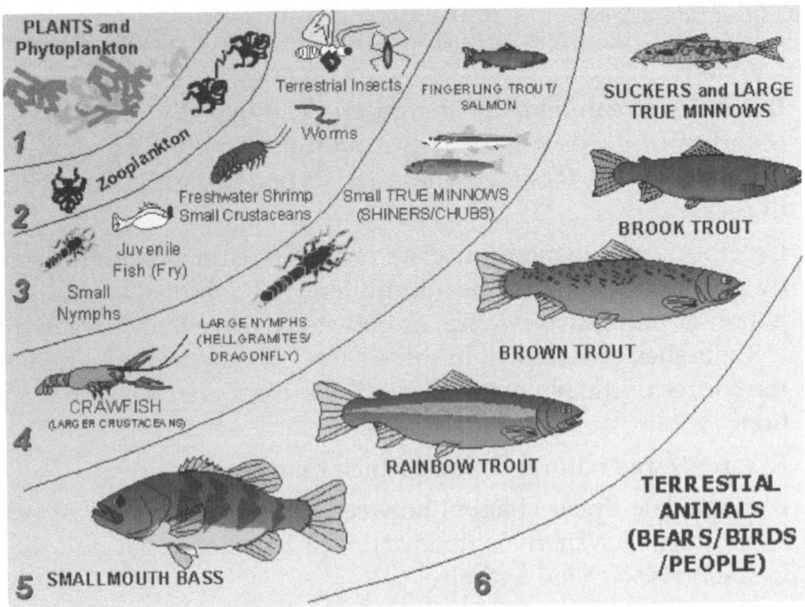

Fig. 8.10: Various levels in stream ecosystem which leads to food chains and food webs

Source: www.combat-fishing.com

from level 4 and 3). Initial level is the sun. Level 1 are plants and phytoplankton, level 2 are Zooplankton, level 3 are small visible animals-usually freshwater shrimp, freshly hatched fish, small aquatic insects and terrestrial insects and worms that feed in the stream. Level 4 consists of fingerling juvenille fishes, small true minnows (such as shiners and chubs), larger crustaceans (crayfish, large shrimps), salamanders, molluscs (clams/mussells), and large predatory aquatic insects (hellgramites, dragonfly larvae). Level 5 is the layer where most gamefish reside, and the most important to anglers. Knowing what animals are on level 3 and 4 will help the angler pick lures and baits appropriate for each stream.

(IV) Rivers as an Aquatic Ecosystem

River (Figure 8.11) is a large natural stream of water emptying into an ocean, lake, or other body of water and usually fed along its course by converging tributaries. River ecosystems are prime examples of lotic ecosystems. Lotic refers to flowing water. Lotic ecosystems can be contrasted with lentic ecosystems, which involve relatively still terrestrial waters such as lakes and ponds.

The following unifying characteristics make the ecology of river waters unique from that of other aquatic habitats.

- Flow in river systems is unidirectional.
- There is a state of continuous physical change in river ecosystems.
- There is a high degree of spatial and temporal heterogeneity at all scales (microhabitats).
- Variability between lotic systems is quite high.
- The biota is specialized to live with flow conditions.

Fig. 8.11: A view of River Ecosystem

Source: www.fs.fed.us

River ecosystems encompass river channels and its floodplains and form a diverse mosaic of habitats with the riparian area at the transition zone between land and water. During flood events, water and sediment are transported onto the floodplain and provide the nutrients that render river ecosystems highly productive. Conversely, floodplains (and other wetlands) constitute important sinks of river nutrients and sediments and, hence, contribute substantially to a river's self-purification. They act as a sponge and regulate the water volume, as they cut off flood peaks and release water during low-flow conditions. Floodplains, especially the riparian areas, provide the river channel with carbon (organic matter) which is essential for sustaining riverine plant, animal and micro-organism communities in many regions.

Looking more precisely at the specific services as shown in Figure 8.12 provided by river ecosystems, their important role for human well-being becomes obvious. Nearly everywhere on earth, people depend on rivers for fresh water supply and sanitation purposes. But there are many more services linked with rivers and floodplains besides these fundamental human needs.

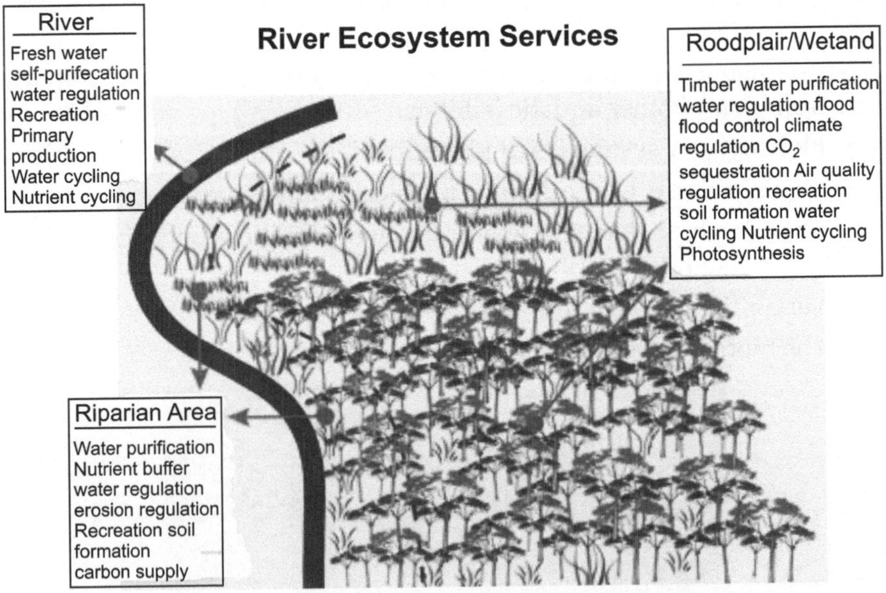

Fig. 8.12: Major ecosystem services in river ecosystem

Source: Harrison, et al., (2010).

Ecosystem services are sometimes valued in monetary terms for use in policy and decision-making. This is relatively straightforward for provisioning services such as water and timber supply where market values exist. However, it is more difficult and often controversial for many regulatory and supporting services for which the direct benefits to people are not as clear. Nevertheless, several studies have provided values for river and floodplain ecosystem services.

Food Chains and Food Webs in River Ecosystem

The energy and matter produced by plants and other autotrophs are distributed to other organisms in an ecosystem through pathways known as food chains and food webs. A food chain is a simple linkage of producers to consumers through feeding relationships. For example, when a small fish eats an aquatic insect, and a larger fish eats the small fish, the two fish and the insect are linked in a food chain. Food webs are more complex, and consist of a network of linked food chains. Organisms commonly consume, and are consumed by, more than one other type of organism. Each organism has characteristic feeding preferences and patterns, and can itself be prey to other consumers. Food webs connect autotrophs, at the lowest feeding level, to the herbivores (primary consumers) and then to various carnivores (secondary consumers).

The trophic level is an organism's position in the food chain as determined by the number of energy-transfer steps required to reach that level. A fish that has consumed an insect, which itself has just consumed algae, is at a higher trophic level than the insect. In rivers, as in the majority of other aquatic and terrestrial systems, the energy at the base of a food web comes from the solar energy fixed by plants (through photosynthesis) growing in the water or on land. Energy derived from terrestrial plants enters the water in the form of plant parts, such as leaves or twigs, or in the form of dissolved organic matter. This material is used as a source of energy by microorganisms such as fungi and bacteria, and by invertebrates. Plants in the river are also important in food web, microscopic algae are often eaten while alive, while larger aquatic plants mainly enter food chains after they have died.

Biomass and Production in River Ecosystems

Organisms use energy to maintain biological functions and to enable growth and reproduction. The organic matter produced by autotrophs and heterotrophs, in excess of what they need to sustain life, adds to the ecosystem's total biomass. The biomass in an ecosystem includes the mass of all living and dead organic matter. Production is the incremental increase in biomass produced by organisms over a period of time. Estimates of biomass and production are one measure that can be used to assess the health of aquatic ecosystems.

Primary production refers to the production of organic matter, such as body tissue, produced mainly by photosynthetic plants. It is expressed as a rate of biomass production for example, the amount of wood produced each year. Secondary production is the assimilation of organic material and building of tissue by heterotrophs, and may involve animals eating plants, animals eating other animals, or microorganisms decomposing dead organisms to obtain the resources (material, energy, nutrients) needed for producing biomass. Secondary production is also expressed as a rate of biomass production, such as the amount of meat produced by grazing cattle each year. In a productive environment, living plant or animal tissue will accumulate over time. Biomass is the amount of this accumulated material at a given moment, while production is the rate of increase in the total biomass. In a river system, biomass may be lost by export (such as downstream transport of biomass), or gained by import from other systems (such as leaves falling into a stream). Estimates of biomass and production can be applied at various spatial scales and to broad or narrow groups of organisms, such as all organisms in a lake, all fish in a lake. Production is often difficult to estimate, since it requires, among other things, accurate measures of biomass repeated at consistent intervals over a long period. High biomass does not necessarily imply high production, and vice versa. For example, the biomass of plankton in a water body may be low, but because plankton grows and reproduces quickly, the plankton population may replace itself relatively quickly, it has a high rate of production. Populations of large, long-lived fish represent a much greater biomass than the plankton; however, the production rate of large fish may be much lower. The rapidity with which living material can replace itself is measured by the production/biomass ratio. This ratio is high for plankton (high production, low biomass) and relatively low for fishes (low production, high biomass), and provides a better indication of energy transfer between trophic levels than instantaneous measures of biomass. *This can best illustrated by figure given below* Figure 8.13.

$$C = W + \triangle B + R$$

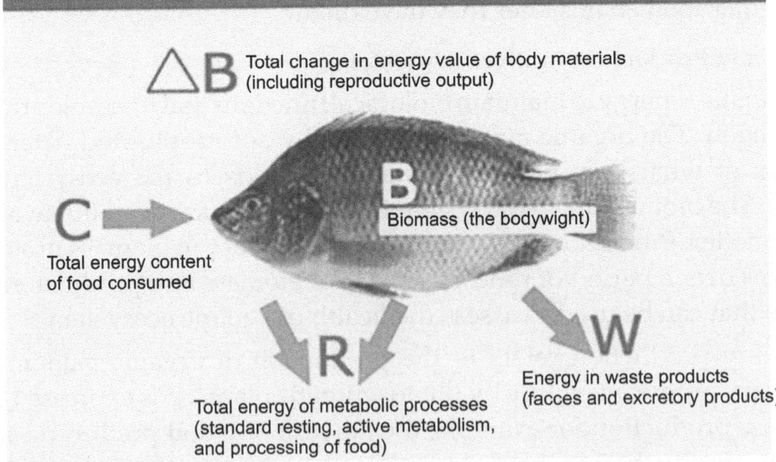

Fig. 8.13: This figure illustrates energy flows related to the accumulation of biomass in an individual animal. Energy is obtained through food, while energy is consumed or lost in metabolic processes (i.e., respiration) and the excretion of wastes.

Source: NTEAP 2007

Marine Ecosystems

Marine ecosystems (Figure 8.14) are among the largest of earth's aquatic ecosystems. They include oceans, salt marsh and intertidal ecology, estuaries and lagoons, mangroves and coral reefs, the deep sea and the sea floor. They can be contrasted with freshwater ecosystems, which have a lower salt content. Marine waters cover two-thirds of the surface of the Earth. Such places are considered ecosystems because the plant life supports the animal life and vice-versa. Marine ecosystems are very important for the overall health of both marine and terrestrial environments. According to the World Resource Center, coastal habitats alone account for approximately 1/3 of all marine biological productivity, and estuarine ecosystems (i.e., salt marshes, sea grasses, mangrove forests) are among the most productive regions on the planet. In addition, other marine ecosystems such as coral reefs provide food and shelter to the highest levels of marine diversity in the world.

Fig. 8.14: An ecosystem is a community of organisms that live and interact within a particular environment.

Source: Ingrid Prats/iStock/Getty.

Oceans as Marine Ecosystem

An ocean ecosystem is a living environment that is characterized by more salt water than fresh water, and it is only marine animals and plants that thrive in such environments. Other aquatic ecosystems include fresh water lakes, rivers and estuaries. An ocean is a body of saline water that composes much of a planet's hydrosphere. On Earth, an ocean is one or all of the major divisions of the planet's world ocean which are, in descending order of area, the Pacific, Atlantic, Indian, Southern (Antarctic), and Arctic Oceans. The word sea is often used interchangeably with "ocean" in American English but, strictly speaking, a sea is a body of saline water (generally a division of the World Ocean) that land partly or fully encloses.

Earth is the only planet that is known to have an ocean (or any large amounts of open liquid water). Saline water covers approximately 72% of the planet's surface (~3.6x108 km^2) and is customarily divided into several principal oceans and smaller seas, with the ocean covering approximately 71% of the earth's surface. The ocean contains 97% of the earth's water, and oceanographers have stated that only 5% of the world ocean has been explored. The total volume is approximately 1.3 billion cubic kilometres (310 million cu mi) with an average depth of 3,682 metres (12,080 ft).

The ocean principally comprises earth's hydrosphere and therefore is integral to all known life, forms part of the carbon cycle, and influences climate and weather patterns. It is the habitat of 230,000 known species, although much of the ocean's depths remain unexplored, and over two million marine species are estimated to exist. The origin of earth's oceans remains unknown; oceans are believed to have formed in the Hadean period and may have been the impetus for the emergence of life.

Physical and Chemical Characteristics of Oceans

Ocean water is a mixture of various salts and water. Most of the water in the ocean basins is believed to originate from the condensation of water found in the early atmosphere as the earth cooled after its formation. This water is released from the lithosphere as the earth's crust solidified. Additional water is also added to the oceans over geologic time from periodic volcanic action.

Most of the dissolved chemical constituents or salts found in seawater have a continental origin. It seems that these chemicals are released from continental rocks through weathering and then carried to the oceans by stream runoff. Over time, the concentration of these chemicals increased until equilibrium is met. This equilibrium occurred when the ocean's water could not dissolve any more material in solution. Similarities between fossilized sea life and organisms living today indicate that the composition of seawater stopped changing drastically about 600 million years ago.

Mainly six elements and compounds comprise about 99% of sea salts (Figure 8.15). Chlorine (Cl^-), sodium (Na^+), sulfur ($SO4^{-2}$), magnesium (Mg^{+2}), calcium (Ca^{+2}), and potassium (K^+). The relative abundance of the major salts in seawater is constant regardless of the ocean. Only the amount of water in the mixture varies because of differences between ocean basins because of regional differences in freshwater loss (evaporation) and gain (runoff and precipitation). The chlorine ion makes up 55% of the salt in seawater. Seawater salinity is made of the parts per 1000 of the chlorine ion present in one kilogram of seawater. Typically, seawater has a salinity of 35 parts per thousand.

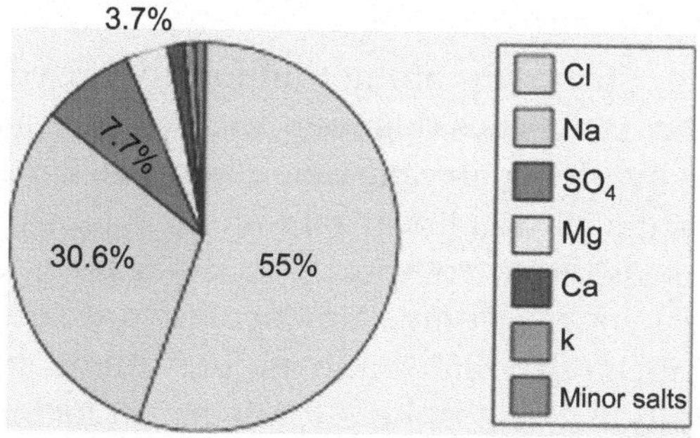

Fig. 8.15: Relative proportions of dissolved salts in seawater.

Source: www.physicalgeography.net

Water is one of the few substances existing on the earth's surface in all three forms of matter. At zero degrees Celsius liquid water turns into ice and has a density of approximately 917 kilograms per cubic meter. Liquid water at the same temperature has a density of nearly 1,000 kilograms per cubic meter. The density of seawater generally increases with decreasing temperature, increasing salinity, and increasing depth in the ocean. The density of seawater at the surface of the ocean varies from 1,020 to 1,029 kilograms per cubic meter. Highest densities are achieved with depth because of the overlying weight of water. In the deepest parts of the oceans, seawater densities can be as high as 1,050 kilograms per cubic meter.

Seawater freezes at a temperature that is slightly colder than fresh water (0° Celsius). The freezing temperature of seawater also varies with the concentration of salts. More salt in the sea, lower the initial freezing temperature. At a salinity of 35 parts per thousand, seawater freezes at a temperature of -1.9° Celsius. Seawater also contains small amounts of dissolved gases. Many of these gases are added to seawater from the atmosphere through the constant stirring of the sea surface by wind and waves. The concentration of gases that can be dissolved into seawater from the atmosphere is determined by temperature and salinity of the water. Increasing the temperature or salinity reduces the amount of gas that ocean water can dissolve. Some of the important atmospheric gases found in seawater includes nitrogen, oxygen, carbon dioxide (in the form of bicarbonate HCO_3), argon, helium, and neon. Compared to the other atmospheric gases, the amount of carbon dioxide dissolved in saturated seawater is unusually large.

Some gases found within seawater are also involved in oceanic organic and inorganic processes that are indirectly related to the atmosphere. For example, oxygen and carbon dioxide may be temporally generated or depleted by such processes to varying concentrations at specific locations within the ocean.

Zones and Depths in Oceans

Like the atmosphere, the oceans are not uniformly mixed but are structured in layers with distinct properties (Figure 8.16). Pressure increases with depth as the weight of the overlying air and water increase. Unlike the atmosphere, however, pressure changes at a linear rate rather than exponentially because water is almost impossible to compress, so it's mass is equally distributed throughout a vertical water column. Atmospheric pressure at sea level is 14.7 pounds per square inch (also referred to as "one atmosphere"), and pressure increases by an additional atmosphere for every 10 meters of descent under water. This gradient is well known to scuba divers who have experienced painful "ear squeeze" from pressure differences between the air in their ears and the seawater around them.

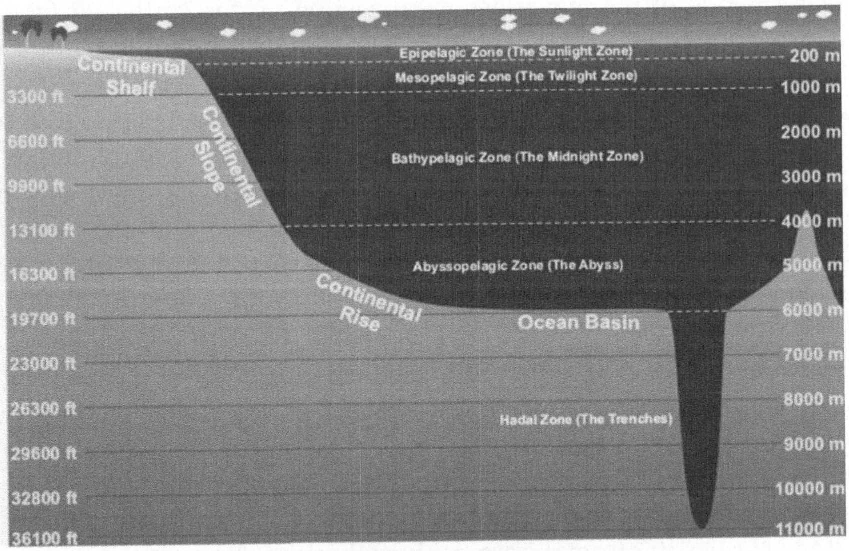

Fig. 8.16: Layers of the ocean

Source: National Oceanic and Atmospheric Administration. National Weather Service.

The Epipelagic, or sunlight, zone (so called because most visible light in the oceans is found here) comprises the first 200 meters below the surface, and is warm and mixed by winds and wave action. Surface waters account for about 2 percent of total worldwide ocean volume. At a depth of about 200 meters, the Continental Shelf (the submerged border of the continents) begins to slope more sharply downward, marking the start of the Mesopelagic, or twilight, zone. Here water temperature falls rapidly with depth to less than 5°C at 1,000 meters. This sharp transition, which is called the thermocline, inhibits vertical mixing between denser, colder water at depths and warmer water nearer the surface. About 18 percent of the total volume of the oceans is within this zone.

Below 1,000 meters, in the Bathypelagic, or midnight, zone, water is almost uniformly cold, approximately 4°C. No sunlight penetrates to this level, and pressure at the bottom of the zone (around 4,000 meters depth) is about 5,880 pounds per square inch. Little life exists at the Abyssopelagic (abyssal) zone, which reaches to the ocean floor at a depth of about 6,000 meters. Together, these cold, deep layers contain about 80 percent of the total volume of the ocean.

The deepest points in the ocean lie in long, narrow trenches that occur at convergence zone points where two oceanic plates collide and one is driven beneath the other. This region is called the Hadal zone. The deepest oceanic trench measured to date is the Mariana Trench near the Philippines, which reaches more than 10,000 meters below sea level. Highly specialized life forms, including fish, shrimps, sea cucumbers, and microbes, survive even at these depths.

Food Chains and Food Webs in Oceans

In an ecosystem, plants and animals are interdependent. Plants, such as algae, produce food using energy from the sun to convert carbon dioxide and water into simple sugars. The alga is eaten by animals, such as fish and prawns. These animals are eaten by large birds. A feeding relationship, where energy is transferred from green plants through a sequence of animals, is known as a food chain (Figure 8.17). The schematic representation of a marine ecosystem food web illustrates some of the interrelationships or ecological pathways between the species that make up the community.

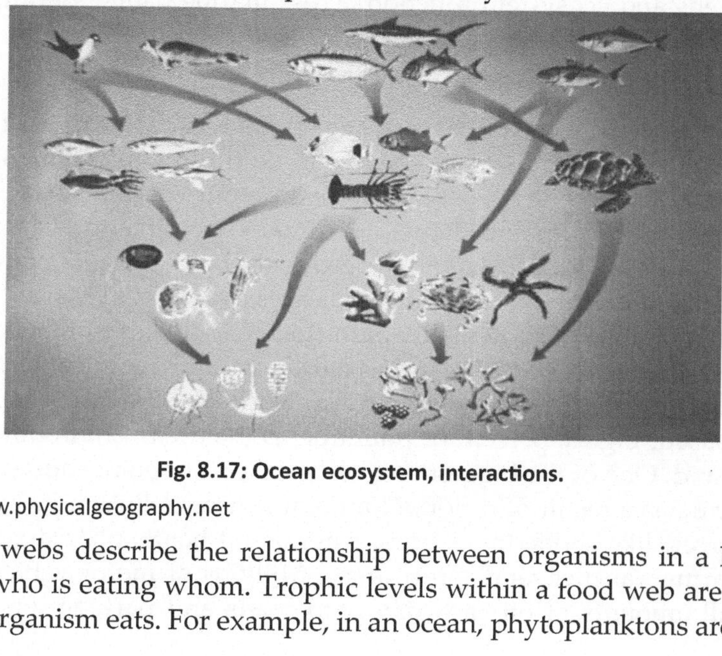

Fig. 8.17: Ocean ecosystem, interactions.

Source: www.physicalgeography.net

Food webs describe the relationship between organisms in a habitat in terms of who is eating whom. Trophic levels within a food web are based on what an organism eats. For example, in an ocean, phytoplanktons are primary producers, mussels and clams are basal consumers (lowest consumers in the food web), crabs are secondary consumers, sea otters are primary predators and great white sharks are top predators. In addition to providing food for higher consumers, species also perform other functions, in their habitat. Organisms that have the same function in a habitat make up functional groups. Functional groups perform jobs such as water filtration, wave buffering, and nutrient recycling. These ecological functions are important for maintaining balance within a habitat and for providing humans with valuable services such as clean water, storm protection and climate regulation. Each ecosystem in the ocean and along the coast has its own set of species that make up different trophic levels and functional groups that co-exist in a healthy, functioning ecosystem. Species composition changes can affect this balance, and alter system functioning.

The most pervasive changes to the marine food web are likely to occur as species move to find a more suitable habitat and invade new spaces, or go extinct if they are unable to find suitable habitat. Species are adapted to the physical and biological features of their environment. As temperature, salinity, pH, habitat and/or currents change, species must be able to adapt to the changes or move to areas that are favorable for reproduction and survival. These large scale changes in distribution will alter the ways organisms interact with one another, the types of biological jobs they perform, and the dominant ecological players in the community. Ocean acidification, increased sea surface and air temperatures, and changes to ocean circulation have significant impacts on food webs and ecosystem function across marine habitats. Although it is uncertain how these changes affect oceans.

Threats to Oceans

Although the world's oceans have a tremendous capacity to assimilate the human race's waste products, as they've done throughout humanity's brief history, we now know that we're overstressing our coastal waters and open seas with too much filth and debris. It is indeed possible to overharvest the oceans' fish and shellfish stocks and to destroy the breeding and rearing habitat of our most important species with our excessive wastes. Marine pollution occurs when harmful, or potentially harmful, effects result from the entry into the ocean of chemicals, particles, industrial, agricultural and residential waste, noise, or the spread of invasive organisms. Most sources of marine pollution are land based. Eighty percent of pollution to the ocean environment comes from the land. One of the biggest sources is called nonpoint source pollution, which occurs as a result of runoff. Nonpoint source pollution includes many small sources, like septic tanks, cars, trucks, and boats, plus larger sources, such as farms, ranches, and forest areas. Millions of motor vehicle engines drop small amounts of oil each day onto roads and parking lots. Much of this, too, makes its way to the sea. Some water pollution actually starts as air pollution, which settles into waterways and oceans. Dirt can be a pollutant. Top soil or silt from fields or construction sites can run off into waterways, harming fish and wildlife habitats. Nonpoint source pollution can make river and ocean water unsafe for humans and wildlife. In some areas, this pollution is so bad that it causes beaches to be closed after rainstorms.

(II) Estuaries

An estuary (Figure 8.18) is a body of water formed where freshwater from rivers and streams flows into the ocean, mixing with the seawater. Estuaries and the lands surrounding them are places of transition from land to sea, and from freshwater to saltwater. Although influenced by the tides, estuaries are protected from the full force of ocean waves, winds, and storms by the reefs, barrier islands, or fingers of land, mud, or sand that surround them.

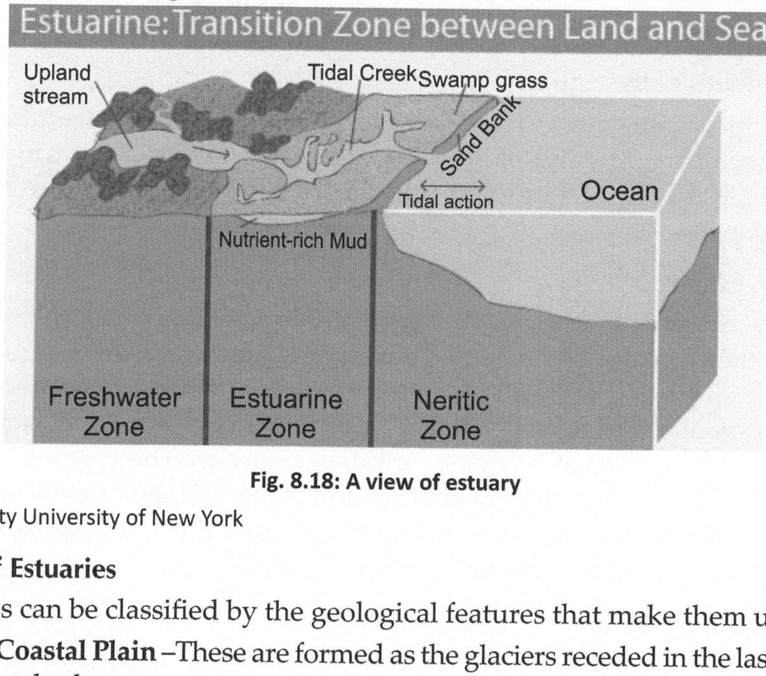

Fig. 8.18: A view of estuary

Source: City University of New York

Types of Estuaries

Estuaries can be classified by the geological features that make them up.

- **Coastal Plain** –These are formed as the glaciers receded in the last ice age and saltwater penetrated river valley, they are also known as drowned river valleys.
- **Tectonic** -Significant tectonic movements lead to the formation of a large depression or basin. As sea water floods in it will meet up with inflowing streams forming an estuary.
- **Bar Built** - Bar-built estuaries are formed by the accumulation of sediment around the mouth of a river. They can occur when sandbars or barrier islands are built up by ocean waves or by the deposition of river sediment at the mouth of the river.

- **Fjord** -Typically long, narrow bays with deep walls that have been cut out by the advancement of Glaciers.

Estuaries can also be Classified by How Fresh and Salt Water Mix in the Estuary

- **Salt wedge estuaries** –These are found at mouths of large rivers (e.g., Mississippi), the large fresh water influx "holds back" salt water at depth creating a salt wedge, little fresh and salt water mixing.
- **Partially Mixed estuaries** –These are deeper than well mixed type but more shallow than Fjord, good fresh and salt water mixing takes place in these estuaries, salinity changes both horizontally and vertically, big tidal influence can be seen.
- **Vertically Mixed estuaries** –These are typically shallow with strong tidal influx of salt water, extensive mixing of salt and fresh water, uniform salinity from top to bottom, water gets saltier the closer you get to the mouth of the estuary.
- **Fjord estuaries** – These are deep, having highly stratified water chemistry, fresh water flows out at surface, salt water flows in at depth, little mixing of fresh and salt water, anoxic conditions are found at depth.

Life in an Estuary

Estuaries are more biologically productive than any other marine ecosystem. As such they can also be home to a large variety of organisms. Large changes in salinity, in particular, mean that estuarian species have to be very adaptable. Hearty organisms like crabs, clams, mussels, and worms are particularly common. Rich arrays of habitats surround estuaries. The type of habitat is usually determined by the local geology and climate. Habitats associated with estuaries include salt marshes, mangrove forests, mud flats, tidal streams, rocky intertidal shores, reefs, and barrier beaches.

The Economics of Estuaries

Estuaries have historically provided the focal point around which coastal communities grew up. Most of the world's largest cities have been built on estuaries. These early developing towns and cities took advantage of the food availability, effective waste disposal, and high quality of life that estuaries provided. Today, estuaries are a tremendous economic resource which provides jobs and resources to coastal communities. Estuaries produce more food per acre than the most productive mid-western farmland, 75% of commercial species depend upon estuaries for their primary habitat, spawning grounds, and nursery areas, 86% of recreational fishing trips occurred within 10 miles of the shoreline.

The Roles of Estuaries in Ecological Systems

Estuaries do far more for our economy than supporting industries and providing jobs. Estuaries provide significant "ecological services" which directly benefit the surrounding communities. For example, estuaries protect landowners from flood waters, improve water quality by filtering runoff, and provide homes for plant and animal species. Some of functions are given below:

- **Habitat**: Tens of thousands of birds, mammals, fish, and other wildlife depend on estuaries.
- **Nursery**: Many marine organisms, most commercially valuable fish species included, depend on estuaries at some point during their development from egg to adult.
- **Productivity**: A healthy, untended estuary produces from four to ten times the weight of organic matter produced by a cultivated corn field of the same size.
- **Water Filtration:** Water draining off the uplands carries a load of sediments and nutrients. As the water flows through salt marsh peat and the dense mesh of marsh grass blades, much of the sediment and nutrient load is filtered out. This filtration process creates cleaner and clearer water.
- **Flood Control:** Porous, resilient salt marsh soils and grasses absorb flood waters and dissipate storm surges. Salt marsh dominated estuaries provide natural buffers between the land and the ocean. They protect upland organisms as well as billions of dollars of human real estate.

Threats to Estuaries

Estuaries are vital links in the life histories of more than two thirds of all our commercially important fishes and shellfishes, most of the near-shore and intertidal sport species, and all anadromous fishes. Pollution of our estuaries is among the greatest threats to our environmental health. Estuarine pollution may be defined as the human introduction to an estuary of any substances such as chemicals and waste products that are hazardous or potentially harmful to the estuarine ecosystem. This includes pollutants that are directly toxic to plants and animals, as well as materials that overload the estuary's capacity to assimilate wastes and thus deplete essential oxygen. Toxic substances commonly found in estuaries include heavy metals, pulp-mill effluents, insecticides, herbicides, and various chemicals and petroleum products. Further stressing estuarine waters are such contaminants as sewage, slaughter house and seafood-processing wastes, tree bark and saw dust from saw mills, wood fibers from log-rafting operations, phosphates and nitrates from detergents and fertilizers, and livestock wastes.

Pollution from upland areas often damages estuaries. Dams can block natural stream and river routes and cut off freshwater from estuaries. When that happens, the fresh and saltwater balance of the estuary is changed and the estuary can be seriously damaged. Development can damage or even destroy estuaries. In the past, many people thought estuaries were wasted land and many estuaries where filled in and built on. Today, we are much more aware of the important role estuaries play in the environment and many people are working to save these areas.

Conclusion

An ecosystem is a natural unit of living and nonliving parts that interact to produce a stable system. An aquatic ecosystem is an ecosystem in a body of water. Aquatic ecosystems include ponds, lakes, streams, rivers, oceans and estuaries. Ponds, lakes, streams and rivers form fresh water ecosystems while as oceans and estuaries form marine water ecosystems. A pond is shallow enough that sunshine can reach the bottom, allowing rooted plants to grow completely across it. Pond ecosystem has two main components. The abiotic components of pond ecosystem are formed as a result of the mixture of some organic and inorganic materials. The biotic components of pond ecosystem consist of producers, consumers and decomposers so is in other ecosystems. Phytoplanktons are the producers of pond ecosystem along with other floating plants. The energy produced by the autotrophs is passed through "eat and being eaten chain to higher organisms. A lake is a body of relatively still water of considerable size, localized in a basin that is surrounded by land apart from a river, stream, or other form of moving water that serves to feed or drain the lake. In lakes, much of the species diversity is concentrated in the littoral zone, near the shore, where algae and plants thrive in the abundant light needed for photosynthesis. A stream is a body of water with a current, confined within a bed and stream banks. Streams are important as conduits in the water cycle, instruments in groundwater recharge, and corridors for fish and wildlife migration. River is a large natural stream of water emptying into an ocean, lake, or other body of water and usually fed along its course by converging tributaries. River ecosystems are prime examples of lotic ecosystems. River ecosystems encompass river channels and its floodplains and form a diverse mosaic of habitats with the riparian area at the transition zone between land and water. The energy and matter produced by plants and other autotrophs are distributed to other organisms in an ecosystem through pathways known as food chains and food webs. Marine ecosystems are among the largest of Earth's aquatic ecosystems. They include oceans, salt marsh and intertidal ecology, estuaries and lagoons, mangroves and coral reefs, the deep sea and the sea floor. They can be contrasted with freshwater ecosystems, which have a lower salt content. Marine waters cover two-thirds of the surface of the Earth. The ocean is biggest among marine ecosystems, principally comprises Earth's hydrosphere and therefore is integral to all known life, forms part of the carbon cycle, and influences climate and weather patterns. It is the habitat of 230,000 known species, although much of the ocean's depths remain unexplored, and over two million marine species are estimated to exist. An estuary is a body of water formed where freshwater from rivers and streams flows into the ocean, mixing with the seawater. Estuaries and the lands surrounding them are places of transition from land to sea, and from freshwater to saltwater. Estuaries are more biologically productive than any other marine ecosystem.

GLOSSARY

Ecosystem: An ecosystem is a natural unit of living and nonliving parts that interact to produce a stable system.

Ecology: Ecology is the study of ecosystems, or how living things relate to the environment and to one another.

Pond: A pond ecosystem refers to fresh water ecosystem where there are communities of organism dependent on each other with the prevailing water environment for their nutrients and survival.

Biotic components: Living components

Abiotic components: Non living components

Producer: These are those organisms which manufacture their own food in presence sunlight.

Saprotroph: Saprotroph is a term used for organisms which obtain nutrients from dead organic matter.

Phytoplankton: Phytoplankton are photosynthesizing microscopic organisms that inhabit the upper sunlit layer of almost all oceans and bodies of fresh water.

Habitat: A habitat is an ecological or environmental area that is inhabited by a particular species of animal, plant, or other type of organism.

Food Chain: A food chain is the sequence of who eats whom in a biological community (an ecosystem) to obtain nutrition.

Food Web: A food web is a graphical description of feeding relationships among species in an ecological community, that is, of who eats whom.

Profundal zone: The Profundal zone is a deep zone of an inland body of freestanding water, such as a lake or pond, located below the range of effective light penetration.

Poikilolthermic: A poikilotherm is an organism whose internal temperature varies considerably.

Aphotic region: The aphotic zone is the portion of a lake or ocean where there is little or no sunlight.

Thermocline: The thermocline is the transition layer between the mixed layer at the surface and the deep water layer. The definitions of these layers are based on temperature.

Wetlands: A wetland is a land area that is saturated with water, either permanently or seasonally, such that it takes on the characteristics of a distinct ecosystem.

Ocean: An ocean is a body of saline water that composes much of a planet's hydrosphere.

Hydrosphere: A hydrosphere is the total amount of water on a planet. The hydrosphere includes water that is on the surface of the planet, underground, and in the air.

Epipelagic: The uppermost part of the oceanic zone, lying above the mesopelagic zone that receives enough sunlight to allow photosynthesis.

Mesopelagic: A layer of the oceanic zone lying beneath the epipelagic zone and above the bathypelagic zone, at depths generally between 200 and 1,000 m.

Bathypelagic: A layer of the oceanic zone lying below the mesopelagic zone and above the abyssopelagic zone, at depths generally between about 1,000 and 4,000 m.

Abyssopelagic: A layer of the oceanic zone lying below the bathypelagic zone and above the hadopelagic zone.

Predators: In ecology, predation is a biological interaction where a predator (an organism that is hunting) feeds on its prey (the organism that is attacked.

Estuary: An estuary is a partly enclosed coastal body of brackish water with one or more rivers or streams flowing into it, and with a free connection to the open sea.

Salt marsh: A salt marsh, also known as a coastal salt marsh or a tidal marsh, is a coastal ecosystem in the upper coastal intertidal zone between land and open salt water or brackish water that is regularly flooded by the tides.

Sea grasses: Sea grasses are flowering plants, which grow in marine, fully saline environments

Mangrove: Mangroves are various types of trees up to medium height and shrubs that grow in saline coastal sediment habitats in the tropics and subtropics.

Environment: The natural environment encompasses all living and non-living things occurring naturally on earth.

REFERENCES

Gupta, R. S. and Zeitlinger, E. D. 2001. The Indian Ocean - A Perspective: A. A. Balkema, a Member of Swets and Zeitlenger Publishers, India.

Kantha, L. H. and Clayson, C. A. 2003. Numerical Models of Oceans and Oceanic Processes. Academic press, Harcourt Science and Technology Company, California.

Robert, G. Wetzel. 1982. Periphyton of Freshwater Ecosystems: Proceedings of the First International Workshop on Periphyton of Freshwater Ecosystems, Sweden.

Scheffer, M. 2004. Ecology of Shallow Lakes. Kluwer Academic Publishers, Neatherlands.

Steinberg, C. and Richard, F. W. 1992. Acidification of Freshwater Ecosystems, Implications for the Future: Report of the Dahlem Workshop on Acidification of Freshwater Ecosystems held in Berlin.

LINKS

wikipedia.org/wiki/Environment_(biophysical)

en.wikipedia.org/wiki/Ocean

wikipedia.org/wiki/Mangrove

lingerdenver.com

en.wikipedia.org/wiki/ Freshwater ecosystem

users.rcn.com/jkimball.ma.ultranet/BiologyPages/F/Freshwater.html

Water Management and Aquatic Ecosystem **Pages 172-183**
Edited by: Dr. Resham Bhalla & Dr. Pawan Kumar 'Bharti'
ISBN: 978-93-86841-96-4
Edition: 2019
Published by: Discovery Publishing House Pvt. Ltd., New Delhi (India)

9

Aquatic Ecology and Plankton Diversity of a Freshwater Lake (L5) at Bharti Island, Larsemann Hills, East Antarctica

[1]Dr. Pawan Kumar 'Bharti'

ABSTRACT

Bharti Island of Larsemann Hills in east Antarctica was selected as a sampling site for the present study. Water sample was collected from a freshwater lake during XXXth Indian Scientific Expedition to Antarctica (ISEA) and analysed for the physico-chemical parameters, major elements, trace metals & major plankton diversity in surface lake water by following standard methodology. The concentrations of metals Cu, Pb, Cd, Zn and Cr were measured using (ICP-OES) Inductively Coupled Plasma Optical Emission Spectroscopy. Total phytoplankton and total zooplankton were found to be 2680 Ind./m^3 and 340 Ind./m^3 respectively. Bacillariophyceae family and Cladocera group members was found as dominant among plankton diversity.

Key words: Aquatic ecology, Water quality monitoring, Antarctic lake, Bharti Island, water pollution

Introduction

Freshwater on Earth's surface is in the form of ice sheets, ice caps, glaciers, icebergs, bogs, ponds, lakes, rivers and streams, and underground as groundwater in aquifers and underground streams. Freshwater is generally distinguished by having low concentrations of dissolved salts and other total dissolved solids. The term fresh water does not have the same meaning as potable water. Much of the surface fresh water and ground water is not suitable for drinking without some kind of purification because of the presence of chemical or biological contaminants. The source of freshwater is precipitation from the atmosphere in the form of mist, rain and snow. Freshwater falling as mist, rain or snow contains materials dissolved from the atmosphere and material from the sea and land over which the rain bearing clouds have traveled.

The Larsemann Hills range is on the Ingrid Christensen Coast in East Antarctica, which includes Bharti Island, Fisher Island, McLeod Island,

1 Antarctica Laboratory, R & D Division, Shriram Institute for Industrial Research, 19, University Road, Delhi-110 007, India

Broknes Peninsula, Stornes Peninsula, and several other islands, promontories, and nunataks. The ice-free area consists of two major peninsulas, four minor peninsulas, and approximately 130 near shore islands. The Larsemann Hills area contains more than 150 freshwater lakes at different Islands and peninsulas. Lakes are important feature of the Earth's landscape which are not only the source of precious water, but provide valuable habitats to plants and animals, moderate hydrological cycles, influence microclimate, enhance the aesthetic beauty of the landscape and extend many recreational opportunities to humankind. The lakes are also used for drinking, irrigation, fishing, eco-tourism, etc. apart from the above advantages (Bharti and Niyogi, 2015a).

Antarctic lakes represent a relatively unique ecosystem in general; however, they remain less intensely studied than lowland lakes, mainly because of their remoteness and the short summer open-water period (Bhat *et al.*, 2011). Nevertheless, Antarctic lakes are sensitive reference systems of global climatic change and other human impacts on a high altitude (Bharti, 2012a). In fact, although remote high altitude lakes are in general protected from direct human impacts, in the last few decades they have been increasingly affected by airborne contaminants, such as acids and nutrients (Rogora *et al.*, 2006), heavy metals and organic pollutants (Carrera *et al.*, 2002).

These freshwater lakes ecosystems have a relatively simple food web and react more sensitively to environmental changes than other lakes, due to the extreme environmental conditions i.e. low temperature, strong radiations, mostly low buffering capacity and low nutrient level (Bharti and Gajananda, 2013). Even minor impacts are able to significantly affect the physical and chemical properties of soft water high altitude lakes, to induce changes in species composition and abundance of the biota and to cause accumulation of trace substances in higher trophic organisms (Hofer *et al.*, 2001). In spite of the socio-economic and ecological importance of these lakes, better knowledge of several ecological aspects is needed for better understanding of their relationships with the environmental variables (Bharti and Niyogi, 2015b). These lakes have received little attention so far in terms of their limnology, diversity, conservation and water management, but they are becoming increasingly important due to the possible consequences of the global climate change (Bharti and Gajananda, 2013). The different problems of the lake include excessive influx of sediments from the lake catchment, discharge of untreated or partially treated waste waters, dumping of solid waste, entry of diffused nutrients source from agricultural and forestry, improper management of storm water, over abstraction, over-exploitation of lake for activities like recreation, fishing, encroachments, land reclamation etc causing lake water shrinkage, shoreline erosion and impacting the lake hydrology, deteriorating water quality, impacting biodiversity, bringing climate changes etc. There is, therefore, an immediate need to know the pollution status of a lake at given time so that necessary conservation activities may be undertaken to regain/ improve the health of water body (Sharma *et al.*, 2010).

The Larsemann Hills area (69°20′–69°28′S, 76°00′–76°30′E) is an ice-free oasis on the Ingrid Christensen Coast of Princess Elizabeth Land, East Antarctica, that includes various Islands and Peninsula, promontories, and nunataks (Fig. 1A). The deglaciated terrain constitutes a transitional zone between marine and glacial ecosystems and includes gently rolling hills, glacially polished and striated bedrock hummocks, scoured surfaces, and broad valleys interspersed with lakes of varying dimensions. Indian scientific studies in the Larsemann Hills started in 2003-04 by various researchers and the present work was carried out from 2010 to 2011 during the construction of the third Indian research station Bharti. To investigate the aquatic ecology, lake water chemistry and characteristics in the area, water sample was collected from a freshwater lake on Bharti Island.

Material and Methods

Study Area

Environmental monitoring and impact assessment studies were carried out in Antarctica during the austral summer seasons of various Indian Scientific Expeditions to Antarctica (SIIR, 2012).

Bharti Island of Larsemann Hills in east Antarctica was selected as a sampling site for the present study. Water sample was collected from L-5 lake of Bharti Island during XXXth Indian Scientific Expedition to Antarctica (ISEA) and analysed for the physico-chemical parameters, major elements and trace metal in surface lake water (Bharti, 2012b). The location map of study area is given in the Figure 9.1A and 9.1B. One sampling point L-5 was selected at Bharti Island, Larsemann hills in east Antarctica. Geo-coordinates of sampling point are given in Table 9.1.

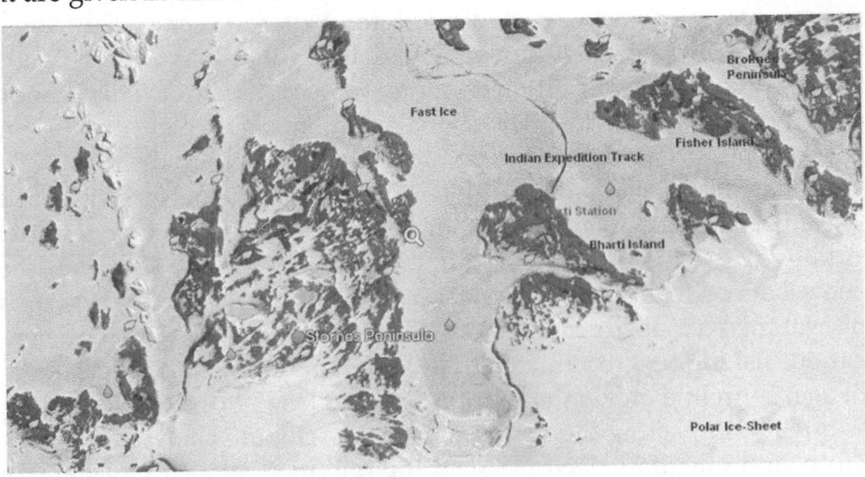

Fig. 9.1 (A-B): Location map of the study area and sampling site

Sampling

The sampling of lake water was carried out in the 1 L PET bottle and stored in a cold storage immediately after preservation by 1 ml 70% HNO_3. The samples were transported to the laboratory after completion of expedition and analyzed for further analysis of the physico-chemical parameters, major elements, trace metals, plankton diversity and microbiological parameters.

Analytical Methods

Temperature and pH of lake water samples were recorded onsite using thermometer and digital pH meter. Standards methods as described in APHA (2005) were followed for the dilution and analysis for various parameters. Laboratory analysis work for metal analysis was carried out with the help of ICP-OES (Inductively Coupled Plasma Optical Emission spectroscopy).

Water sample was collected from sampling station on 16 January 2011. Neatly cleaned and rinsed double Stoppard polyethylene bottles were used for collection of water samples. Bottles were kept in ice box and brought to the laboratory for further analysis. Some of the physico-chemical characteristics of water including water temperature, color, pH were determined onsite using mercury thermometer, visual, digital pH meter respectively. While dissolved oxygen, turbidity and total dissolved solids were analyzed using Orion onsite water quality monitoring kit at the sampling stations. Separate samples were collected in sterile bottles for microbiological studies. Lake water was concentrated using plankton net and collected in a tube for further laboratory studies. Collected plankton were preserved by adding 4% Formalin solution and Lugol's solution. Other parameters including plankton diversity and metals were analyzed in the laboratory following the methods of APHA (2005) & Trivedi and Goel (1984). Plankton counting was conducted with the help of Bogorov / Sedwick Rafter Plankton Counter chambers as described in APHA (2005).

Results and Discussion

Geographical locations of sampling points are given in Table 9.1. Physico-chemical characteristics and trace metals of lake water sample are given in Table 9.2. Lake water temperature was found in very low conditions i.e. 1.0 °C. The lake water chemistry of the area is greatly influenced by chemistry of the host rock rather than precipitation and evaporation (Gibbs, 1970). Numerous examples have appeared in the literatures which indeed support the idea that in an unpolluted environment, where anthropogenic activities are negligible, water quality can be correlated with minerals present in the bed rock (Asthana *et al.*, 2013).

General Physico-chemical Variables

Lake water was found to be free from any colour, odour or turbidity. pH of selected freshwater lake sample was slightly acidic in nature and found to be 5.9. Total hardness of lake water sample was found to be 25 mg/l, while alkalinity was found to be 10 mg/l. Total dissolved solids were recorded 97 mg/l, whereas dissolved oxygen was measured to be 10.9 mg/l. Total organic carbon in lake water sample was found 0.085 mg/l.

Dominant Elements

Chlorides and calcium were found to be the dominant constituents among the lake water contents. Maximum chloride and calcium were found to be 48 mg/l and 6.7 mg/l. Besides these, sulphate (7.0 mg/l), Nitrate (1.1 mg/l) and phosphate (0.025 mg/l) were also detected in L-5 lake water sample at Bharti station, Larsemann Hills.

Table 9.1: Location of Lake's Water Sampling Site at Bharti Island

S.No.	Sample ID	Date	Latitude (S)	Longitude (E)	Altitude (m)
1	L-5	16-01-2011	69° 24′ 26.0″	76° 10′ 59.0″	52

Table 9.2: Results of Lake's Water Sample from Bharti Island

S.No.	Parameter	IS: 10500-1991 Desirable (permissible)	L-5
1	Colour, Hazen unit	5, Max.	<5
2	Odour	Unobjectionable (UO)	UO
3	Turbidity, NTU	5, Max. (10)	<1

4	pH	6.5-8.5	5.9
5	Total hardness (as $CaCO_3$), mg/l	300, Max. (600)	25
6	Iron (as Fe), mg/l	0.3, Max. (1.0)	0.06
7	Chloride (as Cl), mg/l	250, Max. (1000)	48
8	Fluoride (as F), mg/l	1.0, Max. (1.5)	0.08
9	Dissolved Solids, mg/l	500, Max. (2000)	97
10	Magnesium (as Mg), mg/l	30, Max. (100)	3.8
11	Calcium (as Ca), mg/l	75, Max. (200)	6.7
12	Copper (as Cu), mg/l	0.05, Max. (1.5)	<0.001
13	Manganese (as Mn), mg/l	0.1, Max. (0.3)	0.003
14	Sulphate (as SO_4), mg/l	200, Max.	7
15	Nitrates (as NO_3), mg/l	45, Max	1.1
16	Phenolic Compounds (as C_6H_5OH), mg/l	0.002, Max	ND
17	Mercury (as Hg), mg/l	0.001, Max.	<0.001
18	Cadmium (as Cd), mg/l	0.01, Max.	<0.01
19	Selenium (as Se), mg/l	0.01, Max.	<0.005
20	Arsenic as As,mg/l	0.01, Max	<0.005
21	Cyanide (as CN), mg/l	0.05, Max	<0.01
22	Lead (as Pb), mg/l	0.05, Max	<0.01
23	Zinc (as Zn), mg/l	5 Max. (15)	0.01
24	Anionic Detergents (MBAS) mg/l	0.2, Max	ND
25	Chromium (as Cr^{+6}), mg/l	0.05, Max	<0.01
26	Mineral Oil, mg/l	0.01, Max	ND
27	Alkalinity (as $CaCO_3$), mg/l	200 Max.(600)	10
28	Aluminum (as Al), mg/l	0.2, Max	<0.02
29	Phosphate (as PO4), mg/l	0.05, Max.	0.025
30	Boron (as B), mg/l	1, Max (5)	<0.001
31	Total Organic Carbon (TOC), mg/l	-	0.085
32	Dissolved Oxygen (DO), mg/l	-	10.9

(BDL- Below Detection Limit)

Table 9.3: Microbiological Studies of Lake Water Sample from Bharti Island (30th ISEA)

S.No.	Parameters	L-5
1	**Total Bacterial Count/ml** (As per guidelines of IS : 5402-2002, Reaff 2007)	5.4×10^2
2	**Psychrophillic Count/ml** (As per guidelines of IS: 1479 p-3, 1977, Reaff: 2003)	71

3	**MPN Coliform /100 ml** (As per guidelines of IS:1622-1981, Reaff : 2003) Ed 2.4 (2003-05)	No growth observed
4	**Yeast & Mould Count/ml** (As per guidelines of IS: 5403 1999, Reaff: 2005)	Absent
5	**Salmonella/ 25 ml** (As per guidelines of IS: 5887 (p-3) 1999 Reaff: 2005)	Absent
6	**Staphylococcus aureus/25 ml** (As per guidelines of IS : 5887 P-2 1976 Reaff : 2005)	Absent
7	**Pseudomonas spp./10 ml** (As per guidelines of IS:13428, Amn.D, 2005)	Absent

Table 9.4: Plankton Diversity in Lake Water at Bharti Island (30th ISEA)

S.No.	Plankton group	Nos. of Plankton (Ind./ m^3)
A. Phytoplankton		
1	Chlorophyacae	600
2	Basillariophyace	1000
3	Cyanophyacae	80
4	Rhodophyacae	-
5	Others / Unidentified	1000
B. Zooplankton		
1	Protozoa	20
2	Rotifera	-
3	Copepoda	60
4	Cladocera	120
5	Decapoda	-
6	Others / Unidentified	140

Metals

Magnesium was found to be 3.8 mg/l, while iron was found to be 0.06 mg/l in lake water collected from freshwater lake L-5 at Bharti Island. Zinc and manganese were also detected 0.01 mg/l and 0.003 mg/l respectively. Fluoride was found to be 0.08 mg/l in lake water sample. Trace metals like cadmium and aluminum were found below detection level in lake water sample. Similar trend was observed for mercury, selenium, arsenic, lead & chromium metals in lake water sample collected from Bharti Island. Few metals are biologically essential to living organisms in trace quantities in aquatic ecosystems. These trace metals may re-circulate from sediment and became available for biota (Campbell *et al.*, 1988).

Complex Organic Compounds

Phenolic compounds (as C_6H_5OH), Anionic detergents (MBAS) and mineral oil were not detected in lake water sample at Bharti Island in east Antarctica.

Microbiology of Lake Water

Results for microbiological parameters of lake water samples are given in Table 9.3. Total bacterial count and psychrophillic counts were found to be 5.4×10^2 and 71 cfu respectively. No growth was observed for MPN coliform in the sample. Yeast & Moulds, Salmonella, Staphylococcus and Pseudomonas spp. were also found to be absent in freshwater lake water sample. Few similar studies were also carried out by Bharti and Niyogi (2015c).

Plankton

Plankton community consists of two major groups namely phytoplankton and zooplankton in an aquatic ecosystem. Both groups have further various subgroups (families or phylum) having different characteristics, body structure and life cycles.

Under phytoplankton group, Chlorophyceae members (600 individuals/m^3), Basillariophyceae members (1000 individuals/m^3) and Cyanophyceae members (80 individuals/m^3) were observed, while Rhodophyceae members were not found at the time of sampling. Some unidentified or phytoplankton of other groups (1000 individuals/m^3) were also found in the water of L-5 freshwater lake at Bharti Island. Among the Phytoplankton community, Basillariophyaceae and Chlorophyaceae groups were found dominant in the lake water at Bharti Island. Diatoms were found as a major constituent of Phytoplankton. Pinnularia, Nitzschia and Achnanthes were the major diatoms. Frazilaria, Navicula and Hantzchia might be present in Antarctic fresh waters as per some researchers (Gupta, 2002). Besides this, evidences of the presence of Nostoc, Osillotoria, in Antarctic water were also observed by Palanisamy (2010). Few unidentified Phytoplankton genera were also encountered in lake waters during the present study.

In zooplankton group, members of phylum Protozoa (20 individuals/m^3), phylum Rotifera (0 individuals/m^3), phylum Copepoda (60 individuals/m^3), phylum Cladocera (120 individuals/m^3) were observed, while Decapoda members were not found during the sampling period. Some unidentified or zooplankton of other groups (140 individuals/m^3) were also found in the water of L-5 freshwater lake at Bharti Island. Few Daphnia and others unidentified Ciliates were also found in Lake L-5, which indicates presence of some new species of Plankton (Bahrti and Niyogi, 2015b). During the study period in 30th ISEA, the lakes were found in frozen condition so the sample could not be collected for benthic diversity assessment from the deep regions of lake. Results for phytoplankton and zooplankton community in freshwater lake ecosystem are given in Table 9.4 and Figure 9.5 and Figure 9.6 respectively.

After evaluating general physico-chemical parameters, heavy metals and organic compounds in lake water, it has been observed that the water of the selected lake has no pollution load and no significance impact of any anthropogenic activity. Low organic load in lake water indicate the oligotrophic stage of lake ecosystems (Bharti and Niyogi, 2015a; Bharti and Niyogi, 2015b; Bharti and Niyogi, 2015c). In oligotrophic lakes that are low in primary productivity as a result of low nutrient content, the chemistry depends mainly on lithology, precipitation, evaporation and period of sojourn of water in the basin (Shrivastava *et al.*, 2011).

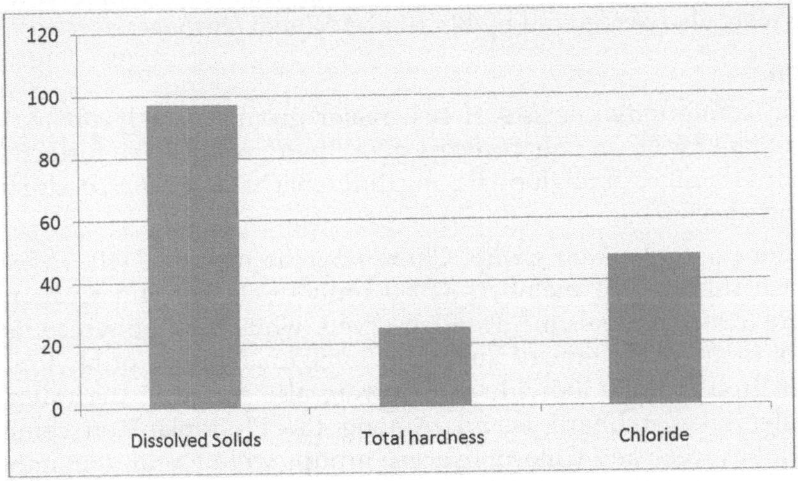

Fig. 9.2: Showing total dissolved solids, hardness and chlorides in lake water (in mg l^{-1})

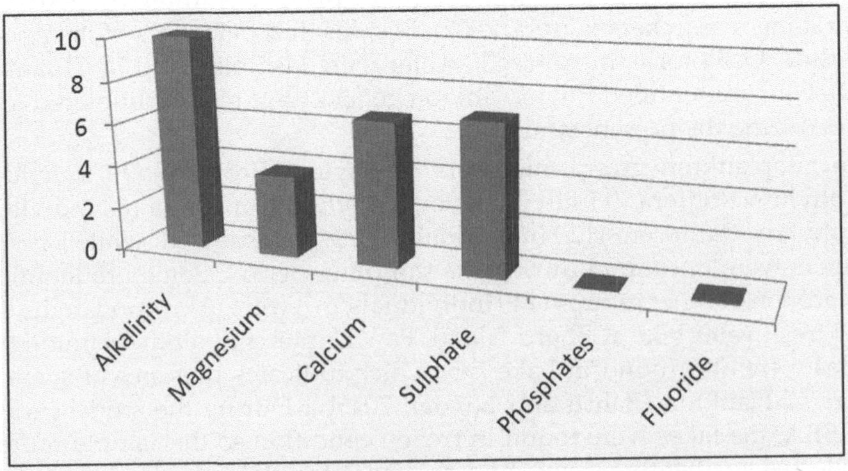

Fig. 9.3: Showing major elements in lake water (in mg l^{-1})

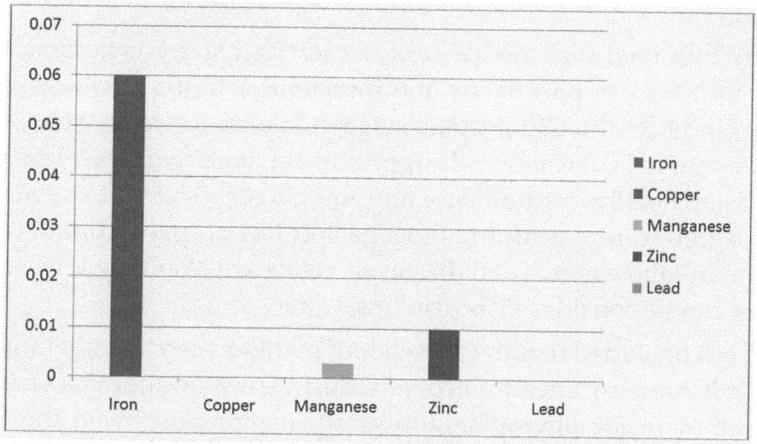

Fig. 9.4: Showing major heavy metals in lake water (in mg l^{-1})

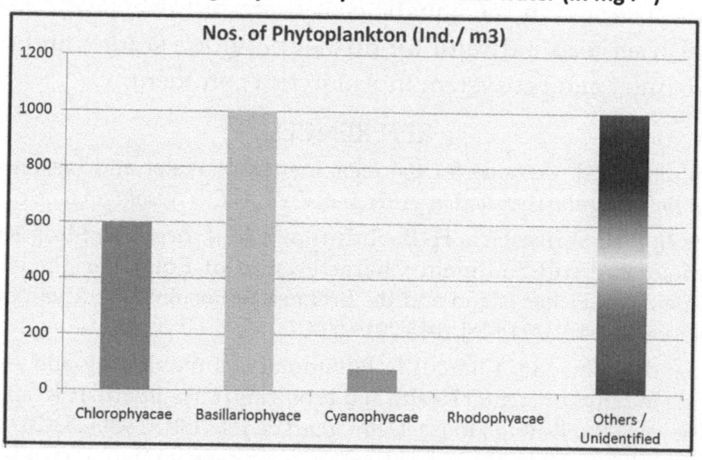

Fig. 9.5: Showing major phytoplankton group in lake water (in Ind./m^3)

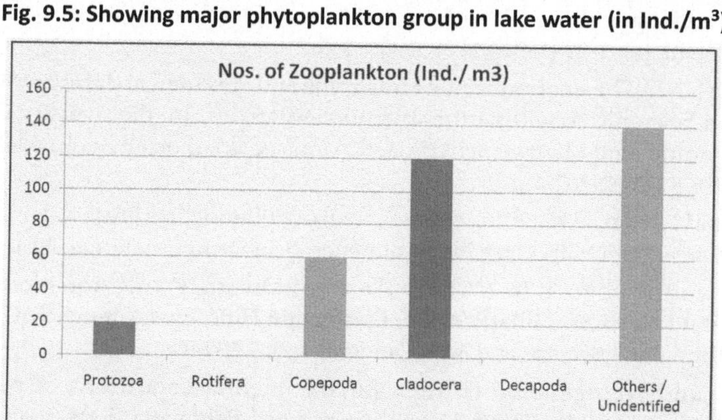

Fig. 9.6: Showing major zooplankton group in lake water (in Ind./m^3)

Conclusion

It has been observed that the water of the selected lake has no pollution load and no significance impact of any anthropogenic activity. Low organic load in lake water indicate the oligotrophic stage of lake ecosystems. High dissolved oxygen content in lake water will support to aquatic organisms. This is indeed very good and healthy condition for any aquatic ecosystem. Lake water sample was found free from harmful pathogens and has no psychrophillic bacterial population in lake water. Total dissolved solids are also very low, so the raw lake water can be considered as drinking water.

It can be concluded that the presence of plankton community indicated the initial establishment of a healthy ecosystem in freshwater lake L-5 at Bharti Island. Abundance of major phytoplankton group members showed the favorable circumstances for photosynthesis in aquatic ecosystem. Phytoplankton and zooplankton observed in the aquatic ecosystem of freshwater lakes of Bharti Island can also serve as indicator for further pollution studies and to know the status of pristine Lake Ecosystem in Antarctica continent.

REFERENCES

APHA (2005): Standard Methods for the Examination of Water and Wastewater. *21st Ed. American Public Health Association, APHA, AWWA, WEF, Washington, D. C.* pp: 1170.

Asthana, Rajesh; P K. Shrivastava, H. B. Shrivastava, M. J. Beg & Pradeep Kumar (2013): Hydrochemistry and Sediment Characteristics of Polar Periglacial Lacustrine Environments on Fisher Island and the Broknes Peninsula, East Antarctica. *Adv Polar Sci,* 24: 4-xxx, doi: 10.3724/SP.J.1085.2013.00XXX.

Bharti, P. K. and Gajananda, Kh. (2013): Environmental monitoring and Assessment in Antarctica, In: Environmental Health and Problems (Eds.- Bharti, P. K. and Gajananda, Kh.), Discovery Publishing House, Delhi, pp. 178-186 (ISBN: 93-5056-263-4).

Bharti, Pawan K. (2012a): Anthropogenic Activities and Global Climate Change, In: Climate Change and Agriculture (Eds.- Bharti, P.K. and Chauhan, A.), Discovery Publishing House, Delhi, pp: 1-22 (ISBN: 9789350561485).

Bharti, Pawan K. (2012b): Environmental Monitoring and Assessment during the Construction of Indian Scientific Base (Bharti Station) in Antarctica, In: Biodiversity Conservation and Environmental Management (Eds.- Khanna et al.), Biotech Books, Delhi, pp. 81-97 (ISBN: 978-81-7622-262-4).

Bharti, P.K. and Niyogi, U.K. (2015a): Assessment of Pollution in a Freshwater Lake at Fisher Island, Larsemann Hills Over East Antarctica. Science International, 3(1): 25-30.

Bharti, P.K. and Niyogi, U.K. (2015b): Plankton Diversity and Aquatic Ecology of a Freshwater Lake (L3) at Bharti Island, Larsemann Hills, East Antarctica. Global Journal of Environmental Science and Management, 1(2): 137-144.

Bharti, P.K. and Niyogi, U.K. (2015c): Environmental conditions of psychrophilic Pseudomonas spp. in Antarctic Lake at Stornes Peninsula, Larsemann Hills, East Antarctica. International Journal of Environmental Monitoring and Protection, 2(3): 27-30.

Bhat. F.A., Yousuf, A.R., Aftab, A., Arshid, J., Mahdi, M. D., and Balkhi M. H., (2011): Ecology and Biodiversity in Pangong Tso (lake) and Its Inlet Stream in Ladakh, India. *International Journal of Biodiversity and Conservation*, 3(10): 501-511.

Campbell, P.G.C., A. G. Lewis, P. M. Chapman, A. A. Crowder, W. K. Fletcher, B. Imber, S. N. Luoma, P. M. Stokes, and M. Winfrey (1988): Biologically Available Metals in Sediments. Publication No. NRCC 27694, *National Research Council of Canada*, Ottawa, Canada.

Carrera. G., Fernandez, P., Grimalt, J.O., Ventura. M., Camarero. L, Catalan, J., Nickus, U., Thies, H., and Psenner R., (2002): Atmospheric Deposition of Organochlorine Compounds to Remote High Mountain Lakes of Europe. *Environ. Sci. Technol.*, 36: 2581-2588.

Gibbs, R.J. (1970): Mechanisms Controlling World's Water Chemistry. *Science*, 170: 1080-1090.

Gupta, R.K. (2002): Morphotaxonomical survey of diatoms in Schirmacher Oasis, east Antarctica. Eighteenth Indian Expedition to Antarctica Scientific Report, Department of Ocean Development, Technical Publication No.-16, pp: 213-226.

Hofer. R., Lackner, R., Kargl, J., Thaler, B., Tait, D., Bonetti, L., Vistocco, R., and Flaim G., (2001): Organo-chlorine and Metal Accumulation in Fish (Phoxinus phoxinus) Along a Northsouth Transect in the Alps. *Water, Air and Soil Pollution*, 125: 189-200.

Palanisamy, M. (2010): Studies on Diatom flora of Schirmacher Oasis, East Antarctica. Twenty-third Indian Expedition to Antarctica Scientific Report, NCAOR, Ministry of Earth Sciences, Technical Publication No.-21, pp: 173-190.

Rogora. M., Mosello, R., Arisci, S., Brizzio, M.C., Barbieri, A., Balestrini, R., Waldner, P., Schmitt, M., Stahli, M., Thimonier, A., Kalina, M., Puxbaum, H., Nickus, U., Ulrich, E., and Probst A., (2006): An Overview of Atmospheric Deposition Chemistry Over the Alps: Present Status and Long-term Trends. *Hydrobiologia*, 562, pp 17-40.

Sharma, M.P.; Arun Kumar and Shalini Rajvanshi (2010): Assessment of Trophic State of Lakes: A Case of Mansi Ganga Lake in India. *Hydro Nepal*, 6: 65-72.

Shrivastava, P.K.; Asthana, R.; Beg, M.J. and Ravindra, R. (2011): Ionic Characters of Lake Water of Bharti Promontory, Larsemann Hills, East Antarctica. *Journal Geological Society of India*, Vol.78, pp: 217-225

SIIR (2012): Long Term Environmental Monitoring Study at New Scientific Base Bharti at Larsemann Hills, 27th, 28th, 29th, 30th ISEA Combined Report to NCAOR, Submitted by Shriram Institute of Industrial Research, Delhi, India.

Trivedi, R. K. and Goel, P. K. (1984): Chemical and Biological Methods for Water Pollution Studies. *Enviro Media Publication, Karad*. pp. 225.

Water Management and Aquatic Ecosystem **Pages 184-190**
Edited by: Dr. Resham Bhalla & Dr. Pawan Kumar 'Bharti'
ISBN: 978-93-86841-96-4
Edition: 2019
Published by: Discovery Publishing House Pvt. Ltd., New Delhi (India)

10 Need of Conservation Strategies for Rehabilitation of Traditional Water System in India

[1]Anshul Sharma and [2]Dr. Pawan Kumar 'Bharti'

ABSTRACT

Water bodies have the high significance value for the human civilization since the ancient time. In many parts of India, there was a proper system for drinking water requirement and supply. Various rivers, ponds, freshwater lakes and dug wells were the prime sources of drinking water. Nowadays, these traditional water bodies are shrinking and dying day by day. Recent research data indicate the decline in the total area of traditional water bodies. Thus, there is a strong need to make a strategy to protect, conserve and rehabilitate these traditional water resources. This article highlights the present status of these rational water resources and suggests some measures for the conservation and protection of theses water bodies.

Keywords: Water resources, Conservation strategies, Rehabilitation, Traditional water system.

Introduction

Water is very much essential for the existence and survival of all life forms on Earth. Hence the human settlements the world over have succeed so long they had enough water for human consumption and growing crops. The Indian subcontinent has witnessed many such early settlements that devised their own systems of water harvesting, which could be either from surface water or ground water. In the medieval age areas dominated by feudal system, some of these systems took more scientific form and surprisingly, many of these water extraction storage and conveyance structures are still in use in some parts of the country. In other parts of the country, especially in the hilly and mountainous terrains, the communities have devised certain means of water tapping and transfer systems that have been used for generations to provide water for drinking and agriculture (Bharti, 2012).

1 Assistant Professor Department of Food Science and Biotechnology, Gachon University, Seongnam, 13120, South Korea

2 Antarctica Laboratory, R & D Division, Shriram Institute for Industrial Research, 19, University Road, Delhi-110 007, India

In India, one may observe regions varying in temperature, elevation and rainfall. As a result, the climate is drastically varying from one place to another for instance, when northern Himalayan regions is compared with that of the southern coastal regions or the dry western and central regions are compared with the west eastern and north eastern regions. Hence, the methods of traditional systems of water utilization have evolved very differently in different places over the years. In general, the main sources of water are:

- Stream and river water
- Rain water (rain water harvesting)
- Ground water

Water Status in India

Water is one of the blessings of mother nature and has unique place as a renewable resource. It forms basis for human existence and progress. For any country, it is mandatory to manage natural resources sustainably for poverty reduction and surge in economic growth. Forefathers in ancient India realized that human civilization couldn't grow without conservation of natural water. Therefore, wisely they nurtured the tradition of water harvesting in different customs in various parts of the country. Depending on the resources available, Indians, over time, developed a range of techniques to harvest every possible form of water. India is traversed by 12 major river systems. Out of total water content available (Figure 10.1), 85% is used for agriculture purpose, 8% for domestic purpose and 5% for industries (FAO, 2003).Water demand for irrigation is projected to rise from 541 BCM in 2000 to 910 BCM in 2025, and to 1072 BCM in 2050 (CWC, 2005). According to World Bank the total cost of environmental damage in India amounts to US $ 9.7 billion annually, of this, 59 percent results from the health impacts of water pollution (Nigam *et al.*, 1995).

Rapid urbanization, industrialization and population growth has impacted enormously our natural resources. Specifically, the water system in India resulted in drying up natural and traditional water bodies, decreased soil moisture content and water tables level. This resulted in deteriorated quality of the water in India. Although India is one of the wettest countries in the world (i.e. it receives about 1150 mm of rainfall annually), but water availability is highly uneven in different parts of the country (Hussain *et al.*, 2014). Over 80% of water used for agriculture related activities considered major source of water wastage and pollution. Near 2020, it is expected that India will be a 'water stressed' country with per capita availability declining to 1600 cu m/person/year.4(Ideally it should be 1700 cu. m/person/year.) (Chaterjee, 2016).

India has about 16 percent of the worldwide population as paralleled to only 4 percent of its water resources. Estimates indicate that surface and ground water availability is around 1,869 billion cubic meters (BCM). Of this, 40 per cent is not available for use due to geological and topographical reasons. With a population of over 1,000 million, the per capita water availability is around 1,170 cu m/person/year (NIH, 2010). In coming years, water scarcity is going to be critical problem. Therefore, on priority basis proper discussion should be there for solution to this.

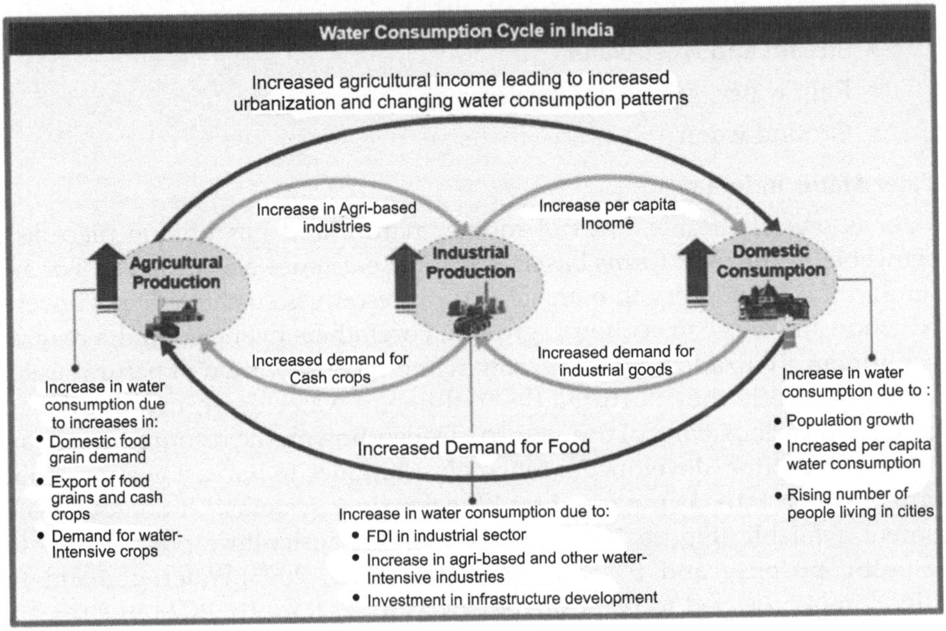

Fig. 10.1: Water consumption cycle in India-agriculture, domestic and industrial production

(**Source:** Grail analysis)

In India, several indigenous water storage systems have been tendered down through generations for use and benefits. They are known by common names in different states of the country like 'Khad', 'Bauri', 'Nawans', 'wells', 'Nalas', 'Dharas', 'Panderas', 'Mangras', 'Khals', 'Chals', 'Guhls' and 'Gharats Dhara'. 'Guhls' are same as 'Kuhls' 'Khatris', 'Pond' (Talab, Talayya, Pokher, Pukur) and 'Zabo'. Even today, a significant rural population depends on natural traditional water resources for subsistence and livelihoods. It is important to heed lessons from what our ancestors and seniors were doing in the past.

In spite of having number of advantages/benefits of these traditional water resources, these diminishing day by day just because of technological advancements. There are number of reasons for this. Facilities of water at home for domestic purpose made the people sluggish to bring water from nearby natural sources. Today's young generation and urban people feel uncomfortable to bring water in containers. Our ancestors had vision also that bringing water from outdoor having an added health advantage also. Such marvelous and widespread life supporting traditional water systems are getting deteriorated in the recent past due to poor maintenance and lack of interest among the users.

In addition, due to changed life style society become unconcerned towards conservation of water, specially people are unaware about the traditional water treasure of India.

By looking at need of water conservation, a number of schemes have been launched like rain water harvesting and ground water restoration but there is need of reformation in our policies for traditional natural water systems which are dying natural death just because of ignorance. Sincere efforts are needed to revive these resources through their proper maintenance, use and education to people for their importance in near future. It is not only duty of government and few good NGO's but our moral responsibility to come forward and should take lead in safeguarding water and traditional water bodies of ancient India.

Security experts are already thinking about ways to tackle the possibilities of water wars in the future. Providing water is absolutely essential for a country's development objectives – job creation, food security, GDP growth and social goals including poverty reduction (UNESCO, 2009). Many conservation techniques have deep historical roots in practice and policy. Increasing emphasis is placed on documentation and adaptation of traditional water conservation technologies in modern rural and urban areas (Agarwal and Narain, 1997). To conserve the traditional treasure, it is not only the central or state government but local panchayat and other people should come forward for rehabilitation. People should understand their moral responsibility and should also educate their children about conservation and preservation of these water bodies.

Strategies for Water Conservation

India's National Water Policy recognizes the importance of providing safe drinking water to its people. It states "Drinking water needs of human beings and animals should be the first charge on available resources". For children, specifically, this right is also enshrined in article 24 of the convention on the rights of the child (CRD) ratified by the Government of India. It has been recommended that water be treated as not just as an `economic good' but as an `economic resource' which is essential for growth and development. But many aspects of the National Water Policy, legislation and regulations and the rights of children under the CRC have not been implementable in the Indian context for various reasons (Nigam *et al.*, 1995).

For greening NRDWP, therefore, the critical components will include:

(*i*) Regeneration and conservation of the resource base through roof rain water harvesting;

(*ii*) Renovation of traditional water harvesting structures;

(*iii*) Treatment of the recharge zones of springs, groundwater aquifers and streams;

(*iv*) Water quality monitoring and treatment to minimize contamination and ensure potable drinking water supply

(*v*) use of renewable energy sources for pumps and higher resource use efficiencies.

Local strategies: In addition, strategies for local areas should be

1. **Awareness Programs:** Several workshops are required at various places of India to educate people about importance of traditional water systems. During the workshop, posters and pamphlets in local language should be distributed to people for better understanding. There should be regular communication to deliberate the issues of water related problems of that particular area.
2. **Identification and documentation of catchment areas:** The identification of the water bodies and proper documentation should be done with the help of inhabitants from neighboring localities from different states of the country. In every village, accountability should be there for the rehabilitation of the water bodies.
3. **Responsibility of local political leaders:** The officials of various departments (Gram panchayat etc.), older wise people along with the local MLA should come forward to take responsibility in creating awareness on importance of water bodies and significance of rainwater harvesting.
4. **Involvement of young brain:** Govt. and private schools should conduct workshops for the young brain of the country to make them aware about the importance of water bodies. There is need to educate them about how we can conserve the ancient treasure.

Revival of Water Bodies

For restore,revive, and rehabilitation of the traditional water bodies, The Government of India has launched a Scheme for Repair, Renovation and Restoration (RRR) of water bodies which has multiple objectives like Comprehensive improvement and restoration of water bodies thereby increasing tank storage capacity, Ground Water Recharge, Increased availability of drinking water, Improvement in agriculture/horticulture productivity, Improvement of 4 catchment areas of tank commands, Environmental benefits through improved water use efficiency; by promotion of conjunctive use of surface and ground water, Community participation and self-supporting system for sustainable management for each water body, Capacity Building of communities, in better water management and Development of tourism, cultural activities, etc. by providing Central Grant to State Governments under a Pilot Scheme directly linked to agriculture during the remaining period of Xth Five Year Plan in January 2005. For preservation and protection of water bodies, Ministry of Urban Development (MoUD) has also issued Advisory which has been sent to all the State Governments for protection of urban water bodies. Main features of the scheme are as (MoWR, 2009).

(*i*) Comprehensive improvement of selected tank systems including restoration.

(*ii*) Improvement of catchment areas of tank.

(*iii*) Community participation and self-supporting system for sustainable management for water bodies covered by the programme.

(*iv*) Ground Water Recharge.

(*v*) Capacity Building of communities, user groups standing committee for Panchayats and State Government/Central Government Agencies concerned with the planning implementation and monitoring of the project.

(*vi*) Increase in storage capacity of water bodies.

(*vii*) Improvement in agriculture/horticulture productivity and increase in recharge of ground water in downstream areas of water bodies.

(*viii*) Environmental benefits through improved water use efficiency;irrigation benefits through restoration of water bodies, supplementation of the groundwater use and promotion of conjunctive use of surface and ground water.

(*ix*) Development of tourism, cultural activities, etc.

(*x*) Increased availability of drinking water.

Conclusion

Obviously not enough, therefore, there is need of encouragement of village inhabitants and individuals to build their own water harvesting and start protecting their traditional water bodies to fulfill their basic domestic requirement for water. Historically, it was seen that there was no problem of water scarcity where the community organizations were strong and the people tried to build traditional water harvesting structures. However, the situation is alarming where the people depended entirely on the state or the government efforts for their water need. This kind of initiative will help indirectly water problems of the are municipality. It will also help to create as sets in the form water bodies and will form the basis for all round development and prosperity. If the world continues to waste water, then not even the best policies and technologies can help to solve water scarcity. It is just because of wisdom of our forefathers who made harvesting of water and its management an integral part of the native culture. Let us come around and multiply this old wisdom for the benefit of all our people especially in the rural areas.

This is the history of our glorious tradition of water harvesting by the village communities and individuals with strong support and encouragement from the state. More importantly this history reflects the ingenuity and wisdom of our forefathers, who made harvesting of water and its management an integral part of the native culture and community life. This meant that these practices were perceived by the common man as his sacred duty and by the communities as part of good local self-governance and social responsibility.

REFERENCES

Agarwal, A. and Narain, S. (1997). Dying Wisdom: Rise, Fall and Potential of India's Traditional Water Harvesting Systems. Centre for Science and Environment, New Delhi, pp. 404.

Bharti, P. K. (2012). Hill-Stream Ecology, Biotech Books, Delhi, pp. 246.

Chatterjee, Kalipada (2016). Water Resources of India, as Accessed on http://climatechangecentre.net/pdf/waterresources.pdf

CWC (2005). Water Data Book. Central Water Commission (CWC), New Delhi as Accessed on /http://cwc.gov.in/main/downloads/Water_Data_Complete_Book_2005 pdf.

FAO (2003). Food and Agriculture Organization, Aquastat, Accessed on http://www.fao.org/nr/aboutnr/nrl/en/

http://www2.warwick.ac.uk/fac/sci/eng/research/civil/crg/dtuold/pubs/reviewed/rwh/eu/c1.pdf

Hussain, J., Husain, I. and Arif, M.. (2014). Water Resources Management: Traditional Technology and Communities as Part of the Solution-Central Groundwater Board, North Western Region, Ministry of Water Resources, Chandigarh, India doi:10.5194/piahs-364-236-2014.

MoWR (2009). Guidelines for Repair, Renovation and Restoration of Water Bodies with Domestic Support Government of India, Ministry of Water Resources 2009, pp. 1-12.

MPHED (2016). Water harvesting-Our old age tradition, Public Health Engineering Department, Meghalaya, as Accessed on (http://megphed.gov.in/knowledge/Rainwater Harvest/Chap2.pdf)

Nigam, A., Gujja, B., Bandyopadhyay. J. and Talbot, R. (1995).Fresh Water for India's Children and Nature', Chapter 1 & 2, by WWF and UNICEF.

NIH (2010). Water Resource India, Annual report, National Institute of Hydrology. Website: www.nih.ernet.in;

UNESCO (2009). World Water Assessment Programme. The United Nations World Water Development Report 3: Water in a Changing World. (http://www.unesco.org/water/wwap/wwdr/wwdr3/pdf/WWDR3_Water_in_a_Changing_World.pdf)

INDEX